# Honey from the Lion

# Honey from the Lion

*Christianity and the Ethics of Nationalism*

Doug Gay

scm press

© Doug Gay 2013

Published in 2013 by SCM Press
Editorial office
3rd Floor
Invicta House
108-114 Golden Lane,
London
ECIY OTG

SCM Press is an imprint of Hymns Ancient & Modern Ltd
(a registered charity)
13A Hellesdon Park Road
Norwich NR6 5DR, UK

www.scmpress.co.uk

British Library Cataloguing in Publication data

A catalogue record for this book is available
from the British Library

978-0-334-04647-9

Typeset by Regent Typesetting
Printed and bound by
Ashford Colour Press Ltd

# Contents

For Rachel, Calum, Beth and Eilidh

I am only a cell in Scotland's body,
struggling to be a brain cell.

*from* The Midge – *Fearghas MacFhionnlaigh*

# Preface

I am grateful for opportunities to try out some of the arguments in this book in seminars at Greenbelt Festival, the Scottish Baptist College, The Lincoln Institute, University of Manchester and the Scottish Evangelical Theology Society Conference.

As with my previous book on ecclesiology, *Remixing the Church*, my hope is to write theology which can find a readership within and beyond the academy; which is accountable to the academy and accessible to a wider readership. The danger remains that of satisfying neither public on either count.

While for you as readers this book will have two lives, one for those who read before and one for those who read after the 2014 Referendum on independence for Scotland, for myself as writer it has only existed in the before. My belief in the importance of contextual theology means that I am unapologetic about having written it 'towards' that unique event, but I hope that the arguments in the book will continue to be of interest within and beyond Scotland, whatever the outcome. If the vote goes against independence, it seems likely that there will still be a further era of devolution and constitutional development. If there is a vote for independence, we will be facing a period of dramatic and daunting change.

The book has been written during a period of considerable upheaval and unsettlement in the institution where I work, in the course of which some treasured colleagues regrettably left for other parts. It was also written without the benefit of study leave, in the face of a busy teaching schedule, alongside active ministry commitments. It is not as 'thick' a volume or a treatment of the issues as I would have liked or as the times deserved. It is, however, a book that I think needed to be written and published when it was. I offer it as an essay in practical, political theology that risks both an unapologetic apology for liberal, civic nationalism and vocal advocacy for Scottish independence. It is intended to stimulate debate and reflection on a topic that is controversial and divisive both within Scotland and the UK and, in general terms, across the world. I look forward to learning from critical readers, who will critique the positions I take, challenge me to deeper engagement with the issues and call me to a more faithful theological engagement with the questions at stake.

My particular thanks to my editor at SCM Dr Natalie Watson for her patience and encouragement and to Harry Smart for invaluable help in getting the final manuscript bashed into shape. Thanks also to Will Storrar and David Fergusson, who were my doctoral supervisors and whose commitment to theology in Scotland has been a continuing inspiration to me.

Doug Gay
*Glasgow*
*September 2013*

# Introduction

## Practical, Political, Poetic, Public Theology

This book looks at the ethics of nationalism from a Christian theological perspective. Some readers, perhaps *many* religious ones, will baulk at the suggestion that there could be such a thing as an *ethical* nationalism, being fully convinced that nationalism is in principle unethical.

I'm aware of the wide range of reactions that the 'n' word can cause; the 'honey' of the title, which has been with me from the start of my work on the book, has been my own way in to the ambivalence of the word 'nationalism'.

There is a story in the Old Testament book of Judges which lies behind both my title and the iconic Tate & Lyle syrup tins that have graced the kitchen tables of Scottish homes since the 1880s.[1]

In the Old Testament book of Judges, Samson the Israelite hero is operating on the cultural and geographical boundaries of Israel and in a context in which we are told 'the Philistines had dominion over Israel' (14.4).[2] Samson's eye roves beyond the women of Israel to 'a Philistine woman' (14.1), and he asks his parents to get her for him as his wife. Their exasperated reply reflects a view held deeply in many cultures through history, that women and men should marry their own kind: 'Is there not a woman among your kin, or among all our people, that you must go to take a wife from the uncircumcised Philistines?'

---

1 I have fond memories of licking the syrup spoon while gazing intrigued at the picture of the lion with bees buzzing around its open belly; an enduring stroke of genius by Abram Lyle and his Victorian marketing team, although I doubt it was 'inverted sugar syrup' which Samson is said to have licked from his fingers back then!

2 All Scripture references are taken from the New Revised Standard Version of the Bible unless marked otherwise.

Old Testament theologian Walter Brueggemann says of the Samson cycle of stories: 'The primary motif in this narrative ... is Samson's complex relationship to the Philistines, Israel's paradigmatic enemy, the quintessential "other" whose narrative function is to serve and enhance Israel's own peculiar identity' (2003, p. 125).[3] At the boundary place of Timnah, where Samson has seen the woman, he is attacked by a lion, and kills it with his bare hands. Returning later to the lion's corpse he finds a swarm of bees have colonized it and made honey. He scrapes it out to eat and to share with his parents. He then makes up a riddle which he uses in a contest with the Philistines. Unable to solve it, they play on the loyalties of his Philistine bride, who cajoles the answer from Samson and relays it to them.

The riddle travels well from Hebrew into English – 'out of the eater came something to eat, out of the strong came something sweet'. The relationship between lions and honey I read (freely) as a metaphor for the central question of political theology and political ethics – the relationship between power and virtue. In the discussion that follows, that question will be explored in relation to questions of *identity*, *legitimacy*, *sovereignty* and *representation*.

While a good many of my readers will have theological or religious interests, I hope the book will find a wider readership among those involved in the current constitutional and public policy debates in Scotland and the UK and those who follow these questions in other countries. One reason for holding out such hopes is the influence, more than two decades ago, of Will Storrar's *Scottish Identity: A Christian Vision* (1990), which was cited by a wide range of commentators in Scottish civil society and further afield. Will was my main doctoral supervisor and is a much valued friend. I hope this book can find as wide and generous a readership as his did, although I fear that public and civic discourse in Scotland and the UK is becoming less hospitable to books that address public policy questions from an explicitly theological angle.

I hope that readers not used to theology who do persist with the book will find that though the theological perspective is unapologetic, the book reflects a desire to find common ethical and

---

3 Brueggemann relates this comment to the work of Jobling, 1998.

political ground between my Reformed and ecumenical Christian humanism on the one hand, and a spectrum of different secular and religious humanisms. Although public discourse has become less hospitable to theology, anyone who has made a serious attempt to read and understand Scottish and British history and the history of political theory[4] will have had to engage with theological themes and concerns as a *sine qua non* of achieving their historical literacy.[5]

For those who are disinclined to read the book as a historical–theoretical document and who read through a more literary critical lens, I hope it will provide a set of colourful metaphors whose sense and reach they can appreciate, even if they have doubts about their provenance. Either way, debates about the place of religious discourse in public life are now moving beyond the era of John Rawls and the 'hard secularist' implications many drew from his proposals.[6] The simplest and best response to Rawls has always been the insistence that when people sit down together to discuss public policy, they are not only allowed to bring their political proposals to the table, they are also allowed to bring their *reasons* for making them (Wolterstorff and Audi, 1997, p. 112). The fact that those reasons may be incommensurable does not mean that the political work of coming to judgement and decision cannot go ahead, although it does, as my Mennonite friends remind me, place the work of peacemaking at the heart of the political process. Jews, Christians, Muslims, Hindus, Buddhists and atheists will often be capable of reaching substantive agreement on political questions, even after travelling to that agreement from different starting points.

One premise of this book is that those starting places do not only provide historical context, they also offer sources of inspiration and imagination as well as practical modes of ethical reasoning. My location within the Christian tradition and the Christian Church is decisive for me. It determines my sense of who I am

---

4 On this, see among others Lilla, 2007; Kidd, 2008; Skinner, 1978.

5 It is not possible to read Scottish history competently without a reasonably well-developed knowledge of Christian theology and the Bible. Ideas of 'covenant' and the 'federal', 'sovereignty' and 'legitimacy', 'law' and the sources of law, 'discipline', 'episcopacy', 'Presbyterianism' all presuppose such a knowledge.

6 In particular, see Stout, 2004; Biggar and Hogan (eds), 2009.

and who others are, and it shapes my perception of and interpretation of the world, as well as providing a context for action.
The increasing 'strangeness' of a Christian theological perspective
within contemporary public discourse will, I think, often just have
to be borne and risked, if it is not to be abandoned or sacrificed. In
saying this, I do not dismiss the desire for 'translation' of religious
perspectives, which Jürgen Habermas has expressed, but nor do
I accept it as a condition of participation in public discourse (on
Habermas, see Junker Kenny in Biggar and Hogan (eds), 2009).
The risk of 'sounding strange' is worth taking because it attests
to a belief that Christian theological language is not capable of
being converted without remainder into some neutral version of
public reasoning. I stand with those, therefore, who argue that the
excess of meaning and reference carried by theological, liturgical
and scriptural language and conceptuality offers a range of possibilities for reading contemporary culture and politics which might
otherwise be lost. While there are times and places for the detailed
work of justifying and defending the Christian doctrines in play
here, my approach will be to deploy them unapologetically in the
service of a Christian political imagination.

In the practice of doing this, I believe that the 'thickness' of
Christian doctrine enables a deep hermeneutics and a deep
poetics,[7] that is to say that it allows *more* to be read and heard
and it allows *more* to be written and said. Because I covet a
readership beyond my own discipline, I have to hope even for
those who struggle to accept theological premises that something
of a hermeneutical and poetic 'more' may still be engaging. If
they, like Habermas, respond to the affective and motivational
power of religious concepts with acts of wary translation, that
is something we can go on talking about. Hopefully we'll have
a better conversation in part because the 'strange talk' has been
thought-provoking.[8] People within my own discipline may ask if

---

7 On the place of poetics in practical theology see Walton in Miller-McLemore
(ed.), 2012.

8 In this way, while remembering T. S. Eliot's warnings about treating the Bible
as 'literature', (*Daily Princetonian*, 24 March 1933), I want to allow that an openness to theology in terms of 'literature' or 'art' may allow a conversation to start. I
may not accept the reduction implied, just as others may not concede in advance the
authority I acknowledge within the tradition, but we can at least engage in thinking

this is really 'practical theology'. The book, like my earlier book on ecclesiology, is not focused on empirical work or field work. However, both books are reflections on practice and both attempt to reframe practice by clarifying key concepts and testing them theologically. In a 1982 essay on 'Ethics and the Pastoral Task', Stanley Hauerwas quotes Iris Murdoch's claim that 'we can only act in the world we see' (quoted in McGrath, 2008, p. 308). We see the world not by aiming our minds and pressing the shutter once, but by looking again and again. The process of trying to say what we have seen, of trying to describe practice, as Pierre Bourdieu points out in his discussion of the 'logic of practice' (1990; cf. Smith, 2009, p. 67), places us within a hermeneutical circle or spiral in which the saying affects the seeing. Our scope for action can be restricted or broadened by the 'saying'. How we produce a 'sayable' world, how we voice and name the world, is a practice in itself; it also creates a context that enables or disables other practices.[9] Many of my key concerns in this book are related to questions I have asked myself about my own practice of voting for a nationalist party in Scotland over a number of decades. I am reflecting on the political practice of that party and other parties both in opposition and in government. I am reflecting on the often vehement opposition to any kind of political nationalism among Christian friends and in wider conversation. I'm engaging the prospect of the referendum on Scottish independence scheduled for the Autumn of 2014 and reflecting on the role that churches, including my own Church of Scotland, might play, in clarifying the ethical dimensions of the referendum choices.

Practices of political debate, of voting, of representation and governance are all in view, as is the consensus among most practical theologians that our discipline is always, somehow, aimed at 'transforming practice' (see Graham [1996] 2002). That the practice in view is 'political' is something that is unremarkable in respect of the last few decades of the Scottish tradition of practical theology. Duncan Forrester, former Professor of Practical

---

through and around theology without having to demythologize or otherwise agree lowest common denominator terms in advance.

9 Cf. Neal Ascherson's profound 2002 book *Stone Voices*, subtitled *The Search for Scotland*.

Theology and Christian Ethics at New College, Edinburgh, did much of his work in this area,[10] as have his successors in that chair, Will Storrar and Oliver O'Donovan. Each of these theologians has worked in their different ways to produce 'contextual theology' – attentive to the surrounding political culture and context.

One factor in the current context, which has so far been little discussed by theologians, but which is clearly of major importance, is the prospect of preparing a written constitution for an independent Scotland. I return to this in Chapter 9, where I offer my own suggestions about how religion should be recognized within any new constitutional settlement.

The aim in what follows therefore is to write practical, political, poetic, public theology, which speaks directly to its context and which readers interested in Scotland's and the UK's constitutional future, or in questions of nationalism, ethics and politics, can be persuaded to engage with, even if they find its theological accent strange.

The book begins by looking at definitions of nationalism and at ways of thinking beyond nationalism. Chapters 2–4 explore an ecumenical political theology, Christian ideas of a good society and theological perspectives on nationalism. In Chapters 5–7 I give a short historical introduction to Scottish nationalism and devolution, discuss the post-devolution landscape and suggest why independence offers an attractive way to engage some intractable problems in Scottish society. Chapter 8 sets out a vision for the future and Chapter 9 addresses constitutional questions.

---

10 On the contribution of Forrester and Storrar to this tradition, see Chapters 4 and 5 of Gay, 2006.

# I

# Rethinking Nationalism as Normal

If you have the temerity to write about nationalism you have first to pull off the trick of sounding as if you know what you're talking about. Then you have somehow to secure the agreement of your readers that what you are talking about is *nationalism*. Neither of these is an easy task. In his innovative, much admired and much discussed study, *Imagined Communities*, Benedict Anderson observed that '[n]ation, nationality, nationalism – all have proved notoriously difficult to define, let alone to analyse' (1991, p. 2).[1] In his preface to the 1991 second edition, Anderson noted that in the intervening eight years, the study of nationalism had been 'startlingly transformed' (p. xi). The literature on nationalism has burgeoned over the past three decades and shows little sign of abating. In this chapter and at other points in the book, I engage some key debates within that literature with an eye to my own distinctive concerns.[2]

Some hotly contested issues in nationalism studies have relatively little bearing on my concerns to explore and test the grounds for an ethical nationalism and I will not engage with or try to adjudicate them here. However, an early objection has to be made to the position of Stephen Grosby in his 2005 Oxford University

---

1 David McCrone, while citing Hans Kohn's 1940s Britannica entry, suggested in 1998 that the study of nationalism was barely 40 years old (1998, p. viii).

2 My own analysis, as a theologian leaning in to the broader conversation, has been influenced by the work of Jonathan Hearn, the US-born, Edinburgh-based anthropologist, and in particular by his study, *Rethinking Nationalism* (2006), which is among the best recent attempts to review and evaluate the field. It has also been informed by the work of the late Adrian Hastings in his important 1997 lectures on *The Construction of Nationhood: Ethnicity, Religion and Nationalism* and by McCrone's account of the sociology of nationalism (1998). My debts to Hearn, Hastings and McCrone will be both clear and acknowledged in what follows.

Press 'very short introduction' to nationalism. Grosby's treatment of nationalism appears to me to foreclose the very conversation I want to open, by insisting, tendentiously, on building ethically unacceptable features into the very definition of the term:

> When one divides the world into two irreconcilable and warring camps – one's own nation in opposition to all other nations – where the latter are viewed as one's own implacable enemies, then in contrast to patriotism, there is the ideology of *nationalism*. Nationalism repudiates civility and the differences that it tolerates by attempting to eliminate all differing views and interests for the sake of one vision of what the nation has been and should be. (2005, p. 17)

Grosby's assertions that 'nationalism repudiates civility', that it 'knows no compromise' (p. 18) and that 'distinctive of nationalism is the belief that the nation is the only goal worthy of pursuit' (p. 5) seem to me not only to be wrong, but in their one-sidedness to be profoundly misplaced in a popular critical introduction designed to introduce students to the contemporary study of nationalism. They do, however, serve as an apt example of why the concept of nationalism incites fear and loathing among many people. My argument will be that nationalism *can* indeed be both imagined and performed in the ways Grosby deplores, but that it need not be and that such ethically objectionable instantiations should not be built into a primary understanding or definition of the term.[3]

---

3 See Benedict Anderson's observation: 'In an age when it is so common for progressive, cosmopolitan intellectuals (particularly in Europe?) to insist on the near-pathological character of nationalism, its roots in fear and hatred of the Other and its affinities with racism, it is useful to remind ourselves that nations inspire love and often profoundly self-sacrificing love' (1991, p. 141).

## Banal nationalism and banal universalism

While we are about the work of what Stanley Hauerwas calls 'swamp clearing', it is worth noting two other common, but unimpressive ways of foreclosing conversations about nationalism. The first is helpfully identified in Michael Billig's concept of *banal nationalism*, by which he denotes the myriad often unconscious and unremarked ways in which national affiliations are marked, symbolized, accepted and assumed by the majority of people in contemporary societies.[4] Billig's analysis sheds light on the way many people, just as they find other people's children more annoying than their own (my comparison, not his), find other people's nationalisms offensive – find them to be 'nationalisms' in fact – while appearing blissfully unaware and benignly accepting of their own. Such attitudes have been highly prevalent within internal UK and Northern Ireland discussions – with Irish, Welsh and Scottish nationalists being seen as 'Nationalists', while 'British nationalists' are seldom identified or perceived in this way.[5] These attitudes, while ethically insubstantial and intellectually indefensible, are surprisingly common, even among those, such as academics (!), who should know better.

A counterpart to this comes in the form of what could be called *banal universalism*.[6] The term takes aim at an uncritical and saccharin appeal to common humanity, to be heard as if accompanied by John Lennon's 'Imagine' playing wearily in the background. The irony of this in a discussion of 'imagined

---

4 Billig, 1995; McCrone speaking of Billig's 'felicitous' phrase comments: 'This perspective is important because it helps us to escape from the orthodoxy that nationalism is a kind of political brainwashing, a sort of false consciousness' (1998, p. viii).

5 Northern Ireland is in a different situation here – with Nationalist and Unionist coded and loaded with a distinctive set of meanings and associations. Despite the Conservative party being officially the Conservative and Unionist Party, outside of Northern Ireland, few people readily espouse and use the Unionist label, even if they remain unionist by conviction. This may be because the Northern Ireland associations have rendered it uncomfortable for people outside of that context.

6 I do not mean this as a catch-all term for all forms of political universalism or cosmopolitanism. Some of these have important roles to play in this discussion, and I will identify my own position with one of them.

communities' lies in the fact that neither the cultural appropriations of it, nor even Lennon's song itself, represent serious acts
of political imagination.[7] The banality here lies not so much in its
background ubiquity as in the way that, like Bonhoeffer's notion
of 'cheap grace',[8] such expressions of universalism do not usually
come at any cost to other political allegiances and identities held
and traded on by those who sing along to them.

We need to avoid both of these (banal) extremes, because both
involve a form of hypocrisy. In the first instance, we refuse to
acknowledge in ourselves what we deplore in someone else.[9] In
the second, we pretend that we have transcended lesser identities
in the name of a higher identity, while still trading on those lesser
identities in our day-to-day living. I will argue in the course of this
book that we need to 'fess up' to our own nationalisms and accept
moral responsibility for disciplining them.[10] A barrier to doing
that, which lies behind both of the evasions just considered, is a
Grosby-like view of nationalism as something inherently unethical. To address that we need to make the case for an alternative
way of defining nationalism as a more ambivalent phenomenon.
In turning to this it is helpful to bear in mind Rogers Brubaker's
contention:

'Nation' is a category of 'practice', not (in the first instance)
a category of 'analysis'. To understand nationalism, we have
to understand the practical uses of the category 'nation', the
ways it can come to structure perception, to inform thought

---

7 I say this as some kind of Lennon fan. The critique of Lennon's position could
also be applied to Virginia Woolf's famous claim in the novel *Three Guineas* (1938):
'as a woman, I have no country. As a woman, I want no country. As a woman, my
country is the world', quoted in McCrone, 1998, p. 124. It can also arguably be
aimed at Tertullian: 'We are cool towards the blaze of glory and dignity and have no
need of political combinations. Nothing is more foreign to us than the res publica.
One res publica we know, of which all are citizens – the universe' (Apologeticus 38),
quoted in O'Donovan, 2005, p. 212.

8 For the origins of this term, see Bonhoeffer, 1960, p. 30.

9 So McCrone, 1998, p. viii: 'The most powerful forms of nationalism are those
which operate its power while denying its existence.'

10 I say more about the concept of discipline and its place within Reformed
theology on pp. 30ff. below.

and experience, to organize discourse and political action. (Brubaker, 1996, p. 10, quoted in McCrone, 1998, p. 3)

## Defining nationalism

From the 1970s, the key fault line in nationalism studies has been between two options usually styled 'primordialism' and 'modernism'[11] and centred on their competing explanations of whether the origins of nationalism were more ancient or more recent (Hearn, 2006, p. 7). The contours of this division are still visible today, although few thinkers willingly self-identify as 'primordialists', possibly because it has a knuckle-dragging ring to it. Jonathan Hearn and David McCrone are among those who do not believe that a 'single, unified theory of nationalism' is possible (Hearn, 2006, p. xii; cf. McCrone, 1998, p. 171), meaning a single, explanatory paradigm which could be applied to all instances of nationalism everywhere. In agreeing with them on this, I also stress that my own concerns in this book lie not with questions of historical origins, but with the contemporary 'performance' of nationalism. However, what has to be possible for the conversation to move forward is some working definition of nationalism, some sense of the nature of the beast. The definition offered by Hearn is valuable because it is both carefully delineated and ethically restrained: 'Nationalism is the making of combined claims, on behalf of a population, to identity, to jurisdiction and to territory' (2006, p. 11) and 'To be nationalism, these three kinds of claims have to come together as a package and be viewed as interdependent by those who make these claims' (p. 12).

It is not surprising that, as a practical theologian, I am drawn to a definition in which nationalism is identified as a practice,[12] and, as a Scottish practical theologian, there are historical reasons to have a particular interest in its being identified as a practice of 'claim-making'. In his earlier *Claiming Scotland*, Hearn offered

---

11 Hastings opts for 'medievalists' and 'modernists' (1997, p. 2).

12 The most common shorthand definition of practical theology is 'theological reflection upon practice'. Note also that Brubaker identifies 'the nation' as a category of practice; see pages 4–5 above.

an original analytic response to questions of national identity via the 'Claim of Right' tradition in Scotland from the seventeenth century to the modern era.[13]

This earlier focus on the metaphor and practice of claiming is now carried over into the heart of Hearn's definition of nationalism. From the perspective of an enquiry into the ethics of nationalism, his definition also seems to be a good fit. It does not pre-load the bases by building in an ethical deficit, but the terminology of 'claim' invites and expects the response of weighing and assessing claims. Those claims may come to be seen as either justified or indefensible, so it does not build in ethical credit either. It directs attention to the nature of the claims being made, but it also implies a need to attend to the process and the criteria by which those claims will be judged. Adopting this as a working definition, I want to explore how Hearn's three claims can be understood in ways that open up a dialogue with practical political theology.

## Nationalism as 'claim to identity on behalf of a population'

Logically, it would seem that a claim to self-determination implies a prior act of self-recognition. In practice the two often come together – we find our being in becoming – we come to know ourselves in the course of living (cf. the social enterprise not-for-profit company We Are What We do). This idea of becoming who we are, of learning to be ourselves, opens the way for a claim to identity to be understood in terms of an identity that is itself still a work in progress. From a theological perspective, in his discussion of 'political institutions' and 'representation' in *The Ways of Judgment*, Oliver O'Donovan comments that 'to see ourselves as a people is a work of moral imagination' (2005, p. 151; for a

---

13 The key dates are 1689, 1842, 1989 and 1991. The mention of four dates and documents may surprise and confuse some here. The first (1689) represents the claim made by the Scottish Parliament in preparation for offering the crown to William of Orange; the second (1842) was produced by the General Assembly in the lead-up to the Disruption; the third (1989) was produced by the Constitutional Convention in their campaign for a devolved Scottish Parliament; and the fourth, 'A Women's Claim of Right for Scotland', was produced by a caucus of concerned women in 1991. Hearn's thesis directs attention to the significance of this resort to 'claim' language in the 1980s and 1990s.

fuller discussion of this, see Chapter 3 below). David McCrone directs our attention away from static, essentialist understandings of identity towards the dynamic processes involved in identity formation, citing Stuart Hall's reading of national identity in terms of a process of cultural *representation* or cultural *production*, as well as Homi Bhabha's idea of the nation as 'narrative'.

Each of these formulations points towards an account of nationalism as a way of seeing ourselves which is also a way of working on ourselves; a way of narrating and representing ourselves politically, socially and culturally (Hall, 1992 and Bhabha, 1990, cited in McCrone, 1998, p. 30). The language of *claiming* captures something of this sense of being in process, of being on the way to something – in this case to a vision, a narrative, a representation of who 'we' are. In the preamble to the US Constitution drawn up in 1787, the famous phrase 'we the people' claims a collective voice for the citizens of the republic as they 'ordain and establish' their constitution.[14] On the terraces at Ibrox stadium in Glasgow, fans of Rangers Football Club have for decades been fond of chanting 'we are the people'. In both cases, context is key to understanding the claims to identity that are being made and in both cases we see that a claim to be 'the people' can also be a work of immoral imagination. The context and character of any such claims have to be interrogated, because forming the *we* of the constitution, like forming the *we* of the football terraces, involves processes of inclusion and exclusion.[15]

The constitution of the other or the *othering* of the other has become such a potent theme in postmodern discourse that we might be tempted to view it as intrinsically immoral. David McCrone is aware of this temptation, as a commentator attentive to the dialectics of identity formation in relation to nationalism; but he is clear that the deeper lesson to learn from thinkers such as Edward Said is that 'All cultures are hybrids, and all identities created in dialectic' (McCrone, 1998, p. 119, citing Said, 1993).

The problem is therefore not in the othering per se, since all distinction involves othering; it lies in what is claimed through the

---

14 http://www.archives.gov/exhibits/charters/constitution.html.

15 African slaves, women and Native Americans in the case of the US constitution; Scotland's Celtic supporting 'Irish Catholics' in the case of (some) Rangers fans.

othering and how. In terms made famous by the French philosopher Emmanuel Lévinas, it has to do with how the other claims us, since the face of the other is Mount Sinai, is the Torah (1985, pp. 85–9). The other, then, in being the neighbour to whom and for whom I am accountable, is the grounds of the possibility that I could love my neighbour. The question of whether a moral or immoral imagination is at work, in our imagining of any given community, turns both on how and why a common bond is claimed and also on how a claimed distinction is responded to. It is certainly possible to imagine a reciprocal relation between 'we the people' and 'you the people', as is found in the BBC's biblical-sounding motto adopted in 1927, 'nation shall speak peace unto nation'.[16]

We see something of this in the language and practice of the 'recognition' of one country by another, when the legitimacy of a new state or regime is recognized after independence or regime change. Since we have returned to 'we the people' language, those of us concerned with overcoming sectarianism in Scotland must also hope that it is possible to imagine a 'second half', a coming age in which 'we are the people' could be understood not by chanting the 'Famine Song', [17] but by affirming that 'you are the people', so the argument of Jim Sillars (1986) that nationalism is a condition of internationalism. (The question of sectarianism and its relation to national identity in Scotland is one I will return to in Chapter 6 below.)

## Nationalism as the claim to jurisdiction and territory

The second component of Hearn's definition of nationalism involves making the claim that 'we the people' should have jurisdiction – that 'we' should have the authority, the right, the ability: to speak the law, to make the law, to administer justice within

---

16 Allegedly a free adaptation of Micah 4.3. This is what lies behind the language and practice involved in the 'recognition' of one country by another, after independence or regime change.

17 The grossly offensive chant by Rangers fans to the tune of the Sloop John B – 'the famine's over, it's time to go home' – perpetuating a rejecting othering of Scottish Roman Catholics on the basis of some of their community's historic links to Ireland. For those not familiar with football/soccer – it is a game of two halves!

a given jurisdiction. Since the term can denote both the right of judgement and the locus of judgement, I will discuss these claims to jurisdiction and to territory together.

Having posited an identity distinction between one and another, between 'we' and 'you'; these further practices of claiming have to do with establishing 'ours' and 'yours'. The project of doing that moves us into the borderlands between jurisprudence and political theory, a hybrid zone for which it is hard to find a name. We might, to make a point, call it *'politymaking'*,[18] it having to do with the judgements about how to establish the boundaries of the *polis*. Such an imagined discipline would consider: how is the *res* in the res publica to be 'reified', in the broader, classical sense of the term not in Marx's sense, to be delineated, to be made something determinate?

This fundamental question of political theory turns out to be profoundly difficult. We are more used to such questions falling within the domain of history and more comfortable with that; history being free to track the contingencies and anomalies of state formation, 'how the boundary lines have fallen' without having to decide in the present, whether or not they have fallen 'in pleasant places'.[19]

Texan theologian Stanley Hauerwas has suggested that liberal political theory, based in universalist notions of human rights and voluntarist understandings of social contract, has particular problems in 'accounting for' borders, in positing land and territory as organizing principles and in giving, therefore, an adequate account of the nation-state (1999). When Hauerwas says 'accounting', the sense he appears to have in view is that of legitimating or justifying. This is surely the further element that needs to be added in to Hearn's definition, that the combined claims characteristic of nationalism, jointly and severally include a claim to 'legitimacy'. Taken together, they claim to answer the questions: *Whose writ should run where, and why?*

---

18 I owe this term to Harry Smart – an improvement on polisprudence, which was not a neologism I expected to catch on – there is some overlap here with debates around failed states and 'nation-building'.

19 The allusion is to the King James Bible's famous translation of Psalm 16.6.

The issues at stake in such a question are nicely illustrated by ongoing debates within the United Kingdom about devolution and independence for Scotland, Wales and Northern Ireland, and about membership of the European Union. Many conservative Unionists are proponents of the Goldilocks principle in relation to the United Kingdom: Scotland is too small, Europe is too big, but the United Kingdom of Great Britain and Northern Ireland is just right![20]

If Hauerwas is right about liberal theory's particular problem with borders (which I believe he is), and if the Goldilocks principle of 'nation-states' is seen to carry less of the 'self-evidence' it presumes to, then we have to set ourselves differently in our engagement with the claims of nationalism.

There has been a tendency, particularly on the Left, to see nationalism as an embarrassingly narrow and primitive dimension of political discourse. On the Christian Left, this has been thought and expressed in strong ethical or theological terms, such that for many nationalism remains a theological and ethical embarrassment, if not an offence. This book is a call to *metanoia*, to a change of mind and stance. It's a call to take nationalism and the ethics of nationalism more seriously because, in facing its apparently embarrassing, antique-sounding claims, we face some of the most demanding anthropological, political and ethical questions about ourselves and how we live together. McCrone put the case robustly in 1998:

> There is no continent, no economic system, no level of development which does not have to come to terms with nationalism. If we had told our predecessors in the middle of this century that studying nationalism was not simply writing history but coping with its many modern manifestations, in all probability they would not have believed us. But then, we inhabit a late twentieth-century world in which many of the old nostrums

---

20 Though cf. McCrone, 1998, p. 176: Daniel Bell's pithy words, 'the nation-state is too small for the big problems of life and too big for the small problems of life'. O'Donovan refers to Aristotle's own version of the Goldilocks argument according to which 'a society is "perfect" when it is not too small to rally against a threat, not too diverse to [not] be interested in doing so' (2005, p. 156).

and doctrines have withered. Socialism has gone; fascism has gone. Nationalism has survived and prospers.

... Nationalism is above all a social and political movement. It manifests itself in rich and in poor countries; it has left-wing as well as right-wing variants; it works with, as well as against, movements of class and of gender. This is a sociological book because it does not reduce nationalism merely to politics. It seeks to look at the social and economic interests which mobilize nationalism, without arguing that it is in any sense epiphenomenal. It is a cultural form of politics which is not simply reducible to material interests. We live in an age of nationalism, but one which spends a lot of its energies denying that nationalism exists. The orthodoxy is that it is a virus left over from an older more vicious age, which, as if mutating itself against all known antidotes, comes back to wreak its havoc on hapless victims. Centres of power employ the commonsense that they are patriotic while their enemies are nationalistic. (p. vii)

In reckoning with the stubborn persistence and the insistent return of nationalism, the tactics of denial and denigration are producing diminishing returns. What we see in the work of both Hearn and McCrone is agreement on the need for more subtle and flexible approaches to 'rethinking' nationalism. Benedict Anderson commented in his 1991 Preface to *Imagined Communities*:

My point of departure is that nationality [nation-ness] ... as well as nationalism are cultural artefacts of a particular kind. To understand them properly we need to consider carefully how they have come into historical being, in what ways their meanings have changed over time and why, today, they command such profound emotional legitimacy. (p. 4)

He goes on to describe as one of the chief perplexing and irritating paradoxes for theorists of nationalism, 'the political power of nationalisms versus their philosophical poverty and even incoherence' (p. 5). It is suggestive to consider this alongside his more famous reference to the 'horizontal comradeship' of the nation

(p. 7) and alongside Oliver O'Donovan's observation in *The Ways of Judgment* that 'the affective dimension is entirely absent from official theories of representation in the modern West' (2005, p. 163).

To invoke the 'emotional', the 'affective' dimensions of nationalism, while contrasting its power with its incoherence, is a sure way to raise the spectre of fascistic nationalism – cue the distancing, denigrating reflexes of the 'scientific' or 'liberal' Left. While there is a case for maintaining a proper degree of suspicion, there are also dangers in a paranoid inability to respond thoughtfully to questions of feeling, belonging and allegiance. What is needed is that we find ways of marrying the rational, the affective and the ethical: that is, keeping our heads, while listening to our hearts and keeping up with our consciences.

## Rethinking nationalism

Finding and legitimating a new way of thinking nationalism entails three related but distinguishable moves.

The first is to make the shift already considered above, from static and essentialist understandings of identity towards a view of the nation as a complex, dynamic work in progress.

The second is to recognize that because the subject is a moving target, attempts to capture and frame it are likely to have a 'fuzzy' quality to them.[21] If nationalism turns out to be a dense, complex and multi-layered phenomenon, then we will have to evolve appropriate ways to study it and to discuss and describe it.

The third move is to respond ethically to the claims being made; to filter, police and discipline them. This is the move we are most concerned with here and we will explore it in more detail as we go on, but it belongs here also because perceptions of the ethical status of any phenomenon affect how that phenomenon is assessed and discussed. The ethical denigration of nationalism and the analytical short-circuiting of the study of nationalism have a mutually reinforcing quality to them. Reicher and Hopkins say:

---

21 I have borrowed this description from Robin Cohen's 1994 work on Britishness and 'fuzzy frontiers', cited in McCrone, 2005, pp. 36, 38; see also 2004, p. 1.

It should be abundantly clear that the division between 'heart' and 'head' does not map onto a particular position. Rather, it provides a resource through which any position can be advanced by the way in which it is mapped onto reason as opposed to unreason. Thus, Scottish unionists see Union as reason undermined by unreasoning nationalism, while Scottish 'nationalists' see independence as reason undermined by an unreasoned reluctance to break the Union. For each, their politics serve as the mental hygiene of the nation. (2001, p. 210)

Accepting their point, I suggest that it is also the 'ethics' of the nation that is at stake and rightly so. We need to bring in the ethical alongside Reicher and Hopkins' cognitive and affective. As I noted previously in response to and in disagreement with Grosby, it matters that we do this at the definitional stage if we are to hold open the possibility that nationalism could in principle be a mentally and morally legitimate option. That possibility then has to be demonstrated in relation to practice, by filling in and making concrete what a reasonable and ethical performance of nationalism might look like, as opposed to an unreasonable and unethical one.

## Nationalism is normal

The path I am following here has already been well marked. My concern here will be with further clearing and securing of the path that Hearn has prepared in order to develop a theological and ethical analysis of it. Building on Michael Billig's work, Hearn suggests that we should view 'the politics of stable democratic regimes as the routinization, rather than the overcoming of nationalism' (2006, p. 145). He expands on this:

I want to argue that in stable democratic regimes this process of nationalism is very deeply embedded in civil society and electoral systems and not simply an elite or state-led process. It is part of the normal functioning of democratic regimes ...
   Liberal democracies do not so much transcend nationalism as domesticate it, routinizing its dynamic by channelling it

through core political institutions. On the one hand, nationalism is seriously altered by this context, de-fanged[22] for the most
part and rendered less dangerous. But on the other hand it is an
indispensable aspect of the state's ongoing need for legitimacy
and inevitable competition between social groups to define the
wider society of which they are members ... Nationalism is a
basic part of how relatively stable democracies legitimate and
re-legitimate themselves. (pp. 165–6)

The points being made here by Hearn are important in reframing
our understanding of nationalism. He moves us away from exotic
and pathologizing accounts towards a thoroughly 'normalizing'
one. To borrow a theological metaphor, we could characterize this
account as having to do with the 'incarnation' of democracy. The
alternative is a conception of the res publica as a permanent ideal
'soul' locked into a form of political docetism, refusing to accept
political incarnation in the material conditions of lived national
identities as they take place East of Eden. By contrast, 'democracy
incarnate' has an address, has majority languages and accents, is
women and men, children and elders, caught up in struggles for
power and resources. It is their work in progress, their ongoing
attempt to define and differentiate their society and to 'domesticate' the processes of claim-making so that they become part of a
process of home-making (or even polity-making).

Hearn's move to normalize nationalism is welcome because it
works to keep the conversation honest, undercutting high theoretical or low partisan disdain for nationalism. To recognize that,
though, is only to travel part of the way with him. What is being
normalized, in his account, is a process of seeking legitimation and
relegitimation. To clarify the terms we are using: 'normalizing'
refers to how common if not ubiquitous this process is, 'seeking
legitimation' has to do with its character as a social, cultural and
political process of asserting the moral credentials of a regime. We
might agree with both of these points about nationalism, but we

---

22 I came to Hearn's book after choosing my own title and metaphor – I had
to include this quote because his imagery here complements mine so well. Michael
Keating in a 2002 paper speaks of an attempt to 'ride the tiger of nationalism' (2002,
p. 1); so a number of us are exploring beastly metaphors!

have not yet broached the different question of legitimacy. A practice of claim-making can be widespread, it can involve repeated
attempts at legitimation in the political sense, but it might still be
wholly illegitimate. The question of legitimacy is the ethical question about whether any given nationalism's claims are morally
justified and morally defensible. With that clarification, we can
move on to consider the sources Hearn draws on to expand his
discussion of legitimation. Hearn cites Beetham's analysis of the
legitimation process in modern states, in which voting and the
rule of law are combined with a justification of rules via shared
beliefs and norms (Beetham 1991, cited in Hearn 2006, p. 166).
He links this characterization of governance to Rogers Smith's
account of how claims of common identity are carried in 'stories '
of peoplehood' (ibid. ), and he concurs with Bobbio in identifying
civil society as a key space of delegitimation and relegitimation
(Bobbio 1989, p. 26, cited in Hearn 2006, p. 167). This allows
him to offer an account of how political parties, in competing
to win votes, make claims to be legitimate representatives of the
interests and values of the entire national population. In a key
passage, Hearn argues:

> In this way, far from transcending nationalism, normal demo-
> cratic party politics keeps national identity on a constant 'slow
> boil'. Nationalism is an essential resource for the maintenance
> of legitimacy in democratic regimes, which harness and contain
> its frequently dangerous energies, while also utilizing them. So
> just as Ernest Gellner argued that nationalism is the demand to
> be ruled by those co-ethnic with oneself, I am suggesting that it
> is also at work in the demand to be ruled by people who share
> one's moral values and beliefs ...
> Billig's account of banal nationalism is celebrated for its
> attention to the mundane ways in which national identity is
> reinforced by a myriad of small daily practices in which it is
> implicit. But his larger point should not be lost and is similar to
> my own. Nationalism is not just residual background noise in
> democratic regimes, it is a key legitimizing resource that can be
> activated and brought into the foreground, for example, during
> times of war and other social crises. (2006, p. 168)

Hearn's analysis is persuasive and helpful, though we need to emphasize again that it is not yet working with an ethical sense of legitimacy.[23] In fact, while I have argued for keeping open the possibility of a legitimate nationalism, it is crucial to note that no such claim can be made about nationalism or nationalisms in general. The ethical assessment of whether the claims of any given nationalism are legitimate will depend on the particular shape of those claims, on the 'stories of peoplehood' that are invoked, on the values and beliefs that are in play. The possibility of nationalism being kept on a slow boil, even the possibility of the heat being turned up in times of crisis are still only descriptions of how regimes seek legitimation and not necessarily objections to their doing that. There may need in any given case to be profound objections to how that is being done. Everything turns on how a particular nationalism is narrated and performed. Before we try to close in on that question, there are other nationalisms that need to be considered, because they also help to undercut and problematize any entirely negative account of nationalism.

## Anti-colonial nationalisms

Despite the appalling trauma of two world wars begun in Christian Europe within a generation,[24] both fuelled by violent and competitive nationalisms, the post-war vehicles for rebuilding new world orders were christened first the *League of Nations* and then the *United Nations*. At the close of the Second World War it became clear that the unravelling of the imperial and colonial projects of the European powers was going to lead to the creation of many new nation-states. The discrediting and delegitimizing of imperialism simultaneously and inevitably had the effect of reactivating and relegitimating nationalisms.

---

23 For example, Gellner's characterization above of the demand is ethically unacceptable.

24 The Baillie Commission of the Church of Scotland commented in 1942: 'We must take deeply to heart the fact that it is what is called Christendom that is now in flames, that the evils from which the world is suffering were generated in the heart of societies which passed as Christian and that the question today arises in men's minds whether the civilization of the West is any longer to be shaped and dominated by Christian influence' (CoS Report of the General Assembly, 1942, p. 544).

As Spencer and Wollman point out, 'the anti-colonial struggle gave nationalism a whole new lease of life in the twentieth century, reinvigorating its appeal across the political spectrum' (2005, p. 14).

Throughout the twentieth century, the Marxist Left had its own tortured series of debates about the relationship between liberation, revolution and nationalism, as it negotiated the gap between a vision of international socialism and its fitful realization in individual locations. The claims of Marx and Engels in *The Communist Manifesto* that 'the working classes have no fatherland' remained officially sacrosanct, but the historical contingencies of the revolutionary struggle led famously to bitter debates about the possibility of implementing 'socialism in one country'.[25]

European colonialism was predicated upon a set of claims to jurisdiction and territory whose illegitimacy was narrated and exposed by a succession of twentieth-century nationalist movements, animated by a range of different political philosophies and ideologies. The United Nations website notes that '[i]n a vast political reshaping of the world, more than 80 former colonies comprising some 750 million people have gained independence since the creation of the United Nations'.[26] The UN General Assembly adopted *The Declaration on the Granting of Independence to Colonial Countries and Peoples* on 14 December 1960.[27] In 2013, we are three years into the UN's Third International Decade for the Eradication of Colonialism[28] with an estimated 2 million people still waiting 'to be decolonized' in 16 Non-Self-Governing Territories (NSGTs) across the globe. The passing of the 1960 Declaration reflected the irresistible momentum of a process then already well underway and gathering speed almost by the hour. Its language and conceptuality exemplify all the problems we have already noted about 'nationalism talk', but they also resist the academic put-down in Anderson's reference

---

25 See van Ree, 2010 for a recent (revisionist ...) discussion of Lenin's position.

26 http://www.un.org/en/decolonization/index.shtml.

27 The Declaration was contained in Resolution 1514 (XV); English text available at http://untreaty.un.org/cod/avl/ha/dicc/dicc.html.

28 First Decade was 1990–2000, second was 2000–10.

to 'philosophical poverty and even incoherence', not just because of the 'political power' he grants to such talk, but because of the ethical force it carries in this context. The 1960 Declaration echoed the language of the 1945 UN Charter which had asserted 'the equal rights of ... nations large and small', the 'end' of living together in peace as 'good neighbours' and the organization's purpose 'to develop friendly relations among nations based on respect for the principle of equal rights and self-determination of peoples'.[29] It recognized 'the passionate yearning for freedom in all dependent peoples' who 'ardently desire the end of colonialism'. It identified colonialism as a denial of freedom, a threat to peace, an impediment to development, a condition of alien subjugation, domination and exploitation and associated it with practices of segregation and discrimination. The positive goals of the declaration were variously identified as independence, progress, freedom, stability, well-being, peaceful and friendly relations, equal rights, self-determination, international co-operation, world peace, free disposal of natural wealth and resources, the exercise of sovereignty, integrity of national territory, free determination of political status and free pursuit of economic, social and cultural development. It spoke too of 'the decisive role of such [dependent] peoples in the attainment of their independence' and the need to act 'in accordance with their freely expressed will and desire' (1960 Declaration). It is hard to conceive in this context of a credible condemnation of most of these goals or to easily dismiss their pursuit as philosophically incoherent. Tracing the growth of UN membership from its founding 50 to today's 193, it is impossible to ignore the ethics and politics of how its expansion is overwhelmingly bound up with the recognition of 80 former colonies as independent peoples.[30] We are involved in something like a vicious circle here. Those who discount the value and coherence of nationalism are often even more vehement in their denunciation of the poverty and incoherence of colonialism, but nationalism in relation to colonialism could almost be seen as akin to Derrida's

29 UN Charter 1945, quotations from Preamble and Chapter 1; http://www.un.org/en/documents/charter.

30 This figure rises if countries within the former USSR and under its direct influence are seen as also subject to a form of 'colonialism'.

*pharmakon* – it is both cause and cure, both poison and antidote. Colonialism is the projection of power by distorted, domineering nationalisms, but its power is typically challenged and brought to an end through the agency of mobilized, 'liberation nationalisms'.

The North American political theorist Bernard Yack picked up a witty and perceptive point by Gellner and extended its force when he wrote:

> The late Ernest Gellner once quipped that Marxists have been forced to come up with a 'wrong address' theory of history in order to explain the success of nationalism: history had a message for classes that somehow got delivered to nations by mistake. Liberal theorists are only beginning to face up to their similar disappointment. History, they believed, had a message for individuals, but that message somehow got delivered by mistake to nations. The age of liberal individualism has also been the age of nationalism; liberal practices have been realized, for the most part, within the framework of national communities. (Yack, 1999, p. 115)[31]

Gellner's and Yack's observations are telling because they satirize both liberal and Marxist dismay about nationalism. As a theologian it is tempting to add Yoder and Hauerwas to the list and associate them with a similar wrong address theory in relation to the Church. I will return to a discussion of church and catholicity in a later chapter, but for now I want to stay with the dilemmas posed by the *pharmakon* of nationalism and to explore the concepts of cosmopolitanism and internationalism, which might provide the pharmacological criteria for naming something as either poison or antidote.

## Thinking beyond nationalism

The discourse of cosmopolitanism emerged from Greco-Roman classical and Judeo-Christian sources (cf. C. Taylor, 2007, p. 192) and was both held and qualified in particular ways within

---

31 I owe this reference to Jonathan Hearn (2006, p. 91).

medieval Christianity before its flow was first diverted into the various channels of the European Enlightenment and then further canalized by groups within the European Left.[32] In the post-colonial era, new kinds of critical pressure have been applied to dominant strands of this discourse, questioning both its Euro-centric character and its 'subaltern' credentials. From its origins, it can be seen to have existed in a complex and interdependent relationship with more local and 'national' affiliations, and in the post-Enlightenment and postcolonial eras its relationship with nationalism remains in play.

The Greek Cynic Diogenes' famous claim to be a *kosmopolitēs*[33] was developed by a series of Greek and Roman Stoic thinkers.[34] In an important discussion of the influence of Stoic cosmopolitanism on Kant, Martha Nussbaum notes:

> Even in its Roman incarnations, this proposal is not, funda-mentally, a proposal for a world state. The point is more radical still: that we should give our first moral allegiance to no mere form of government, no temporal power. We should give it, instead, to the moral community made up by the humanity of all human beings. One should always behave so as to treat with equal respect the dignity of reason and moral choice in each and every human being. And, as Marcus holds, this will gen-erate both moral and legal obligations ... No theme is deeper in Stoicism than the damage done by faction and intense local loyalties to our political lives. (1997, p. 8)

However, Nussbaum also observes how Stoic thinkers stress 'that to be a world citizen one does not need to give up local identifica-tions and affiliations, which can frequently be a great source of richness in life'. Nussbaum cites Hierocles' and Cicero's image of

---

32 In a frankly astonishing presentation in Glasgow in 2012, David Inglis spoke of the canon of cosmopolitanism in contemporary sociology/critical theory as con-taining nothing much between the Stoics and Kant. Cf. Inglis and Delanty (eds), 2011.

33 Martha Nussbaum comments that Diogenes (b. 412 BCE) seems not to have had a well-developed political sense of what he meant by this term; see 1997, p. 4, n. 11.

34 Zeno Cicero (b. 106 BCE), Seneca (b. 4 BCE) and Marcus Aurelius (b. 121 CE).

human life as lived within concentric circles, beginning from the self and expanding outwards to the whole of humanity. Within this vision of human being, our task as citizens of the world will be 'to draw the circles somehow toward the center', to see the other as like ourselves. In that way, to use Cicero's phrase, borrowed from Terence: *'Homo sum: humani nihil a me alienum puto'* ('I am a human being; I think nothing human alien to me') (p. 9).

This way of thinking insists on the priority of the universal, while allowing local duties, allegiances and responsibilities their proper place. Nussbaum argues that it is this 'deep core' of ethical commitments to the other within Stoic cosmopolitanism that is appropriated by Immanuel Kant as a 'regulative ideal' and moral motivation for virtuous social and political life: 'the idea of a kingdom of free rational beings equal in humanity, each of them to be treated as an end no matter where in the world he or she dwells' (p. 12). She suggests that as for Cicero and Marcus, so for Kant the cosmopolis acts as a 'virtual polity' that makes implicit claims upon us, regardless of whether there is an actual political organization corresponding to it (p. 12).[35] It does this in part by its role in shaping 'passional enlightenment', creating the enlightened passions or well-ordered loves that are capable of including the other, the alien and the enemy within a common vision of embodiment and historical destiny (p. 20). For Nussbaum, this Stoic vision of moral education is directly relevant to contemporary drives that would educate children out of racist, sexist and classist attitudes and behaviours into politically correct (she stands by this term) and liberal mores. Its role as a regulative ideal should also be reflected in our law codes and institutions (p. 24).

Nussbaum's veneration of the classical sources has been vigorously challenged by, among others, Sheldon Pollock. Pollock, in a

---

35 Nussbaum's article contains an interesting struggle against the alliance between providence and cosmopolitanism, which she concedes is a key feature of both Stoic thinking and Kant's position. She resolves this through what is to my mind a strained appeal to moral voluntarism, suggesting that in a 'disorderly and unfriendly' universe, to elect (my word) a universal and moral community is a particularly noble and impressive response. She struggles too with Kant's anthropology and the debt it owes to 'Augustinian Christianity' in its portrayal of competing states driven by warring passions.

postcolonial reading of Roman 'practices of culture and power', reads Stoic admiration for the 'cosmopolitan' as the ideology of those who 'had been able to transform the kosmos into their polis' and who responded brutally and genocidally to those unwilling to be assimilated in some acceptable way (Pollock in Breckenridge et al. (eds), 2002, p. 25). Pollock's essay, however, struggles to articulate a way beyond the 'bad, bitter and sad' choices offered by contemporary cosmopolitanisms and vernacularisms.[36] Tom Nairn (1993) had already walked a similar line on cosmopolitanism, but had also offered up a remarkable elegy and epitaph for an older vision of proletarian 'internationalism', which was finally shown to have been lost by the events of 1989. In its place, Nairn argued, was appearing a homogenizing 'internationality', as the forces of capitalism dissolved traditions and effaced frontiers that stood in the way of the business strategies of multinational corporations (1993, p. 157). For Nairn, the only way back to a meaningful 'internationalism' would now have to be by way of 'nationalism'.[37] A Nairn *bon mot*: instead of the Macedonians resigning themselves to progress, progress will now have to resign itself to being Macedonian (p. 158). In these changed times, 'socialists will have to decide what type of capitalists they will become, and internationalists will have to decide what sort of nationalists they will become' (p. 164). Nairn still relished the analytic potential of 'historical materialism', but saw that the old-style projects of political Marxism were dead. Resistance to exploitative and imperialistic capitalism would, he suggested, have to be rebuilt and that would have to happen by the 'anarchic' potential of democratic nationalisms resisting *imperium*. In this way internationalism could be reset as a moderating and mediating inter-national force within the global system, rather than a profound transnational class-borne solidarity (p. 167).

36 See Bruce Robbins' comments on Pollock's essay in his insightful review in *The Journal of Asian Studies* 62:1 (2003), pp. 192–4.
37 He gives an ironic embrace to Lenin's conceptualization of nationalism as 'medieval particularism' (ibid.).

## The nature of the beast?

Nairn's ironic, post-cosmopolitan, post-internationalist 'national-ism' displays his determination, in defiance of Eric Hobsbawm's warnings, to paint nationalism red (Bell and Miller (eds), 2004, p. 17); although, he also wants to stripe it with some anarchist black. Despite Ronald Turnbull's criticism of his 'unbelieving', utilitarian nationalism (Chapter 2 in Bell and Miller (eds), 2004), Nairn's vintage revisionism belongs within a range of contemporary rethinkings of nationalism. In the post-1989 world, no attempts to transcend nationalism escape suspicion or critique. Marxist internationalism, the internationality of multinational capitalism and Nussbaum's liberal cosmopolitanism are all candidates to be indicted for their failures to respect and protect difference.

If there are chronic problems with rethinking the 'national' from above, Robert Young suggests that some postcolonial theorists are adopting a contrasting strategy:

> [P]ostcolonial intellectuals, particularly from India, have tried to think of the nation differently, to propose alternative accounts of the nation which begin not with an idealized version of how it might be, but with how it is, highlighting the ways in which the nation can work as a force of oppression. This means thinking the postcolonial, or the postimperial, nation in terms of its fragments, those parts and those peoples who do not easily belong to it, who exist at the margins and peripheries of society. They are the means through which the nation relates to itself. (Young, 2003, p. 63)

A final contrast can be drawn between this turn to the 'fragmentary' and the current prominence of Alain Badiou's and Slavoj Žižek's work.[38] Badiou and Žižek have both tried to chart a way forward for the Left that can address the 'relativism' of

---

38 Ken Jackson's article on 'The Great Temptation of "Religion": Why Badiou has been so important to Žižek' (*International Journal of Zizek Studies* 1:2, 2007) offers one of the more accessible introductions to this notoriously complex set of academic conversations.

deconstructive strategies and the infinite regressions of cultural fragmentation and particularism. Both of them have advocated a secular appropriation of New Testament Pauline thought. In the past decade, Paul's capacity to think beyond old dualities – Jew/Greek, male/female, slave/free – to the universal vision of a new single, 'spiritual' humanity has been resurrected. Suddenly, and to the surprise of most New Testament scholars, Paul has appeared at the centre of radical, critical debate.

## Work in progress

It might be too optimistic to claim that the rethinking of nationalism and cosmopolitanism remains work in progress; better perhaps to think of it as work in disarray. With the rhetoric of postmodernism growing quieter by the day, postcolonial theorists have reinjected more ethical–political energy into the debates, but caught between the hapless Left and the shameless Right, 'nations and nationalism' remain vexing topics for theorists and theologians alike. Some of that vexation, for the internationalist and cosmopolitan aspirations of the Left and for the catholic confessions of Christian theology, includes attempts such as this, to articulate an ethical, liberal, civic and democratic nationalism. In the following chapters, I try to add some of my own vexatious reasoning to the mix.

# 2

# Ecumenical Political Theology

In his theological study of traditions of economic thinking, Stephen Long mentions a comment of R. H. Tawney which had a lasting influence on Tawney's student, Ronald Preston. Tawney had suggested that the social teachings of the Church had ceased to count because the Church had ceased to think (quoted in Long, 2000, p. 29). Long's own work has been part of a reversal of that, although theological work on economics still lags behind other areas of political theology. Today the Church is, or the churches are, busy thinking again about the nature of politics, society and the state. There are new theological conversations underway about politics and the political that hold great promise for the future. That said, there are two key challenges still to be met. First, the conversations developing within particular theological and ecclesial traditions need to find better ways of attending to one another's insights and integrating them within an 'ecumenical' political theology. Second, we need more examples in which we develop a synthesis of practical theology and political theology, pushing the conversations to engage with concrete political issues and public policy challenges. This book is a modest attempt at trying out both of those things.

Some of the issues central to the first challenge were explored in Jeffrey Stout's important study, *Democracy and Tradition* (2004), where he attempted a pragmatic defence of democracy as itself a vital tradition in response to what he named as liberal overdefence of it by Rawls and traditionalist disdain for it from Hauerwas, Milbank and MacIntyre. My concerns here are different. Attending to the three main ecclesial traditions of Western Christianity: Roman Catholicism, the Reformed Churches and the Anabaptist

Churches, I want to sketch the outlines of an appreciative ecumenical inquiry into their strengths and charisms for political theology and to suggest how each of them contributes something distinctive to the Christian idea of a society.[1]

## Catholic social teaching

The first tradition is that of (Roman) Catholic social teaching. In Mark 12, we are told that Jesus sat down opposite the treasury and watched. Jesus witnesses the crowd putting money into the temple treasury and comments to his disciples on the significance of their gifts, in particular 'the two small copper coins' given by a poor widow:

> 'Truly I tell you, this poor widow has put in more than all those who are contributing to the treasury. For all of them have contributed out of their abundance; but she out of her poverty has put in everything she had, all she had to live on.' (Mark 12.43–44; cf. Luke 21.1–4)

'Jesus sat down opposite the treasury and watched' (12.41). As readers we are drawn into this deliberate act of watching; we are asked by Mark to watch with Jesus. As we look over his shoulder, we see how this Jesus watches where money comes from and goes to. He witnesses the coins ring in the collection box, and as he does so he not only figures the totals, but also computes the percentages. These two calculations require two different knowledges to be brought together. One is the thin knowledge of how much is given, which can be reckoned by anyone able to count and applauded by anyone concerned to maximize income. The other is the 'thicker' reckoning of how much can be afforded, which requires a political knowledge of who has what, a calculus of relative wealth and poverty and an ability to identify the have-*lots* and have-*nots*. In case we fail to discern the political edge of this story, a glance back to the preceding verse leaves little room for doubt in its graphic description of those who 'devour

---

1 Its ecumenical reach is, however, limited to Western traditions and biased towards the global North.

widows' houses' (Mark 12.40). The Jesus of Mark 12 is a Jesus who, in the words of Marvin Gaye (no relation), knows 'what's goin' on'; who knows, as they used to say where I lived and ministered in Hackney, 'how people stay'. To compare the treasury of the Jerusalem temple with HM Treasury or the US Treasury is mostly just a play on words, but the image of Jesus' attentiveness is striking. Our attention is directed to the Jesus who watches 'the treasury', and to the awareness he brings with him about 'how people stay', which allows him to interpret what he sees. Jesus' actions here offer an important model of informed attentiveness for Christian theologians and disciples, prompting us to question which 'treasuries' we should be sitting down in front of.

In his classic and prophetic 1944 study, *The Great Transformation*, Karl Polanyi wrote of the dangers inherent in 'the running of society as an adjunct to the market'. This, he said, produced a tragic inversion in which '[i]nstead of economy being embedded in social relations, social relations are embedded in the economic system' (Polanyi, 2001, p. 60). Deploying the same metaphor in a theological vein, some 50 years later Stephen Long wrote in *Divine Economy*:

> Once the narrative phenomenon of embedding is lost, traditional moral rules about economics either become unintelligible or are transmuted to serve new interests. This is precisely what has occurred within the Christian tradition: rules such as the just wage, the prohibition of usury and specific forms of the admonition not to steal are no longer viable for us. All we have are the fragments of these rules, but we lack the narrative context within which they could be intelligible. For these rules to make sense, we must recover the theological narrative out of which they arise. (Long, 2000, p. 231)

Reflecting on the post-2008 economic crisis, in the light of Mark 12, we could say that 'Bankers need tellers'.[2] In their book

---

2 Someone who works in a bank was traditionally called a 'teller'; the Old English word 'tell' has to do with order, with counting, with giving an orderly account, and from those beginnings it moved to being a word associated with stories, with narratives.

*Calculated Futures*, Methodist theologian D. Stephen Long and Jewish economist Nancy Fox express this well:

> Theology and social analysis are always already linked. When we are doing theology we are already doing political and economic analysis. When economists are doing economics they are also doing theology. The question is which theology is being done, not if it is being done. Everything is theological.
>
> To use God for political or economic ends is to take God's name in vain. That everything is theological then means something different from this; it means that everything which is creature, by virtue of being creature, bears some sign, some mark, some relation to the Creator and theologians must narrate all those creatures within the divine economy. (Long and Fox, 2007, pp. 6–7; see also Long, 2000)

Our economic activity, our market activity, our financial dealings – these are all profoundly theological. They do not have self-evident, free-standing, scientific, technical meanings which simply speak for themselves. They are only given meaning when they have tellers; they need to be placed within a bigger story of what and who they are for. The move is from tellers to *telos*. Within my own denomination, the Church of Scotland, we were once very used to asking this kind of question: Q: What is man's chief end? A: To glorify God and enjoy Him forever (Westminster Shorter Catechism). It is a question that is reworked in the title of a book by the brilliant American agriculturalist, novelist, poet and philosopher Wendell Berry, *What are people for?* (1991). Although rendered by Berry with lovely compressed bluntness, it is a classic question that comes to us from Aristotle, Augustine and Aquinas and one that is central to the evolution of Catholic social teaching. At the heart of Catholic social teaching lie the twin concepts of human dignity and the common good, concepts of the 'me in we' and the 'we in me' thickened and developed in 17 encyclicals since 1891. Framed within the grand narrative of creation and redemption and confessing grace's renaturing of denatured humanity, Catholic social teaching deploys a comprehensive and coherent vision of integral human development, parsed in terms of solidarity, subsidiarity and sustainability. My point as a Reformed theologian in honouring this body of teaching is not to suggest that it stands alone, is infallibly correct or that it has not been paralleled and supplemented at many points by various strands of Protestant theology. It is to recognize it both as a profoundly important resource for all the churches, and to acknowledge that despite characterizations of it as 'our best kept secret' (DeBerri et al. (eds), 2003) it has a cultural currency within contemporary public policy debates in many countries, which far outweighs any other example of Christian social teaching. Marked rhetorically by a high sense of its own authority, the weight of tradition gives Catholic social teaching a low centre of gravity. The English writer Paul Vallely, writing of the aimless drift of the European Left post 1989, proposed Catholic social teaching as an alternative position, which (alone?) possessed the 'comprehensiveness' necessary to fund a critique of capitalism (1998, p. 2).[3] Staying with economic themes, a key example is the 2009 encyclical *Caritas in Veritate*, which is unsurpassed in contemporary theology as a powerful and stable performance of the narrative embedding of the economic within the social, and of the social within the theological. A telling and encompassing vision of the divine economy. I am familiar at first hand with one example of ecumenical appreciation and appropriation of this, in the work of the Church of Scotland's Commission on the Purposes of Economic Activity, established in the aftermath of the international financial crisis of 2008.[4] In its focus on the *ends* of economic activity, the Church of Scotland's 2012 Commission showed its debt to this long-term sight line of Thomistic theology. It was given a nice articulation during the Commission hearings by the theologian Chris Wigglesworth, when he said 'The economy is for God, which means it is also for my neighbour and it is for my neighbour, which means it is also for God.' The charism of Catholic social teaching is not one it possesses exclusively or displays invariably, but is one it

---

3 In the same volume, another English Roman Catholic commentator, Clifford Longley, praised the richness and 'coherence' of Catholic social teaching (Vallely (ed.), 1998, p. 98).

4 The Commission, chaired by Professor Charles Munn, met between 2010 and 2012 and submitted its report to the General Assembly in 2012.

embodies consistently in ways that constitute a resource for the whole Church catholic and reformed. If the strength of Catholic social teaching lies in its capacity for displaying key principles within a grand narrative, it has been suggested, again in relation to the post-2008 financial crisis, that its weaknesses may lie in the breadth and openness of the orientation it gives and its reluctance to wrestle with more detailed social policy implications.[5]

## Reforming discipline

Turning to the second example, I suggest that the particular charism of the Reformed tradition is to be found in its understandings of stewardship, vocation and 'discipline'. In my own tradition of Scottish Presbyterianism, the word 'discipline' has deep resonances. The manifestos of the first and second generations of the Reformation in Scotland were known as the First and Second Books of Discipline, with John Knox and Andrew Melville as their lead authors. It is this sense of discipline that is powerfully expounded by Charles Taylor in the second chapter of *A Secular Age*, in which he speaks of the rise of the disciplinary society. Taylor tells a story in which the influences of nominalism, neo-Stoicism and Calvinism are brought together in a moment of cultural bravura, fuelling an extraordinary self-confidence about the capacity to remodel society (2007, p. 121). In Taylor's account, this is held together with a key theme from his earlier work in *Sources of the Self*, that the Reformation dramatically revised understandings of vocation away from the specialized callings of the religious orders towards what he calls 'the affirmation of ordinary life' (1989, p. 209). This account of Reformed social vision is not without its own internal tensions. Calvinist theology has been conspicuously aware of both total depravity[6] and human finitude, conscious therefore that human beings will often make wrong, selfish and anti-social choices. Given this, it is

---

5 See Linda Woodhead's comments in a guest blog post for *The Tablet* in November 2012, http://www.thetablet.co.uk/blogs/401/17.

6 This much misunderstood doctrine is not a form of theological miserabilism which holds that everything in life is as bad as it could possibly be, but a sober recognition that all areas of human life are affected by human sinfulness.

notable that Taylor recognized this tradition as having generated such zeal and confidence about the project of reforming European societies in the early modern period. In Scotland this vision first animated and then was challenged by the reforming visions of the eighteenth-century Scottish Enlightenment and reasserted itself in the early nineteenth century in Thomas Chalmers' vision of the godly commonwealth. Its understanding of stewardship was destabilized in Adam Smith's account of economic life and debased in the context of British imperial expansion, which saw large numbers of Scots/Calvinists/Presbyterians on the make.[7] Such examples of basic Calvinist beliefs biting back illustrate the way in which a Reformed social vision takes shape in the face of demanding tensions between aspiration and limitation. The literature of every Calvinist country will, like that of Scotland, abound in testimonies to the personal hypocrisies and indisciplines of those who would reform and discipline others. Without gainsaying these, such counter testimony does not mean there were no positive social effects of Calvinism in these countries.[8] In the area of economic life, a confidence about social discipline over the Scottish financial sector still had residual currency and cultural visibility into the twenty-first century. It finally died in 2009, with the effective bankruptcy of both the Bank of Scotland and the Royal Bank of Scotland. If the sixteenth- and seventeenth-century versions of this disciplinary dream suffered from Calvinist hubris, the late twentieth- and early twenty-first-century retreat from regulation[9] evidenced a disciplinary deficit. The acids of right-wing scorn and the canker of left-wing ineptitude combined to eat away at public confidence in the need for effective regulation and the capacity of the state to provide this. Today, as Western economies struggle to re-regulate and re-stimulate their economies, the need to rediscover the Reformed charism of discipline is pressing once again. In keeping with a Reformed alertness to both total depravity and human finitude, a new attention to regulation must be shaped by a double awareness of the ethical deficits that create the

---

7 For the ugliest side of this, see Whyte, 2006.

8 See p. oo below for Beveridge and Turnbull's critique of anti-Calvinist inferiorism in Scottish culture.

9 Begun in the Thatcher/Reagan years and continued in the Blair/Brown years.

need for regulation and the hermeneutical deficits that lead to bad regulation. Recalling Taylor's naming of Reformed vocation as 'the affirmation of ordinary life' we need to reaffirm the strategic spiritual vocation of the accountant, the regulator, the financial controller. Bringing together this and the previous tradition, we could say that bankers need 'tellers', but they (and we) also need auditors, those authorized to listen attentively to accounts of our corporate behaviour. The good society needs both a narrative framing that embeds the market within a vision of social relations and a disciplinary vigilance that responds to the ever-present failures of understanding and virtue.

## Radical witness

My final ecclesial example comes from the traditions of the radical reformation, for a long time neglected and marginalized in mainstream Protestant ethics, but today an extremely influential strand, taken seriously across the ecumenical spectrum.[10] We could speak of a number of charisms associated with this tradition, but the one I have in mind here is the characteristic Anabaptist stress on the witness of distinctive and exemplary corporate practice.[11] Here the Reformed sense of the need to restrain evil across society as a whole is balanced by a new stress on the capacity of the Christian community to generate virtuous examples. The drive on the part of Catholic social teaching and Reformed theology to discipline the whole of society is eschewed in favour of an ecclesial ethic, which first of all calls the Church to be the Church.[12] Instead of emphasizing discipline as a whole

---

10 Largely due to the prominence of John Howard Yoder's work and helped by Stanley Hauerwas' championing of it and James McLendon's work over the past three decades.

11 Though cf. *Caritas in Veritate* 37: 'Space also needs to be created within the market for economic activity carried out by subjects who freely choose to act according to principles other than those of pure profit, without sacrificing the production of economic value in the process. The many economic entities that draw their origin from religious and lay initiatives demonstrate that this is concretely possible.'

12 The phrase 'let the church be the church' was first coined by J. H. Oldham in the preparatory papers for the 1937 Oxford Conference on Church, State and Society; see Visser 't Hooft and Oldham, 1937.

society goal, the stress is placed on the self-discipline of groups of Christians. In economic terms this can enable them to generate mutual and co-operative models that restrain the profit motive, offset the drive for personal enrichment and reduce the degree of inequality resulting from how an enterprise operates. In his mini-classic, *Body Politics*, John Howard Yoder argued for a pattern for human sociality in which the Church prefigures the world:

> [T]he pattern we shall discover is that the will of God for human socialness [sic] as a whole is prefigured by the shape to which the Body of Christ is called. Church and world are not two compartments under separate legislation or two institutions with contradictory assignments, but two levels of pertinence of the same Lordship. The people of God is called to be today what the world is called to be ultimately. (Yoder, 1992, p. ix )[13]

One of the five key practices Yoder explores in the book is that of 'disciples breaking bread together'. Having highlighted the significance of sharing bread in the Eucharist as an economic act (p. 20), he speaks of a 'mediation or bridging over' from ecclesial practices to social structures:

> This kind of 'mediation' is not a mental or verbal operation of translation or conceptual bridging, but rather the concrete historical presence, among their neighbours, of believers who for Jesus sake do ordinary social things differently. (p. 74)

The influence of this tradition has been illustrated and extended in the work of Texan Methodist/Anglican theologian Stanley Hauerwas, most famously in his book *The Peaceable Kingdom*, where he argues that 'the nature and form of the church is the center of any attempt to develop Christian ethics' (2003, p. 95), and that 'the church does not have a social ethic; the church is a social ethic' (p. 99).[14] Hauerwas' championing of the work of

---

13 This is one of a number of places where Yoder's debt to Karl Barth shows through – 'the church is the world already turning to God'.

14 Duncan Forrester calls this 'one of Stanley Hauerwas' most suggestive and problematic epigrams' – 'it is a very attractive notion, suggesting that Christian

John Howard Yoder was a key trigger for James Gustafson's (in)famous paper on 'The Sectarian Temptation'. This much cited article, which appeared in 1985, argued that Hauerwas was engaged in a retreat from responsible Christian concern for society into an idealized ecclesial location, where purity came at the expense of irrelevance.[15] A further major critique of Hauerwas and Yoder was launched by Jeffrey Stout in *Democracy and Tradition* (2004), where Stout registers his concern at the growing influence of their work within North American theology. Despite these significant theological disagreements and also because of them, interest in and appreciation of Anabaptist theology continues to grow across many Christian traditions. In a world where Christianity is so often co-opted or compromised, the charism of difference has a particular attraction. To live it out authentically is not a sectarian device to keep your hands clean, but a different and often costly way of getting your hands dirty. Those of us from traditions that have often succumbed to the Constantinian temptation or the Erastian temptation have things to learn from those who have not.

## Ecumenical social theory

So far I have traced the outline of what we might call an 'ecumenical' vision of the good society. I have suggested the traditions of Catholic social teaching offer a narrative account of the ends and goals of society, while Reformed political theology furnishes a broad understanding of vocation and stewardship and a dynamic stress on enacting discipline and regulation. Anabaptist

---

ethics must be embodied in the life of a community, that ethics is not a possession of the Church but the gift to the Church which constitutes it as Church' (in Nation and Wells (eds), 2000, pp. 195 and 205).

15 The honour of having provoked or at least focused this best known and most widely repeated criticism of Hauerwas belongs to a Scottish theologian, Duncan Forrester, whose appreciative remarks about Hauerwas at a meeting of the Society for the Study of Christian Ethics, made to the North American theologian James Gustafson (who had been Hauerwas' doctoral advisor at Yale), led Gustafson in 1985 to write his highly critical paper, 'The Sectarian Temptation: Reflections on Theology, the Church and the University'. See Gustafson, 1985, p. 83.

traditions stress the importance of witness and a communitarian drive to generate virtuous examples that can act as models for a good society. Within the landscape of contemporary theology, these traditions are keenly aware of one another and are increasingly influencing and inflecting one another. My aim here is to support and encourage those ecumenical synergies, recognizing that while there are still many critical debates to be had, each of these traditions brings something essential to the table. In particular, reflecting on my own location, as someone whose thinking has been enriched by my encounters with Catholic social teaching and Anabaptist theology, I want to re-commend the contribution of the Reformed tradition, which is I think less valued and valorized in contemporary political theology than the others. My thinking about the importance of a Reformed stress on discipline was stirred by reflection on the post-2008 economic crisis in which failures of regulation relating to banks and money markets were a key factor. Since then and with great credit to the work of Christian Aid in the United Kingdom, campaigning on issues of international tax avoidance, transfer pricing and tax havens has helped to give these issues a new political visibility. Both of these are areas that call out for Reformed accents on stewardship, on the vocation of 'ordinary' Christians working in these sectors and on the promotion of social discipline via the proper enforcement of tax legislation and regulation of the financial sector. The Fall 2013 issue of North American *Comment* magazine was devoted to the theme 'We Believe in Institutions' and featured an editorial with that title by James K. A. Smith.[16] Smith's instincts on this (as in much else) are I think right. Rising generations have good reasons to be cynical about many of the institutions they observe and interact with, but not to believe there are non-institutional ways to achieve the changes they want to see. Radical social change will need institutions to bring it about. An ecumenical political theology of institutions in the spirit of this chapter will ask what they are for, will be both ambitious for and cautious about what they can achieve and will work to create church institutions that are models of virtuous institutional life. As the

---

16 http://www.cardus.ca/comment/print_issues/4026/.

Christian commentator and activist Jim Wallis once wrote of and to the Church, in words I first read in my teens more than 30 years ago, which have stayed with me and come back to me often, 'We have nothing more to share with the world than what we are sharing with each other' (1981, p. 130).

# 3

# Something Sweet
# The Christian Idea of a Society

Early in the project and with some reluctance, I realized this book would need to say something about the nature of 'sweetness'. My reluctance was not because this was an unwelcome subject, but because it is a daunting subject. It goes to the heart of what a political theology defines as a good society. In Chapters 4–7 I offer a qualified defence of nationalism, both in general terms and in the particular case of contemporary Scotland. A key part of that defence will involve the claim that nationalism can be the friend and not the enemy of the good society.

This chapter can only offer a small contribution to the vast, ongoing work of elaborating a Christian social theory or social vision. However, it seems necessary to the argument of this book that some account is given of what might count as honey, before we scrape around for it inside particular lions. It also matters to my own project as a practical theologian, that the account I give is one that is communicable and explicable, that will preach, that can be used within catechism and play a part in the formation of young people.

In a 1939 essay, T. S. Eliot famously explored *The Idea of a Christian Society*. My reshuffling of his title does not mean I am abandoning all of his concerns, but it does reflect a change of emphasis within political theology. My title is more ambivalent about Christendom and its legacy and more conscious of the need to shape pluralist spaces, where people of different faiths and no faith can live side by side. When our time is compared to Eliot's, it seems clear that Christians today must assume less, dictate less, presume less. But Eliot, complex figure though he was, was already more aware of the challenges of secularization than we might imagine. Like Tawney, he too wanted the Church to think, and in fact did himself think alongside Tawney as part of a working group of the Conference on Church, Community and State held at Oxford in 1937. Granted the great weakness that they were all white Western males, was there ever a more fascinating or impressive group of Christian intellectuals assembled to work on anything as those in the section of that conference considering questions of 'Economic Order': R. H. Tawney, V. A. Demant, John MacMurray, T. S. Eliot, John Baillie, Paul Tillich and Reinhold Niebuhr (Visser 't Hooft and Oldham (eds), 1937). Eliot's involvement there and in 'The Moot' (a wartime discussion forum organized by the remarkable Christian thinker and ecumenical networker J. H. Oldham) is a testimony to the seriousness he attached to the task of thinking Christianly about every area of society. His reputation as a conservative and an elitist does not do justice to the depth of his commitment, including his explicit sense of economic commitment, to the well-being of every group within society (see Eliot, 1939; Kojecky, 1971; Clements, 1999). Eliot and the 'Oldham groups' he was part of were impressive not only in terms of the intellect and learning they brought to their subjects, which were engaged with theoretical, philosophical and theological depth and rigour, but also in their determination to focus on concrete policy questions and their interest in working across a wide range of policy areas (Clements, 1999, pp. 315ff.).[1]

A consciousness of presuming less on the creation of a 'Christian society' should not excuse a less serious engagement with a Christian idea of society. Within the UK, the theological landmarks of John Milbank's *Theology and Social Theory* (1990) and Oliver O'Donovan's *The Desire of Nations* (1996) were examples of theological thinking confident about its own take on fundamental sociological questions regarding the nature of a(ny) society. Luke Bretherton's *Christianity and Contemporary Politics* (2010) engages appreciatively and critically with their work, but also displays a new appetite for engaging with and reflecting on more concrete practices within contemporary politics, such as

---

1 See also Moot papers in the John Baillie Archives, Edinburgh University Library.

community organizing, fair trade and treatment of refugees and asylum seekers. In holding together engagement with the tradition of political theology and attention to policy, his work offers an important model for others.

## Biblical poetics and politics

In the opening pages of *Theopolitical Imagination*, William Cavanaugh writes:

> Politics is a practice of the imagination ... and engages the imagination just as art does ... The political imagination is simply the condition of possibility for the organization of bodies in a society ... To identify politics and religion as acts of the imagination is to recognize their historical contingency and thus give hope that things do not necessarily have to be the way they are. (2002, pp. 1–2)[2]

In the poetics of the second creation account in Genesis, when Adam awakes to see Eve, his response 'This at last is bone of my bones and flesh of my flesh' (Gen. 2.23) is a cry of recognition which leads to the union in which woman and man become 'one flesh' (Gen. 2.24). East of Eden, one flesh takes on the new shapes of Cain and Abel and human beings have to learn the language of mother, father, brother, sister. In its fifth chapter, the book of beginnings begins its first mythic genealogy – from Adam to Noah, Eden to Flood. In this scriptural frame, the act of self-recognition is impossible without narrative and the first narrative is a narrative of kinship – out of many stories of begetting, one story of 'us' is born and grows. The power of Old Testament narratives, in particular the primal sagas of Genesis 1—11, to shape a theopolitical imaginary is something that can be traced through 1,500 years of theology, art and literature, from Augustine's *City of God* onwards. I will explore this in more detail in relation to nations

---

2 That theme of imagination had been given powerful articulations as 'hopeful' and 'prophetic' from within biblical studies in the 1970s and 1980s, in Walter Brueggemann's work on the theme of exile (1978, 1985).

and nationalism in the next chapter. Here I want to approach the project of a Christian social imaginary from a different angle.

Christian theology, in its social and political imagination, is profoundly shaped by the Hebrew Bible, the Old or First Testament of its Christian Scriptures. The Genesis of all things, which produces the genesis of human society, begins with the narrative of humans being created in the *imago Dei*, male and female. The primal *us* has sexual difference and complementarity[3] inscribed within it here, as well as the possibility of touch, connection, communication, hospitality, service, companionship, sex, procreation, co-operation, co-working, gift. These things are made possible by the presence of the other. YHWH looks on all that is made and says it is good. To be male and female is good, to be embodied and 'other' is good, to be fruitful and multiply those personal, sexual, differentiated bodies into families and societies is good. Genesis offers to the Jewish and Christian imaginations the narrative basis for a rich celebration of sociality, which is rooted and grounded in a single humanity, a single human race, all of whom are made in the divine image.

It offers also the commission, which is the original 'mission' of humanity, to 'be fruitful and multiply, replenish the earth and subdue it and have dominion' in the King James language to which Lynn White famously linked a mindset which was leading to ecological crisis (1967). In the KJV translation of these verses a certain (male oriented) buccaneering, questing, explorer quality adheres to this talk of subduing the (whole) earth and exercising dominion, but the accompanying canonical narrative of Genesis 2 offsets this, in its portrayal of the domestic, horticultural, local and familial scale of the commission. Growing in Eden are trees 'pleasant to the sight' as well as 'good for food' – this garden is a place for walking as well as working (Gen. 3.8).

---

3 This term is now caught up in evangelical culture wars, especially in the USA. Scot McKnight offered a witty and rueful account on his blog in July 2013 of how its meaning was appropriated by the religious Right, so that those of us who used to be complementarian as opposed to hierarchical (because it meant egalitarian) are now egalitarians, because the meaning of the term has shifted. I am an egalitarian, but still believe this word captures something significant about human identity, so refuse to give it up to the Right. See http://www.patheos.com/blogs/jesuscreed /2013/07/01/who-says-whats-an-egalitarian/.

The nascent good society of Genesis 2 lasts no longer than Genesis 3, at the end of which humanity is driven out of Eden, the return barred by the angels with the flaming, turning sword.[4] East of Eden, home must be improvised in new ways, subject to new dynamics of distortion and new conditions of vulnerability. Even so, in the continuing narrative God is still close at hand, seeing, speaking, calling, blessing, judging. The later Genesis narratives trace the call of Abraham, the promise of the Land and the journey into Egypt. The tribal society whose story has been unfolding along with that of the God of Abraham/Sarah, Isaac/Rebekah and Jacob/Rachel/Leah, having found a providential refuge within a larger and more powerful society, finds itself at the beginning of the book of Exodus at the mercy of a new king 'who did not know Joseph' (Exod. 1.8). In the face of imperial oppression and genocide, the Exodus texts bear witness to a God who says 'I have observed ... I have heard ... I know their suffering ... I have come down to deliver ...' (Exod. 3.7–8). The political power and significance of the book of Exodus is a recurring motif in the Hebrew Bible. The liberating God is revealed to also be the law-giving God, as a not always grateful Israel struggles to love the gift of law it has been given by YHWH. Both the removal of oppression and the gift of law are presented as crucial to the functioning of a good society. The promise of land, the experience of freedom and the exercise of law combine in a potent social-political imaginary for the exodus nation 'let go' that they may worship God.

## Fullness of life

Near the beginning of *A Secular Age*, the philosopher Charles Taylor, a Canadian and liberal Catholic, observes:

> Every person and every society lives with or by some conception(s) of what human flourishing is: What constitutes a fulfilled life? What makes life really worth living? What would we most admire people for? (2007, p. 16)

---

4 As Ellul says, 'these cherubim have very little to do with Raphael's pink, chubby little cherubs. These cherubim are terrible fighters' (1970, p. 4).

Taylor summarizes this via what I presume is an intentional echo of John 10.10, in his use of the term 'fullness'. The Christian idea of a society is framed eschatologically, is in Cavanaugh's terms imagined, at its genesis and in its consummation, by means of visions of fullness and blessing, of peace, joy and love. This is a point so well known and so long made, so deeply inscribed into the art and literature of Western culture that it functions effortlessly to generate common clichés and to underwrite popular jokes. Within the wider culture, the garden to the city, Genesis to Revelation motifs occupy an ambiguous status, capable of being mobilized within a range of different rhetorics, from the satirical to the sublime. Their capacity to do this reflects their 'classic' status and their persistence within what Charles Taylor terms a social imaginary, in which although their meanings are now 'buffered', their imagery is still highly visible (2007). Their continuing currency also reflects the difficulty their secular substitutes have, the secular narratives of human evolution and progress, in mobilizing human responses that are both engaging and ethical.[5] These are experienced as 'unbuffered' in the sense of the most proximate accounts of 'how things are', and as capable of evoking fascination and wonder, but they are not experienced as 'meaningful' in the way the Christian accounts were. Every grand narrative will have its shadow side, a new problem it creates while it is solving an old one, but evolutionary narratives almost by definition, when they are presented without a religious frame, are disposed to seem blank, flat and empty, if not downright menacing.[6]

Clifford Geertz famously defined culture as 'the ensemble of stories we tell ourselves about ourselves' (1973, p. 448), offering an image that sits well alongside Cavanaugh's acts of imagination or Taylor's social imaginary. To ask about our political culture involves asking for the stories we tell ourselves about what it means to be a good society. We are back to Berry's question 'What are people for?' and to the ideas of society that our

---

5 Jürgen Habermas, in what is hailed by many as a late change of tack, has spoken of the value of religion in providing motivation for social solidarity; see Maureen Junker-Kenny's discussion in Biggar and Hogan (eds), 2009.

6 Cf. Charles Taylor's conception of the modern secular outlook of 'homogenous empty time' (2007, p. 124). I am of course not arguing a creation*ist* position, but a mainstream Christian understanding of creation by evolution/evolution as creation.

answers to that question lead us to. Here I offer four comple-
mentary social visions which, woven together, seem to me to
approach the Christian (which in scriptural terms always means
Jewish + Christian) idea of a society. Christians hope and pray for
a society that is:

- beloved and joyful
- free, just and equal
- landed and lawful
- complex and peaceful.

## Beloved and joyful

Two recent Glasgow Professors of Divinity, one Protestant and
one Roman Catholic, have written theologies centred on love:
George Newlands' *Theology of the Love of God* (1981) and
Werner Jeanrond's *A Theology of Love* (2010). Without love,
theology is nothing and without love, despite what Reinhold
Niebuhr says, politics is also nothing.[7] I could go on expanding
the list, in the way of Paul in 1 Corinthians 13, but will stop at
one more, the Augustinian insight that society is nothing without
love.[8]

The first love is divine love. To see Scotland in true scale to
the infinite, not for MacDiarmid but for me, is to see it as part of
*The Divine Comedy*, moved like Dante and all of human being,
by 'the love that moves the sun and other stars'. Calvin notes
that people are not easily persuaded that God loves them (1958,
p. 193), and Scotland in recent years has not been easily persuaded that Calvinists love it. That God is love and that God loves
the world is the presupposition of all Christian attempts to learn
and to think the world. The love of God is what moves us to love
God and one another – 'We love because [God] first loved us' (1
John 4.19). Paul's insistence in 1 Corinthians on rehearsing a list

---

7 In *Moral Man and Immoral Society* (1932), Niebuhr famously argues that love
can only be the standard for personal relationships, while social relationships need
to be addressed in terms of justice.

8 'One of the great achievements of Augustine's *City of God* was its capacity to
frame moral anthropology as social philosophy' (Gregory, 2008, p. 50).

of things that will mean nothing without love is just the kind of relentless 'note to self' that political animals need to be regularly returned to, particularly if they also aspire to being theological animals. The language of love is a solvent for all kinds of inhuman constructions, legal, political, economic, sociological, which we find ourselves given to. When it is given to us and when it moves us, we are forced to reconsider what it means to make something of ourselves and of others, by the reminder of how lovelessness amounts to nothing. The domination of politics by men and the patriarchal desire to police a separation of public from private space have not provided much room in discourse or practice for love in politics. Feminist theologians and philosophers have led the way in rejecting that policing and making room for love in their own discourse (see McAfee, 2011; Harrison, 1990). The vital connection is there in the *shema* and in Christ's restatement of it. It is notable that in Matthew 22, the lawyer's question to Jesus comes just after another Pharisee question about the lawfulness of paying taxes to the Emperor (22.17). His response, that we give 'to the emperor the things that are the emperor's, and to God the things that are God's' (22.21) is given on the way to the answer about the greatest commandment in the law:

> He said to him, '"You shall love the Lord your God with all your heart, and with all your soul, and with all your mind." This is the greatest and first commandment. And a second is like it: "You shall love your neighbour as yourself." On these two commandments hang all the law and the prophets.' (Matt. 22.37–40)

It all hangs on this. The community sent in Genesis 1, given to one another in Genesis 2 as bone of each other's bones, flesh of each other's flesh, are addressed also in the narrative of Genesis 4. Here YHWH says to Cain, 'Where is your brother?' and Cain's sullen, fearful response, 'Am I my brother's keeper?' is met by YHWH saying *you are*: 'your brother's blood is crying out to me from the ground'. In the Genesis imagination, we are sent to keep one another in life and in love. The stewardship of creation is also a stewardship of one another. We are called, in the exquisite words of the wedding service from the Anglican *Book of Common Prayer*, to cherish one another. There is a Christian humanism (Howard and Packer, 1999) here which has profound political implications. Of the many places we could go to illustrate this, Daniel Berrigan's widely cherished *Advent Credo* is one of the most powerful and poignant, with its passionate series of refutations and affirmations:

> It is not true that we must accept inhumanity and discrimination, hunger and poverty, death and destruction ...
> *This is true: I have come that they may have life, and that abundantly.* (2004, p. 211)

There is ample and chilling testimony in history to the political power of an operative, popular anthropology. Violence or discrimination against 'others' within society is very often accompanied by a denial of their full humanity on the grounds of their having the 'wrong' ethnicity, religion, gender, sexual orientation, physical or mental capacity. Conversely, movements for political reform typically make a powerful anthropological appeal to bring about change that will recognize the full humanity of those who are suffering. The anthropological question, as a question inherent in Geertz's narrative set, is supremely important because it defines where our politics come from. It roots politics in the stories we tell about ourselves and, the external, reciprocal face of culture, what we tell ourselves about each other. Christian theology provides narrative resources to name *them* as us, to name *them* as neighbour, to name *them* as the enemy who yet must still be loved. These are the narrative resources, rooted in Judaeo-Christian thought, which have joined those from classical philosophy to underwrite the development of Western traditions of jurisprudence and human rights. The power of the biblical imaginary lies in the capacity of our encounters with Scripture to continually exceed and correct our existing attempts to create the good society. We find ourselves continually revisiting the tensions of Deuteronomy 15, where we move from the promise/imperative of verse 4, 'there shall be no poor among you', to the grim realism of verse 11, 'the poor shall never cease out of the land'.[9] The history of Christendom, as it is told in large compass by Oliver O'Donovan (1996) and John Milbank (1990), is the story of myriad national, international and local attempts to practise a politics that is haunted by these narratives by design. The history of radical Christian critique of Christendom as represented in Andrew Bradstock and Christopher Rowland's reader of *Radical Christian Writings* (2002) is the story of a host of acts of prophetic counter testimony seeking to practise a politics that is also haunted by these narratives by intent. Both are fruits of Christian mission and essential elements of the Christian idea of a society.

If the perception of organized Christianity in Scotland as austere and unloving is one of the great wounds of the churches, another is its reputation for being joyless. The sad irony is that to the question of what people are for, the answer of the Westminster Shorter Catechism was always insistent: that we are made for *joy* (see Nouwen, 1986). To rehearse this is a powerful act not just of theological confession but of political imagination. This should have been one of the great political gifts to Scotland of the Reformed tradition, to catechize women and men in an ecstatic anthropology, an anthropology of fullness, with the Reformation accent on Genesis 1 tying this to the unity of humanity. We are one human race, made for joy in God. The reality is that we have struggled to learn our own catechism. The common and at times lazy diagnosis has blamed Calvin/ism and Knox. Edwin Muir, in his poem 'Scotland 1941', lamented the curtailing of popular celebration in rural Scotland with his brusque account of how 'Knox and Melville clapped their preaching palms/ and bundled all the harvesters away'. There are, however, other strands within Reformed DNA that can and have led believers from that tradition in a different direction.[10] In a sermon on 1 Corinthians, Calvin said, 'There is not one blade of grass, there is no colour in this world that is not intended to make us rejoice' (Sermon 10 on

---

9 The verse Jesus quotes in words we know best in the English of the KJV as 'you have the poor with you always'.

10 See also Donald MacLeod's fine article on the cultural legacy of Scottish Calvinism and how it has been variously, but mostly negatively portrayed: http://www.freescotcoll.ac.uk/files/Articles/Scottish-Calvinism.pdf.

1 Corinthians). The novelist Marilynne Robinson has spoken of the striking sense in Calvin that 'the aesthetic is the signature of the divine'.[11] That this aspect of the Calvinist inheritance has been too little explored and understood in Scotland is the fault first of its Reformed churches and their theologians and only secondly of inferiorist 'revenge-ism' from hostile critics (see Fergusson in Forrester and Gay (eds), 2009, pp. 23–35). We are still waiting for a serious theological exploration of Calvinist aesthetics in relation to Scottish history and culture (see F. B. Brown, 2003; also Davie, 1978, p. 119). While we are waiting, those of us in the Reformed tradition can try to re-catechize one another and to make up for lost time. We have things to learn here from the traditions of Dutch Calvinism, both in The Netherlands and as they have been developed in North America at centres like Toronto's Institute for Christian Studies and at Calvin College in Grand Rapids (e.g. Wolterstorff, 1980; Seerveld, 1980 and 2000). What has to be recovered as part of our birth right and offered belatedly (and humbly) to Scottish culture is a sense of how the Christian idea of a society marries the aesthetic with the ethical; in its promotion of the ecstatic, the joyful and the beautiful as essential dimensions of what people are *for* and in its insistence that this is what *all* are made for, not just some. Berrigan's lyrical affirmation can be extended: *it is not true that beauty or art, leisure or 'culture' are for a privileged and discerning few/ this is true: that we are all made for beauty and for joy.*

## Free, just and equal

Christian ideas of society have a rich tradition of drawing on both the Exodus imagination and the prophetic witness of the Old Testament against oppressive kings and enslaving empires. These narratives offered very direct denunciations of oppression and injustice. They disclosed a picture of a God, described by Japanese theologian Kosuke Koyama as a 'hot God' (1999), no cool detached deity, but the Exodus God who saw, heard, knew

---

11 In interview with Andrew Brown, http://www.theguardian.com/commentis free/andrewbrown/2009/jun/04/religion-marilynne-robinson.

and came down to liberate. The hot God was also a holy God, but a Scripture such as Leviticus 18 reveals that with this profoundly 'social holiness'[12] being holy as God was holy meant not gleaning fields to the edge, not lying, withholding wages, discriminating against the poor, prostituting your daughters or oppressing the aliens in your midst. From Leviticus to Amos, in worship songs, laws, poetry, wisdom sayings, historical reports and eschatological visions, examples could be multiplied of the divine demand for justice, the divine denunciation of the oppressor, warnings to the rich, consolations and hope for the poor. The Gospels too were rich in revolutionary pickings, from Mary's Magnificat, through Jesus' call of fishermen as disciples, in the Nazareth manifesto and beatitudes, in the widow's mite or the parable of Dives and Lazarus, or through Jesus' scandalous table fellowship with prostitutes and sinners. Last, not least, the Apocalypse fulfils Mary's prophecy, bringing down the mighty, burning down Babylon and destroying the Beast for ever, while Jerusalem descends like a bride. Andrew Bradstock's and Christopher Rowland's reader in *Radical Christian Writings* (2002) is a feast of appropriations of such Scriptures by those hungry and thirsty for righteousness, from the Lollards to the Diggers, from Sojourner Truth to Martin Luther King, from Dorothy Day to Gustavo Gutiérrez.

Even the more abstract formulations of theology provided rich inspiration through the centuries for those who wondered why the wicked prospered. The doctrine of creation in the *imago Dei* and redemption in the *imago Christi* would continually reassert themselves as subversive ideas and identities, capable of being claimed and asserted by those struggling for freedom and equality. The singularity and universality of Pauline theology included all in its indictment and allowed no one human credit for their own justification: 'all have sinned and come short of the glory of God'; 'as in Adam all died, so in Christ shall all be made alive'. Ecclesiology and pneumatology also had influential political effects. Theologians as different as Oliver O'Donovan (1996) and John Howard Yoder (1992, pp. 60ff.) have pointed to the political significance

---

12 Mennonite theologian Alan Kreider develops this idea in the book of the same name (2008).

of New Testament accounts of early church meetings. Both have written about the significance of 1 Corinthians 14, from which Yoder draws his understanding of 'the Rule of Paul' and in which both he and O'Donovan find insights that feed through Puritan and dissenting traditions into ideas of democratic deliberation and parliamentary democracy. Presbyterianism and congregationalism, with their democratic leanings and federating dynamics, built support for ideas of equal political voice (though not for a long time for women) and designed models of governance that could be scaled up and adapted for use at state levels.

Out of the clash and synthesis between the classical ideas of the Greco-Roman world, the rich resources of Scripture and a 1,000 years of Christian theology and practice were forged the tradition we have come to call liberal and the tradition we have come to call democracy. Robert Song offers a compressed summary of the 'family resemblances' that characterize liberalism: 'The most central of these are a voluntarist conception of the human subject; a constructivist meta-ethics; an abstract, universalist and individualist mode of thought and a broadly progressivist philosophy of history' (1997, p. 9). Oliver O'Donovan would not endorse the tradition in those terms, but is insistent about its importance for political theology:

> The liberal tradition ... has right of possession. There is no other model available to us of a political order derived from a millennium of close engagement between state and church. It ought, therefore, to have the first word in any discussion of what Christians can approve, even if it ought not to have the last word ... We cannot simply go behind it; it has the status of a church tradition, and demands to be treated with respect. (1996, p. 238)

Political liberalism and the ideas of liberal democracy need such theological allies and defenders, of whom Nicholas Wolterstorff is another prominent example, because they are the subject of intense criticism from many angles. The common factor behind most critiques of liberalism is some form of the argument that it fails to discern or display a substantive conception of or commitment to 'the good'. To go back to Eliot, Roger Kojecky observes:

The liberalism he so often deprecated is regarded as a modern substitute for the traditional Christian world-view involving fragmentation into many autonomous areas ... liberalism was an enemy just because it exalted many goods, while denying their source or sanction, the supreme good. (1971, p. 115)

The example of Scottish philosopher Alasdair MacIntyre is often cited because his hostility to liberalism remains intact through his journey from Marxism to Roman Catholicism, although the reasons for it change shape.[13] For Marxist, feminist or postcolonial critics, liberalism is damned by comparing its claims to embody freedom with its historical record of social exclusions and collusions with capitalism and colonialism. For Green critics, it has failed to respond to ecological priorities. Muslim critics share many of the concerns of Thomists about supreme goods, while Mennonite or Quaker critics abhor its capacity to tolerate violence. Small wonder then that Robert Song claims 'one of the primary negative responsibilities of political theology must be the critical evaluation of liberalism' (1997, p. 1).The trouble with this troubled debate, however, is that it can sometimes feel like a phoney war, conducted mainly by people who benefit daily from the continuing influence of liberalism on their own *Sitz im Leben*. Churchill's over-quoted defence of democracy as the worst system apart from all the others yet tried is the stock response of pragmatic conservatives to the rainbow coalition of liberalism's critics. It still earns its moment of pompously acerbic rebuke within what can be a dangerously self-indulgent stoning session, but this is not just a phoney war. We should not pretend that the Christian idea of a free society can be easily or simply expressed today or set much store by those who claim it can. Oliver O'Donovan names the challenge of the present moment as 'to think of other liberalisms, different possibilities of combination and development than those which have woven our contemporary bondage' (1996, p. 228).[14] The entitlement of

---

13 MacIntyre's *After Virtue* (1981) has been one of the most influential texts, not least for theologians, in the development of a critical evaluation of liberalism; in the Scottish context it has influenced Beveridge and Turnbull (see p. 105–6 below).

14 The projects of Song, Fergusson, Stout, Gregory and Wolterstorff share similar conclusions.

liberalism's critics and, above all, of its victims to both impatience and rage over its failings does not mean he is wrong. Moments in history when new constitutions are produced or proposed offer concrete opportunities to make our best attempts at weaving a free-er and fairer liberalism. They also remind us how hard this is to do. The 'thicker' account of virtue that many theological critics see as central to rethinking liberalism will not be secured by even the best constitutional draft. It will, I believe, have to be mostly a thickening from below, which relates both to the survival and extension of 'complex' space (see the discussion below on pp. 60–64), to the holding open of discursive spaces in which serious thinking can take place[15] and to the building, Yoder style, of real-life communities (including church communities) in which we taste the sweetness of freedom.[16]

The brief discussion of liberalism attempted here has already invoked themes of justice and equality, as will the discussion of land and law below. Christian ideas of justice in society relate to a wide range of social contexts: the balance of housework between husbands and wives, the avid concerns of the Hebrew prophets for proper 'weights and measures' and public officials who do not take bribes, patterns of landholding, access to housing, wage levels and wage differentials, combating ethnic or religious dis-crimination, opportunities for people with disabilities, personal and corporate tax rates, law enforcement and criminal justice. In all of these and many other areas, the (social) holiness of God's people and the hallowing of God's name (Long, 2010, p. 38) on earth is at stake on a daily basis as is our obedience to the command 'to do justice, and to love kindness and to walk humbly with your God' (Mic. 6.8).

Like the phoney and real wars of liberalism, Christian ideas of justice and equality exist in a tension between damning

---

15 Cf. Jacques Ellul's discussion of the vocation of the Christian intellectual in Chapter 4 of *The Presence of the Kingdom* ([1967] 1948), entitled 'The Problem of Communication'; sadly and ironically both universities and political parties in con-temporary Scotland/UK are often poor examples of such spaces, with limited reach into the wider community.

16 Luke Bretherton's discussion of community organizing and his reflections on the work of London Citizens makes important contributions on all three of these fronts. See Bretherton, 2010, Chapter 2, 'Local'.

simplicity and daunting complexity. So while O'Donovan can say unequivocally:

> The equality of human beings is an aspect of the doctrine of creation. It locates every human being equally to every other as one summoned out of nothing by the creator's will, one whose life is a contingent gift, created for fellowship with others and answerable to judgment. (2005, p. 41)

He also makes the equally blunt assertion that 'the fate of all revolutionary equalization is to make human life unlivable' (p. 42). Christian ideas of justice, he argues, involve a sensitivity to the need for 'attributive justice', which will 'elaborate differences' in the strategies and judgments necessary for just outcomes to be achieved (p. 42). The distinction is one guaranteed to activate hermeneutics of suspicion among those hot for social justice and wary of O'Donovan's often austere defence of liberalism. However, the more I read O'Donovan, the more I find him an unreliable ally for conservatives, who is willing to cut through neo-liberal evasions to set out positions that have radical implications for social policy:

> The criteria of human equality establish the minimum demand, the demand on the threshold, which takes priority over all other possibilities of attributive justice ... The opportunity to live and the opportunity to participate in a society are metaphysically foundational; they correspond to our universal created nature as human beings; they can seriously and unqualifiedly be demanded from fellow human beings. On this account 'equality of opportunity' ... is a definite social disposition of material resources, to achieve which we may have to take definite action. (2005, p. 48)

Such definite action includes government intervention in economic life to restrain both deliberate and unwitting wrongs, because 'markets do not regulate themselves. They *adjust* themselves, but like the brutish and short-sighted Leviathans they are, they trample people beneath their feet while they do so' (2005, pp. 64–5). Perhaps more than anyone else in this conversation, O'Donovan forces us back from mere sloganizing, to acknowledge the demanding nature of political theology. I often go back to his statement in the Introduction to *The Ways of Judgment*: 'The Gospel proclamation I take to be in its essential features, luminous, the political concepts needed to interpret the social and institutional realities around us obscure and elusive' (2005, p. x).

So it is with the Christian Idea of a Free, Just and Equal Society. But the light shines in the darkness.


## Landed and lawful

Another dimension of the biblical imaginary which informs Christian ideas of the good society is that of *land*. Walter Brueggemann asserts that '[l]and is a central, if not *the central theme* of biblical faith' (1977, p. 3).[17] The fundamental confession about land that permeates the Hebrew Scriptures, and through them Jewish and Christian imaginations, is that the land belongs to God, the maker of heaven and earth. This is the blunt, bold affirmation of Psalm 24.1, 'The earth is the LORD's, and the fullness thereof', and of Psalm 95.4–5, 'The sea is his, and he made it: and his hands formed the dry land.' This global affirmation is not only liturgically rich, but it also has profound political and jurisprudential consequences. In the Hebrew Scriptures, the land never ceases to belong to God. As Chris Wright points out, even when the land had been given to Israel (and other nations) for their use and blessing: '*the land was still God's land*. [God] retained the ultimate title of ownership and therefore also the ultimate right of moral authority over how it was used … The clearest statement comes in Leviticus: "the land is mine and you are but aliens and my tenants" (25.23)' (1983, p. 56). Based on this ongoing insistence on divine ownership of (all) land, a rich theology of the landed society is developed. Both in the Genesis 2 creation story and in the creedal testimony of Deuteronomy 26.5–10, 'A

---

17 He earlier notes Paul Tournier's suggestion of a dialectic around place, wherein the task of those not having a place is to find one and the task of those having a place is to leave it (1968, cited in Brueggemann, 1977, p. 1).

wandering Aramean was my ancestor ...', the land is understood
as God's *gift* to Israel. Its possession is not to be presumed upon,
but received with gratitude and shared with generosity (p. 51). If
the land is presented as gift to those already in possession of it,
the land is also offered as *promise* to those who are still seeking
it. The promise made to Abraham and Sarah of a home-land is
expanded through the experience of the Exodus to become the
promise of a free-land. With gift and promise comes *provision*.
The land in Genesis 1 and 2 is given as good for food; it is the
material base of Israel's life, a fact continually remembered in
festivals and liturgies of thanksgiving for harvest. It is the land
'flowing with milk and honey' (p. 52).

It is also, in terms that must be confronted head on, disputed
land acquired by conquest, from which others have been driven
out and to acquire which others have been slaughtered. The fact
that there may be an infinite regression here, in which those dis-
placed had themselves acquired it by tooth and claw and those
displacing been previously victims of genocidal oppression, does
not dissolve the theological agonies or anxieties that inhere in our
reading of the Old Testament.[18] Land is central. It was in Israel's
Babylonian exile that one of its scribes wrote the words, 'Listen;
your brother's blood is crying out to me from the ground' (Gen.
4.10). It was in recently unified Germany, in the 1930s, that the
late nineteenth-century nationalist vision of *Blut und Boden* was
given deadly articulation by the Nazis, glorifying the rural Ger-
man peasantry and their relationship to the soil, while planning
for a programme of eugenics to 'purify' the nation (Lane and
Rupp, 1978). Land is central. We have nowhere to live but the
land. There is no way back to Eden where the land is quiet. We
have to live East of Eden where we can hear its cries.

In his commentary on Deuteronomy, J. A. Thompson observes
soberly that 'it will be harder to leave the old ways than to
leave the old land' (1974, p. 74). He is pointing beyond Exodus
to the need for law. A land or society to which we applied the
fourteenth-century English term 'lawful'[19] is one where the vision

---

18 http://www.churchofscotland.org.uk/news_and_events/news/2013/the_
inheritance_of_ abraham_revised_report_released.

19 http://www.oed.com/view/Entry/106420.

of fullness includes an appreciation for its being 'full of law'; a condition opposed to that of being empty in the sense of being 'lawless'.[20] The Hebrew Bible is all over law, revelling in its capacity to celebrate the gift of law in all of its life-giving, health-giving, society-protecting dimensions. Most famously in Psalms 19.10 and 119.103, the psalmist hymns the beloved law as sweeter than honey in his mouth.

The mindset here can seem remote to twenty-first-century liberal democracies, where the more common refrains are complaints about excessive regulation and bureaucracy. Such complaints are put into perspective by the examples early in this twenty-first century of countries such as Somalia, the Democratic Republic of Congo, Iraq and Afghanistan, which all in their different ways reveal the terror of lawlessness. When law fails, the gun rules. Without the law of society, there is no honey in the lion, only the law of the jungle where might is right.[21]

When we enter the realm of 'law-talk', we are moving in space that lies between the two loci of grand narrative and social discipline outlined in the last chapter. Law-talk in general discourse, within Scottish and British society at least, suffers from a narrowing of horizons, being too often reduced by a loss of the narrative embedding which would make the ends and goals of law visible. Some would argue that it suffers, too, from inflationary trends within 'rights-talk', which works to reduce a broader, social vision of law to competing visions of individual rights.[22] For others, human rights discourse remains a crucial way of connecting society to its best ideals and aspiration.

If we take bearings again from the biblical imaginary, building on the previous discussion of land, we find that in the Old Testament with the land comes *law*. Law seeks to create new ways to

---

20 http://www.oed.com/view/Entry/106432.

21 Among these examples, the invasion of Iraq was itself arguably a breach of international law. In both Iraq and Afghanistan, the issues of failed states and 'nation-building' have been the subject of much debate and concern. Although I do not consider these questions directly in this book, there are obvious links to be made between them and the subjects addressed here.

22 On this, see Joan Lockwood O'Donovan, 'Historical Prolegomena to a Theological Review of "Human Rights"', *Studies in Christian Ethics* 9:2 (1996), pp. 52–65; c.f. Wolterstorff 2010 and Gregory 2008 who defend the achievements of human rights language.

live in the new land. In his study of Old Testament ethics,[23] Chris Wright argues that 'it was the historical land-gift tradition which generated *individual property rights* in Israel':

> The gift of land 'percolated' so to speak, down to the lowest social level, so that each individual household could claim that its right to the land it possessed was guaranteed by God himself. Thus, inheritance language was used of the small portions of land belonging to each household, as well as of the territory of whole tribes or the whole nation. They too were held as the gift of God. (1983, p. 54)

Wright draws our attention to the rarely visited 'Sasine Register' sections of the Old Testament, Numbers 26 and 34 and Joshua 13—19, which describe the division of the land according to tribes and clans of Israel. He notes:

> To us these detailed lists seem tedious and interminable, but for Israel they enshrined a fundamental principle: the land was intended to be equitably shared out, so that every household had its part in the national inheritance. (p. 54)

This is an example of a broad articulation of law, underpinned by a powerful theological and ethical narrative, which in turn becomes part of the social imaginary of those who live in, on and from the land. The generation of a sense of 'right' or entitlement[24] is an important part of Brueggemann's 'prophetic imagination' because it becomes an integral part of how people imagine the good society. Wright powerfully connects the 'tedious and interminable' lists of Numbers to the prophetic cry in Isaiah 5.8 against those who abuse land rights, 'who add field to field, until there is room for no one but you, and you are left to live alone in the midst of the land'. There must have been many

---

23 Wright's book (1983) owes a good deal to the insights and approach of the pioneering work of Norman K. Gottwald in *The Tribes of Yahweh*, although Wright brings his own judgements to the material.

24 My grumble is against inflationary understandings of 'rights' not against a proper place for them within an overall legal economy. For a defence of rights language, see Wolterstorff, 2010.

times in Christian history when it was a deeply uncomfortable thing for some to hear that passage read aloud in church, and a conscientizing and inspirational moment for others.[25] Law here offers an iteration, an articulation of the land-gift tradition in relation to the whole society. What is striking about ancient Israel is that its legal traditions in relation to land do not stop here. If Numbers 26 exemplifies the narrative pole of jurisprudence, the Jubilee legislation of Leviticus 25 exemplifies the disciplinary and regulatory pole. It was because the land belonged to God that it could not be finally alienated from those to whom God had given it. This theological understanding set limits to the market in land that Israel was allowed to establish. The consequence was a broad but still ethically ambitious framework for promoting and (crucially) restoring equality, which was premised on a realistic assumption that the working of the economy and the functioning of a market in land would always lead to inequality and with that the threat of landlessness for future generations. The imaginative power of the Jubilee provisions lies particularly in their concern for future generations and their insistence that future generations will also have a claim on this land-gift of YHWH. That claim can be threatened within a generation, but the Jubilee intent is that it cannot be finally and permanently sold from under children and grandchildren. It should not be lost in perpetuity, either because of the misfortune, wickedness, laziness or foolishness of the current generation of owners or because of the commercial skill and strength of those who buy their land from them when they are in trouble. One of the most powerful and poignant narrative expressions of prophetic imagination in relation to this Jubilee provision comes in Nehemiah 5, when there is 'a great outcry of the people and of their wives against their Jewish kin'. The outcry is against those who are exploiting the desperation of the people in a time of famine and forcing them to mortgage fields and vineyards. What is particularly striking and moving about this passage is the appeal to the effects of the situation on the younger generation:

---

25 In the UK context we can cite the Levellers and the Diggers (see Bradstock and Rowland, 2002, for selections from Winstanley); in the US context, first nations populations and African American slaves; in the Latin American context, indigenous people deprived of land.

Now our flesh is the same as that of our kindred; our children are the same as their children; and yet we are forcing our sons and daughters to be slaves, and some of our daughters have been ravished; we are powerless, and our fields and vineyards now belong to others.

I [Nehemiah] was very angry when I heard their outcry and these complaints. After thinking it over, I brought charges against the nobles and the officials ... And I called a great assembly to deal with them. (Neh. 5.5–7)

The vision of a lawful society is given a fine articulation in relation to contemporary economic issues in Daniel K. Finn's *The Moral Ecology of Markets* (2006), where Finn patiently makes the case in relation to neo-liberal champions of the 'free' market that all markets have rules and are surrounded by legal 'fences' of different kinds (p. 119). Finn's work is an important example, along with the teaching on economics offered in the 2009 encyclical *Caritas in Veritate*, of how to give substance to the narrative front-end of law-making. It remains striking, however, how difficult it is in contemporary Western societies such as Scotland/the UK to present ideas about a just distribution of 'land' that are not seen as anachronistic retrievals of communism. I have two brief thoughts about how we might address this. The first is that while crude, state-determined allocations of property do indeed have the smack of Bolshevism, there are other key areas of contemporary economic life where an imaginary shaped by Numbers 26 and Leviticus 25 would seek to order the market differently. In relation to housing policy, housing subsidy and their associated taxation policies, a desire and determination to protect basic minimum standards (not least for the sake of new generations of children) and to remove incentives to excessive accumulation are a minimum requirement. While *public* housing has had a mixed record (particularly when its allocation, management and maintenance has been linked to the political fortunes of particular administrations), *social* housing in the UK, delivered through housing associations and housing co-operatives, has a strong record of quality control and of tenant and member

bullsh*t in
the 21st century under
neoliberal markets

participation in management. Public investment and subsidy in social housing of this kind remains a priority if decent housing for the poorest in society is to be available. In relation to preventing excessive accumulation, there is a growing awareness in the light of the international prevalence of systematic and cynical tax-evasion measures that we need to rebalance tax towards land and property, which cannot be hidden or offshored as other types of capital can.[26]

My second thought reflects the third 'Anabaptist' strand of the ecumenical model presented in the last chapter. It recognizes that there are limits to what can be achieved prescriptively by law and even that there are times when a society can be 'full enough' of enacted law, such that further attempts to introduce change via the direct action of the state will be ineffective and counter-productive. Those of us who dream of radical social change, but live in democracies where most people will not vote for it, rather than turning to the cynical agit-prop of the hard Left or the cynical self-interest of neo-liberalism, can invest in the project of building a third-sector movement of social enterprises, where a more just pattern of ownership, trade and distribution is built from the bottom up. If we 'love the law' as the psalmist did, if we feel called to what Mennonite theologian Alan Kreider has dubbed 'social holiness' (2008), if we get a taste for ways of living that are 'sweet' with divine justice and grace, then we should invest in them, along with our congregations and denominations (if we are Christians), our families and friends.

*Paradoxia?*

## Complex and peaceful

The last section, with talk of housing associations, co-ops and third-sector organizations (among which should be numbered 'community organizing' initiatives), moves us towards an important recent theme in political theology, the critique of monolithic or 'simple' conceptions of sovereignty, the state and political 'space'.

---

26 See among others the Mirrlees report on the future shape of taxation: http://www.ifs.org.uk/mirrleesReview, and in a Scottish Context Andy Wightman's proposals for a land value tax: http://www.andywightman.com/?page_id=1027.

The impetus came from John Milbank's essay 'On Complex Space', in which he opposes a medieval imaginary of complex or 'gothic' space, constituted by an array of social bodies with overlapping powers, responsibilities and jurisdictions, to an undifferentiated modern conception of simple space (1997).[27] Milbank's account, with its 'advocacy of complex space'[28] re-attached to socialism, offers a positive reassessment of the neglected twentieth-century traditions of guild socialism associated with the Anglican political theologian Neville Figgis, as well as G. D. H. Cole and Harold Laski. Luke Bretherton draws together these and other strands in his important 2013 review essay on 'Sovereignty', in which he sets them alongside the work of seventeenth-century Calvinist jurist Johannes Althusius, twentieth-century Calvinist accounts of 'sphere sovereignty' from Abraham Kuyper and Herman Dooyeweerd and accounts of 'subsidiarity' drawn from Catholic social teaching.[29] Bretherton asserts the need to develop this tradition into new forms of Christian 'consociational' thought:

> Central to the Christian consociationalist tradition is the sense in which we do participate in a cosmic order that can disclose to us some measure of meaning and purpose. It is this cosmic social imaginary that distinguishes the theological consociationalism of Figgis, Kuyper and Maritain from their secularist counterparts, notably Emile Durkheim and Paul Hirst. This consociational tradition with its distributive and federal conception of sovereignty, offers a rich yet underexplored thickening of more Trinitarian and Augustinian responses to political and economic absolutism. It is the combination of one

---

27 In Milbank, 1997. There are connections to be made here to feminist critiques of how social space is characterized as either public or private; though feminist gothic usually means something rather different.

28 '"The advocacy of complex space" seems to me to be the key distinguishing mark of Christian social teaching in the nineteenth and twentieth centuries – whether Catholic, Calvinist or Anglican – in so far as it in any significant way distances itself from modern social reality' (Milbank, 1997, p. 271).

29 Bretherton's essay is Chapter 12 in Adams et al. (eds), 2013; for more on the reception of Althusius's thought in a Scottish context and on how it can be fitted into a tradition of thinking sovereignty in Scottish political theology from George Buchanan, through Samuel Rutherford, Steuart and Mackenzie, see Jackson, 2003, pp. 98, 111, 117.

or more strands of consociational thought with a Trinitarian theological anthropology and an Augustinian eschatology that needs to frame contemporary theological accounts of sovereignty if they are to move beyond critique to constructive conception. (Bretherton, in Adams et al. (eds), 2013, p. 274)

The work of Milbank and Bretherton and the older traditions they are drawing on holds out the promise of Christian theology contributing something crucial to a post-Marxist, anti-capitalist rethinking of the nature of sovereignty and state. To stay with the title metaphor of this book, we can invoke the broken lion and speak here of a certain 'breaking' of the idea of sovereignty. Referencing a different political symbol from the bestiary, Rousseau spoke of Hobbes' achievement in 'reuniting the two heads of the eagle', by refusing to allow the spiritual to evade or divide the sphere of sovereign power.[30] The argument offered here that the Christian Idea of a Society should have something of the character of a 'complex' society is an argument for the need to break open that singular Hobbesian vision of simple space. In Milbank's case, he argues that once the simple logic of subsuming the parts under the whole is rejected, we are thrown into the (political) work of negotiating association and exchange, of creating common (holy) order (1997, pp. 279–80). In the context of this discussion, we could read this as an alternative way of framing the issue of when a political unit is recognized to be the right size. If the work of negotiating association is a political task, then we escape the logic of the 'natural' or the self-evident and we have to negotiate the 'con' of our sociality. Who do we want to associate *with* and why? If we are not following a progressive Enlightenment logic of the consolidation of simple space into a single cosmopolis, then patterns of association could shift over time. We might decide to enter unions, but might also decide to leave or reconceive them. Such decisions could, in Milbank's terms, be fresh acts of human political imagination, which continued the unfinished work of building the 'neo-gothic' space of

---

30 Social Contract IV, 8(13). I owe this quote to Luke Bretherton, in Adams et al. (eds), 2013, p. 263.

human community. The decisive issue here would seem to be discernment. When is complexity a humanizing characteristic of a political system, which bears witness to the proper ends of life, and when is it an anachronistic survival of elite privilege or local chauvinism?

Having aligned myself with this argument, I have to admit to doubts about how far the process of constitution writing for newly independent states is able to recognize and inscribe this kind of complexity. The appetite for democratic control and demand for self-determination will tend to override such gothic pretensions in the name of a clean, geometric modernity, free from asymmetric detail and monstrous stone pillars that cut off sightlines. But that is too pessimistic for at least two reasons. First, complexity happens and can be recognized and welcomed even where it has not been 'designed in'. Second, if the inspiration of gothic is more than an antiquarian fantasy, then we should anticipate that the future will witness the advent of new and creative ways to design in complexity and to practise subsidiarity.

The final theme I will discuss here is the Christian idea of a peaceful society. The relationship between complexity and peace can be seen in the work of John Milbank, whose participationist ontology of peace offers an Augustinian vision of the reconciliation of difference in a *concentus musicus* (in Ward (ed.), 1997, p. 268). Stanley Hauerwas, who is an admirer as well as a critic of Milbank's work, insists that the counterpart to such an ontological vision must be a vision of discipleship that is committed to the practice of pacifism and non-violent resistance (1999, p. 231).

Within contemporary Scottish and European societies, the relationship between religion and peace is one many people have strong convictions about. A feature of both the popular recoil from organized religion in European societies and of hostile attitudes to Islam is the widely embraced and expressed opinion that religion is a cause of violence. Within Scotland, the growing tendency of people to identify as 'no religion' is one legacy of the history of sectarian conflict between Protestants and Catholics.[31]

---

31 We still await the 2011 Census Data for religious affiliation in Scotland, but predictions on all sides are for those ticking the no-religion box to increase.

William Cavanaugh, in *Theopolitical Imagination*, offers a bold challenge to what he calls 'the soteriology of the modern state', which he argues has become part of a standard narrative of western historiography, in which the role of the state is to save us from the Church:

> The story is a simple one. When the religious consensus of civil society was shattered by the Reformation, the passions excited by religion as such were loosed and Catholics and the newly minted Protestants began killing each other in the name of doctrinal loyalties ... The modern secular state and the privatization of religion was necessary therefore, to keep the peace among warring religious factions. (2002, p. 20)

From this, he argues, comes the Hobbesian vision of a single sovereignty, which consigns religion and the Church to a private sphere, where its capacity to cause violent division can be minimized (p. 36). Cavanaugh's alternative narrative rejects both the 'religion as *cause* of the Wars of Religion' thesis and the privatization of the Church conclusion which has been drawn from it.

Common to all three theologians is a conviction that embrace of the secular soteriology of the state is a dangerous wrong turn and that liberalism ultimately harbours a greater potential for violence, because it lacks both the imaginative capacity to think difference and the ethical resources to maintain unity. On the one hand, I have strong sympathies with their analysis and with the theological importance they place on the Church as a public, political community. However, as a practical theologian, I also recognize that the mistrust of organized Christianity in Scotland and the UK has not come from nowhere. The salutary vision offered by David Fergusson at the close of his study of *Church, State and Civil Society* was of a church needing to accept its diminished role within society and to rebuild the credibility and plausibility of its witness through its capacity to participate in public conversations, its example of loving service to society and its critical support of the state and social institutions (2004, p. 194). He was also clear that all of this would depend upon congregations which were living out the gospel:

Within this more complex differentiated setting, the social contribution of the church will itself be varied. Discernment will be required on when to offer support for change, to contest existing practices, to engage in dialogue and to form alliances. In different ways the church will find itself functioning both as lubricant and irritant within the systems of its host society. This public voice of the church will require to be established upon a strong congregational base. Apart from this, it will sound increasingly hollow and strident, while lacking the resources in energy, intellect and personnel to participate effectively in the public domain. (p. 192)

One of the key programmes within the contemporary Church of Scotland is the Place for Hope ecumenical programme sponsored originally by the Women's Guild, to train individuals for the work of mediation and conflict resolution within the Church. In seeking to manifest the fruit of the Spirit which is peace, as with its journey towards joy, my own church is discovering its need to be recatechized about some very basic dimensions of Christian living.

## Conclusion

Advocacy for the Christian idea of a society by those who seek to articulate such an idea will involve appeals made, within a common democratic conversation about the common good, to taste and see the sweetness/goodness of constantly reformed and reiterated social visions. In one of the best recent books on political theology, Luke Bretherton has issued a bold call to Christians to humble and hospitable political engagement in common politics, pointing out that the situation of Christians today is one in which 'the church no longer has priority and Christians are not in control'. Following Augustine and Brueggemann, he reads this through the text of Jeremiah 29, where 'the Israelites are to learn in exile what they failed to learn in Jerusalem' (Bretherton, 2010, p. 5). This is well and powerfully said and I have been deeply affected both by Brueggemann's ongoing readings of that motif and by Bretherton's recent rereading of it. I would also set alongside it the task of not forgetting in exile what was done well in Jerusalem. That is the task that John Milbank and Oliver O'Donovan have contributed to at a time when the instincts for repentance of a postcolonial theology were threatening to sweep away many Christian achievements in their disgust for Christendom's failures.

Christian political theology still has a part to play within Scotland and the UK in public deliberations over the common good. It can and should bring its gifts to the table, charisms of narrative, discipline and witness. But as it does so, Scotland's churches face something of the same challenge today that J. H. Oldham set before those who were preparing for the 1937 Oxford Conference on Church, State and Civil Society. They need first to re-apply the Christian idea of a society to their own life. Let the Church be the Church. Let it think and serve and bear witness in the way of Jesus Christ. Let it model what it dreams of Scotland becoming.

# 4

# Honey from the Lion?

# A Theological Account of Nationalism

Nationalism is a subject which attracts disciples and heretics.

(McCrone, 1998, p. ix)

In this chapter I begin to develop a theological account of nationalism, an account that explores whether and how a version of nationalism can be conceived that is compatible with the Christian idea of a society explored in the previous chapter.

## Biblical imagining – primal sendings

Throughout the discussion so far, I have stressed the importance of the books of Genesis and Exodus for a Christian theo-political imagination. My engagement with the biblical material is primarily concerned with how it functions in relation to the biblical canon, with literary critical interpretations of the material and with its reception: the history of interpretation and of the cultural and historical effects of biblical interpretation (cf. Ellul 1970, p. xvii). The historical-critical issues around ideas of people, nation, nationality and political identity in ancient Israel have their own academic domains within biblical studies (see Liverani, 1992; Christensen, 1992). I am not seeking to intervene in or adjudicate complex archaeological or historical questions, although I am aware of how the problem of anachronism bears on how specific terms are deployed.[1]

---

1 There is of course a certain circularity here as, for example, Liverani's useful entry on 'Nationality and Political Identity' in *The Anchor Bible Dictionary* (1992)

In the previous chapter, we explored elements of the accounts of creation and fall in Genesis 1—4 and I want to return to those here, before reading on through other key passages in the book of Genesis. Recalling Geertz's focus on 'the stories we tell ourselves about ourselves', it is in the work and play of reading Scripture that a Christian imaginary is formed. For Christians, it is as we read these ancient narratives and find ourselves addressed by God in them that we learn our own names, learn who and whose we are and what and who we are for. When we hear and tell the creation story of Genesis 1 as a story about ourselves, we learn that we are a sent people. We realize that the original mission of humanity is life. We are sent to live, fully and fruitfully, stewarding and multiplying. For myself, as someone raised within what might generously be called a 'claustrophobic' conservative Christian tradition, raised in feverish mistrust of body and world, art and politics, on escapist soteriology and rapture eschatology, to relearn the name of God as the God of Life and to relearn creation as a (co)mission to live still has an overwhelming potency and poignancy. To learn this is to believe and know God as one who wants women and men to be, who loves their life/lives, who means them to live and to find fullness of life. To learn this in the context of Genesis is to learn it as a universal affirmation, God's will for everyone born, and it is to learn it as a global affirmation, God's will for everyone born everywhere. The Genesis imagination knows of only one kind of human and presses the conclusion that we should only ever make a singular use of the language of race. We are all, as Hamish Henderson says, the Bairns O' Adam[2] and, as C. S. Lewis says, the Daughters of Eve.[3] The *imago Dei* given in creation undercuts and overcomes all other distinctions and the injunction to 'fill the earth' admits of no exclusions. This primal sending to fill the world affirms the value of every person

draws on modern theorists of nationalism such as Kohn, Deutsch and Gellner in attempting to define what such anachronisms might consist of. To the extent that theories of nationalism and the nation alter, so the attempt to define anachronism may also be put in need of revision.

2 Hamish Henderson, 'The Freedom Come All Ye' – lyrics, recordings and staff at http://www.educationscotland.gov.uk/scotlandssongs/secondary/thefreedomcome allye.asp.

3 Lewis famously uses this term in *The Lion, the Witch and the Wardrobe*.

and every place within creation. It evokes the Puritan saying that 'every place is immediate unto God'. There are no parts of the world or peoples of the world that are in principle God forsaken (not even England).

The second Genesis sending, the sending out of the garden, when humans are forced to improvise home East of Eden and 'away from the presence of God', is a sending out into a world marked by death and violence and insecurity (Ellul, 1970, pp. 1–18). Every place in this scenario is equally alienated from the presence of God. The poet Edwin Muir spoke of what has been unseen by humanity 'since Eden locked the gate that's everywhere and nowhere' (Muir, 1963). There are no parts of the world that will, in the terms of Genesis 6—7, escape the flood, or that are in principle closer to God than others (not even Scotland …).

Through these two sendings, we are offered a double theological verdict and presumption about every place (and person) on earth – that every human society is both affirmed and judged, that every place is a space of both vocation and alienation. This is of course nothing more than an iteration of a classic Pauline, Augustinian, Thomist, Calvinist confession that the world is both created and fallen. Such an iteration is needed because humans and Christians in every age have found it terrifyingly easy not to see themselves and their neighbours or enemies within such an uncompromising universal frame. To tell and hear these stories as stories about ourselves is to be on our way towards a Christian cosmopolitanism,[4] which is resolute in its insistence that there are certain privileged stories that will always 'trump' all other stories. The narratives of creation and redemption are always trump cards within Christian political theology. Just as the *imago Dei* characterizes the whole of humanity in creation, so this image, as it is restored and renewed in redemption, leads also to an insistence on the other great singular of one Church, entry into which is by virtue of one baptism. In the end, for Christians, ecclesiology is always more determinative than biology and water is always thicker than blood. The dogmatics of creation and redemption are already in themselves the ethics that outlaw racism and ethno-

---

4 I agree with Luke Bretherton (2010, p. 134) in his use of this phrase, although not in his comments on nationalism, which I regard as far too sweeping.

centrism. God's Holy Spirit bears witness with our spirits that we are not made for such discriminations.[5] Stories that tell us that we are so made are, as Daniel Berrigan reminds us, the wrong stories: 'it is not true that ...'.

## Nationalism after Babel

Genesis 5 presents a first poetic genealogy from Adam to Noah. After the narrative has dealt at length with the Flood and with only minimal attempts to accommodate the interlude of Babel, to which we now turn, Genesis 11 returns with a second structural genealogy, carrying the narrative from Noah to Abram. While Genesis 10 introduces the *goyim* in passing, reporting breathlessly 'the clans of Noah's sons ... within their *nations*. From these the *nations* spread out over the earth after the flood' (Gen. 10.32 NIV), Genesis 12 moves the project of nation-making centre stage, with the divine promise to Abram which will be returned to constantly in Scripture as the beginning of Israel's story: I will make of you a *goy hagadol* – 'a great nation' (Gen. 12.2).

Standing between Noah and Abraham in the narrative, however, interrupting and disrupting the account of the post-flood dispersal of the nations, is the extraordinary story of the city and tower of Babel in Genesis 11. Conventionally read in terms of a divine curse and as an alternate 'fall narrative', these nine verses have a massive and ongoing legacy within art and literature as well as within theology and biblical interpretation.[6] They are significant for developing a political theology of nationalism, particularly in the light of an alternative and increasingly common hermeneutical approach that reads the story as one not of curse but of blessing. Within this interpretation, the 'curse' of Babel is read as an act of divine providence that reinforces the diversity of creation and reflects the divine mandate to fill the earth. On this reading, what is cursed is not the linguistic and cultural divers-

---

5 These are indeed examples of what Bretherton calls 'false and destructive patterns of binding and loosing' (2010, p. 134) – but they should not be simply equated with nationalism, nor should nationalism simply be equated with such patterns.

6 In 2013 the second multi-million-selling album by Mumford & Sons was called *Babel*, so the motif is still operating freely within popular culture.

ity that ensues from the divine scattering, but the imperialistic, even fascistic project of *ein Volk, eine Sprache*. The poet Fearghas MacFhionnlaigh, in his epic poem *The Midge*, in a series of 'Adam as' stanzas, reflecting on the nature of fallen humanity, speaks of 'Adam as Tower of Babel, the Alcatraz of languages'.[7] This image suggests that God's way of frustrating and resisting this demonic form of unity is through releasing the blessings of Babel,[8] the gifts of linguistic and cultural diversity, which become resources that enable resistance to imperialism. The creational mandate is given an expanded reading by means of the Babel narrative in terms of a stewardship of cultural diversity. This is a mandate affirmed by the Holy Spirit at Pentecost, who is revealed as the Spirit of translation (Sanneh, 1989), giving birth to a Church whose catholicity transcends cultural difference without abolishing it. It is a providential mandate whose value within history is dramatized and celebrated by the great vision of Revelation, in which heaven itself displays, without reduction, every tribe and language and people.[9] Christian theology has long wrestled with questions of how to relate these trajectories of universality and particularity. Eric Gregory comments that while Augustine at first held that the special relations of the biological family or civic commonwealth were a result of the fall:

> Augustine abandons this early view in favor of a more nuanced mediation between the universal and the particular. Even in Paradise, he comes to think, 'there would have been relatives and kindred even if no-one had sinned' (Retr.I.12). To use current vocabulary, Augustine provides an early discussion on the proper relationship between cosmopolitanism and particularism as it relates to citizenship. Providence and finitude affirm

---

7 *The Midge*, printed in *Cencrastus* 10 (1982), pp. 28–33 – it was reading this extraordinary poem aged 19 that influenced my own turn to Scottish nationalism.

8 For this reading see Yoder, 2001.

9 Rev. 5.9; Rev. 7.9: 'It is also important to note Augustine's eschatological affirmation of this plurality. Plurality and separateness of identity are not simply providential aspects of creation or a mark of sin that will be overcome in the drawing together of the Eschaton – as if Pentecost was simply a negative undoing of Babel' (Gregory, 2008, p. 261).

special relations, even if love continually expands the circle of neighbourly concern. (Gregory, 2008, p. 354)[10]

## Nation as vocation?

While we are not there yet, we are edging closer to the possibility that some kind of 'nationalism' could be a legitimate and even necessary part of the human vocation. We approach this if we begin to think the idea of cultural diversity is something created by God, which God looks on and says 'it is good'. Its goodness echoes the goodness of the whole creation but it also represents a form of providential goodness; something that is provided by God, given into the human historical future, in the face of human evil, to defend human flourishing. It is given, in particular, to protect the weak and those who are most likely to become the victims of totalizing and homogenizing empires. When peoples are subject to either invasion or to exile, with the loss of a free *place* that was their own, linguistic and cultural diversity protects a free social *space* within which to maintain and mobilize resistance.

This narrative dogmatics implies a narrative ethics. If we follow this trajectory of reading Scripture, the universal scope of this blessing implies an ethic of equal regard. It summons us to an ethic of neighbourliness, which binds us into loving our neighbour's culture, language and place as we love our own. There is a pluralism here that is saved from being relativistic by the double judgement referred to above, the sense that all cultures take their place on the earth in relation to both a divine affirmation and a divine judgement. In the words of Lamin Sanneh:

Christianity is first and foremost a pluralist religion ... As Paul affirmed, there is no respect of persons with God (Rom 2:11) and nothing in itself is unclean (Rom 14:14). The positive sides of these statements are equally valid: all persons are precious in God's sight (1 Pet 2:4) and all things indeed are pure (Rom

10 See also p. 295: 'Augustine's evolving view of providence, however, appears to include a particularized notion by which one's friends and immediate community can be seen as providential gifts of God.'

14:20). In the same fashion, no one is the exclusive or norma-
tive pattern for anyone else and no one culture can be God's
favourite. (1989, p. 30)

My stewardship of my culture involves both celebration and penitence and I should also welcome and expect that from others in
their stewardship of their culture. Furthermore, I am my brother's
and my sister's keeper. I am charged not to do violence to your
culture, but to be hospitable to its difference from mine. As the
Welsh theologian and missiologist Dewi Hughes puts it, I am
charged to keep, not to 'castrate', your culture (2001).[11]

## A Mirror for national self-imagining?

So far I have used the imaginative resources of Genesis and
Revelation to trace a broad Christian orientation that holds a
resisting pluralism in tension with an embracing universalism or
cosmopolitanism. I am working within a hermeneutical circle/
spiral, which is produced by, held within and accountable to the
traditions of the Christian Church. I read these texts as someone
who has been baptized, as someone who belongs within the one,
holy, catholic and apostolic Church, which means that I read as
someone who has been told who I am by those who passed on the
faith to me. My primary identity, given by grace and inhabited
in a faltering way, is that I am a Christian. The rite connected to
that identity, of baptism, is accompanied by the confession that
'in Christ there is neither Jew nor Greek, male nor female, slave
nor free'. Through that rite, Christians believe that they have been
called to the centre of their identity, since to be in Christ is the
identity that 'goes all the way down'. As Stanley Hauerwas says,
'the Church is not a character in the world's story, but the world
is a character in God's story, made known through the story of the

---

11 Cf. Ronald Turnbull's comments on Ernest Gellner: 'Nationalism [for
Gellner] also serves to guarantee "cultural diversification".' Gellner's rather cursory
argument as to why this is desirable is that 'pluralism is some kind of insurance
against both tyranny and political folly' (Gellner, 1964, p. 178, quoted in Bell and
Miller (eds), 2004, p. 46).

church' (1998, p. 192). In worship, Christians relearn the world, which means they also relearn their own identities in relation to their primary identity as disciples and their primary allegiance to the lordship of Christ. Christian discipleship therefore involves a continuous process of testing and weighing the claims we are making or are party to making, to identity, place and power, to see whether they are incongruous for disciples of Jesus Christ.

In that process of relearning the world, of weighing and testing claims, the Church reads and reflects on Scripture under the guidance of the Holy Spirit. It receives the Scriptures of both Old and New Testaments as its rule of faith and life and from the beginning has found the task of relating the two testaments to be a demanding one. In James 1.22–25 hearing the word of God is compared to looking in a mirror in which we see what we are like. When we live into that disclosure, when we try to be doers of the word, living out what we have heard, we are blessed. While James' use of the mirror image is not without ambivalence, the same image is deployed more negatively by the Mennonite biblical scholar Willard Swartley. Swartley asks about:

> Our willingness to be changed by what we read, to let the Bible function as a 'window' through which we see beyond self-interested ideologies, and not a 'mirror' which simply reflects back to us what we want it to show. Biblical interpretation, if it is worthy to be so called, will challenge the ideology of the interpreter. It can and will lead to change, because people do not come to the text thinking as God thinks, or even as the people of God thought in serving as agents of divine revelation. Interpreters [must] listen to the text carefully enough not to like it. [When they do so] it powerfully demonstrates that the text's message has been heard and respected. (1983, p. 86)

As we move from the poetic sagas of Scripture into the historical books, the way in which the text shapes our political imagination begins to change. Born of the promise to Abraham and Sarah, a blessing carried by Isaac is stolen by Jacob and then reaffirmed by God after the wrestling match at Peniel, along with a divinely inflicted wound and the new name Israel. These few wandering Arameans are in stark contrast to the power of the Egyptian empire, into whose control they are forced to migrate in the face of famine. For Israel in Egypt's land, the combination of being fruitful and multiplying and of being ethnically and religiously distinctive leads to a ruthless, oppressive and ultimately murderous response from Pharaoh. YHWH responds to the cries of the oppressed by opening the way for Exodus and renewing the promise to the freed people of law and land. Reading from the twenty-first century, we cannot help but read for the other or enemy within, the slave 'nation', the object of 'genocide', the formulation of law and constitution.

The nation wandering in the wilderness, judged and divided, yet not abandoned, is finally led by cloud and fire to the edge of the Promised Land. But the land promised is not empty; it now has to be entered and conquered. Other 'enemy' 'nations' have to be driven out. Israel, until now oppressed by external powers or divided by internal conflicts, now becomes a warring, invading power itself. The lion of the tribe of Judah bares its teeth and prays to the Lord of Hosts for victory.

The conquest of the land produces borders and enemies, it calls for patterns of settlement and systems of governance, it leads to new shrines and new laws. From the restless coalition of tribes in the time of the Judges to the deeply sceptical accounts of the advent of monarchy, to the valorizing of the Davidic era and extolling the fame of Solomon, the chroniclers of Israel tell a story of gradual 'state' centralization, in which monarchy and cult become focused on Israel's 'capital' Jerusalem. Within this story the key dramatis personae emerge as Chris Wright's triad of 'God, Land + People' along with those in Scripture who occupy the roles of prophet, priest and king.

Adrian Hastings, in his study *The Construction of Nationhood: Ethnicity, Religion and Nationalism* (1997), highlighted the crucial role played by this biblical model (and mirror) in the emergence of European national identities:

The Bible, moreover, presented in Israel itself a developed model of what it means to be a nation – a unity of people, language, religion, territory and government. Perhaps it was an almost terrifyingly monolithic ideal, productive ever after of all sorts of dangerous fantasies, but it was there, an all too obvious exemplar for Bible readers of what every other nation too might be, a mirror for national self-imagining. (p. 18)

Hastings does take sides in the struggle alluded to above between the modernists and primordialists, believing the modernist account of nationalism to be untenable not least because of its failure to take seriously the influence of religion:

> Religion is an integral element of many cultures, most ethnicities and some states. The Bible provided for the Christian world at least, the original model of the nation. Without it and its Christian interpretation and implementation, it is arguable that nations and nationalism, as we know them, could never have existed. (p. 3)

In partial agreement over the role of language, literature and the vernacular, but also in strong disagreement with Benedict Anderson over dating of the crucial shifts, Hastings argues:

> [E]thnicities naturally turn into nations or integral elements within nations at the point when their specific vernacular moves from an oral to written usage to the extent that it is being regularly employed for the production of a literature and particularly for the translation of the Bible. (p. 12)

Integral to this move is that those caught up in the production of vernacular literatures and vernacular Bibles come to imagine themselves politically 'through the mirror of the Bible, Europe's primary textbook' (p. 2).

By the mid-sixteenth century something new had started to happen. People in England, Scotland and across Europe went to church and heard someone reading a vernacular Bible to them. They began to hear and increasingly to read for themselves 'the frequent and emphatic biblical reference to nations and the world as a world of nations'.[12] The Bible, for Hastings, was a key

---

12 The English Bible, it is not exaggerated to claim, has ensured a standard use of the word 'nation' from the fourteenth to the twentieth century. Where the Vulgate

nation-building tool; it built the concept of the nation in people's imaginations by exposing them to 'the regular implication that the world consists of a number of nameable peoples' (p. 17).

Hastings' case is that Europe (another construction of course) learned itself, made itself and attempted to make itself 'Christian' in part through what it did on the basis of hearing of a world of nations in the mirror of the word. The question then arises, was this an outcome incongruent with the gospel? My view, in keeping with the argument of Chapter 1 about nationalism as claim-making, is that such a self-imagining and such a process of nation-building are *not* intrinsically wrong, disordered, 'false and destructive'.[13] For sure, Adrian Hastings acknowledges that the picture of Old Testament Israel as presented in Scripture might offer an almost terrifyingly monolithic ideal, capable of generating dangerous fantasies. Which is to say, in the terms we have been using, that it could inspire fantasies of building Babel. That it could, but it might not, and need not is at the heart of the argument of this book.

Here we are back in the territory of Chapter 1 where we considered the tendency to scapegoat other people's nationalism while ignoring one's own. We are well used to the Augustinian–Calvinist tradition in political theology warning us that every temporal political arrangement is going to be finite and flawed and at some level incongruous, a poor fit with aspects of the gospel.[14] The task in offering a theological account of nationalism is to bring the criteria presented in the previous chapter – criteria for what constitutes the good society and makes for fullness of life – into dialogue with the particular claims made by any particular nationalism. Eric Gregory makes the point that 'an Augustinian

---

had translated the Greek 'ethnos' as 'natio' it was rendered 'nacioun' in English. While the Vulgate certainly does not employ it with any technical precision, the regular implication that the world consists of a number of nameable peoples is clear enough (see Hastings, 1997, pp. 16 and 17).

13  Again I echo Bretherton's problematic definition, though there is an argument within political theology that all social formations other than the Church are intrinsically disordered; see, for example, Healy, 2000, p. 17.

14  Cf. Gregory, 2008, p. 32: 'Here I follow Robert Markus's argument about the pirate story: "The point Augustine is making is not that societies are morally equally bad or neutral or all equally deficient, but that none can claim the only true justice, which is to be found only in the heavenly City" (CS, 63).'

ethics of citizenship can be *perfectionist*[15] without trading in sentimentalism, Pelagian notions of achieved *perfectibility* or elitist conceptions of undemocratic politics' (Gregory, 2008, p. 9). It can and must aspire to ends with which it does not believe the earthly city will achieve a perfect fit in the time of the *saeculum*.

The degree of ethical incongruity will shape a Christian response to any existing political arrangement. One of the resources from the Old Testament that vividly illustrates this process of adjudging claims is the story in Daniel 5 of Belshazzar's Feast and 'the writing on the wall': 'Thou art weighed in the balances. and art found wanting' (Dan. 5.26 KJV). While that judgement is applied to Babylon, the city that along with Babel becomes a key biblical figure for rebellion against God, the prophetic tradition within the Old Testament is just as capable of applying it to Israel and to Jerusalem. So (and this is crucial) the mirror for national self-imagining did not simply show early modern Europe an image of Israel in its Davidic and Solomonic prime; the hearers of the vernacular word also heard the searing verdict of God on Israel which was delivered by Jeremiah:

> I have forsaken my house, I have abandoned my heritage;
> I have given the beloved of my heart into the hands of her enemies.
> My heritage has become to me like a lion in the forest;
> she has lifted up her voice against me – therefore I hate her.
> (Jer. 12.7–8)

For South Africa in the apartheid era, where the majority of people were denied constitutional means to participate in the governance of their society, a broad-based struggle was required to promote radical constitutional change in the face of a nationalism that made racist and white supremacist claims. The political grouping that was at the forefront of this struggle, led at its breakthrough moment by Nelson Mandela, also had the word 'national' in its name: the African National Congress. The claims made by this anti-colonial, anti-imperialist anti-racist party were of a wholly

---

15 That is, can aspire to an ideal or perfect condition (without believing this is achievable in this life).

different nature to those made by the racist National Party, but in both cases there were a set of claims that were coincident. Despite the ANC's strong legacy of and commitment to pan-African political projects, it was still claiming freedom and constitutional change for a unitary state, with defined borders, which would have a name, a capital, an anthem and a flag. It was a very differently articulated and performed nationalism, driven by a different set of claims. Archbishop Desmond Tutu (1994) coined the phrase 'rainbow people' to define this early in the history of a democratic South Africa, and it was taken up by Mandela in a 1994 speech when he claimed that '[e]ach of us is as intimately attached to the soil of this beautiful country as are the famous jacaranda trees of Pretoria and the mimosa trees of the bushveld – a rainbow nation at peace with itself and the world' (Manzo, 1996, p. 71).

The biblical counterpoint to building Babel is building Jerusalem, where Jerusalem is understood as the city whose builder is God. The direct reference here is to Hebrews 11, the early Christian theological panorama of Israel's history, which was a key scriptural template for Augustine's *City of God*. Even where a people understand themselves, as Israel did, to be living out of and into a divine promise, they are also living into the divine call. This is the third great missionary sending of Genesis, the call to Abram: 'Go ... to the land that I will show you' (12.1). The writer of Hebrews echoes the wonderfully curt 'and he went' of Genesis 12: 'he set out, not knowing where he was going ... For he looked forward to the city that has foundations, whose architect and builder is God' (Heb. 11.8, 10). The search for a homeland (Heb. 11.14, 16), for the city of God, is read by Augustine as an erotic project that animates and a blessed vision that judges life in every homeland, every city:

> Two cities, then have been created by two loves: that is, the earthly city by love of self extending even to contempt of God and the heavenly city by love of God extending even to contempt of self. (*City of God* 14.28)

Much subsequent theology and a host of literary and poetic improvisations around it have followed Hebrews, Revelation and

Augustine in turning Babel–Babylon and Jerusalem into historical threats and promises for peoples in all places and times. The most famous English language reference is to William Blake's anti-capitalist vision of building Jerusalem in England's green and pleasant land, but Bob Marley's poetics of Zion and Babylon express the same mix of longing and lament.[16] Marley reads his part in the (enforced) African diaspora through the metaphor of Babylonian exile, while also expanding the metaphor of Babylon to cover every global situation of white oppression. The Babylonian captivity has haunted theological and literary imaginations down through the centuries. Augustine's injunction to those living within the City of God to 'enjoy the peace of Babylon' (*City of God* 19.26) has remained a compelling image for many theologians and has been popular again in recent decades as a metaphor for the position of the Church in post-Christendom contexts. It is a rich and suggestive image through which to read the times, but there is also a suspicion that its contemporary appropriation by mainly white, Western, European or North American males may represent a degree of finding comfort in being numbered among the oppressed. There is no question that it has been preferred poetically and politically to the ethically risky territory of Ezra and Nehemiah's post-exilic project of rebuilding the city and reclaiming the land.[17]

Looking back with a sceptical historical critical eye on issues of 'nationality and political identity' in the Old Testament, Liverani reflected in his 1992 *Anchor Dictionary* article on 'a kind of paradox':

[T]he national unity of Israel was the result, not so much of a political unification, but of the political disaster of the Exile and the return. The national self-identification was achieved, not when the material conditions were more stable and peaceful, but as a reaction against vicissitudes and conditions conceived in order to destroy any national feeling in the melting-pot of the

---

16 For example, 'Babylon System' from the 1979 album *Survival* by Bob Marley and the Wailers.

17 An example of Swartley's mirror reading? Eliot alludes to the rebuilding project in *Choruses from 'The Rock'*.

imperial state. As a consequence of this paradoxical situation, the features that were privileged in the shaping of the nationality, that were conceivable outside of the land were the unity of cult (the Solomonic temple was never so important in Israelite ideology than after it was destroyed) the common law of divine origin, the historical traditions (providing a model for national recovery) and the assumed ethnic unity (in the form of extended kinship ties).

Lacking territory, political unification and independence, land and kingship were projected into the future (and the past ...) as necessary to 'be the nation again'.[18]

> All the differing attempts which took place in the postexilic period, from the building of the Second Temple to the constitution of the Hasmonean kingdom, were conceived of as a restoration of the past and necessarily produced the myth of a lost national identity and history. But this 'former stage' of the national unity never occurred in reality in the forms later presumed in order to fit the political programs of the postexilic community. So the Israelite nationality assumed its form in the very period of its disintegration, as something projected in the past and in the future – but undergoing 'presently' to [sic] a state of crisis ... From the model of the national state emerged that of a religious community devoid of any political power and competence and reusing the previous projects of national recovery as a metaphor for the eschatological salvation. (Liverani, 1992, pp. 1035–6)

His judgements may be provocative in some respects, but the accusation of a mythologizing reuse of the past is a telling one and one recognizable in nation-building projects throughout history: the stories we tell ourselves about ourselves. Unless we really are Mennonites, and perhaps even if we are, we may need to pay

---

18 Those familiar with the populist anthem 'Flower of Scotland' will recognize the reference.

more attention to Israel's post-exilic dilemmas as a way of testing our theo-political instincts – holding up a different kind of mirror to our national imaginings.

## Augustinian civic nationalism

In the end, since nationalism is a practice of claim-making, each and every nationalism needs to be given a thorough Augustinian interrogation about the kind of loves that are embodied in the claims it makes. At a minimum, the only kind of nationalism that a Christian is justified in supporting is one that makes three renunciations. For the power of nationalism to be sweetened it must renounce imperialism, essentialism and absolutism (or, if you like, the world, the flesh and the devil).[19]

- To renounce imperialism is to renounce domination and to practise recognition of the other.
- To renounce essentialism is to renounce a biological nationalism based on the *ius sanguinis* or law of the blood in favour of a habitat-based nationalism, based solely on the *ius solis*, on the law of territory. (This point is well made by Adrian Hastings, 1997, p. 34.)
- To renounce absolutism is, in the language of the Barmen Declaration, to place the state under God, asserting God's sovereignty over the state and the state's accountability to God.

These three renunciations represent a 'breaking' of nationalism and with that they also signal a breaking of the power of the state, by which I mean a marking of how power must give way to virtue. In *The Desire of Nations*, Oliver O'Donovan (unlike Hauerwas who simply refuses this task) suggests a way to think theologically about the state. In his chapter on 'The Obedience of Rulers', he argues that the provisional character of the state is revealed in a christological understanding of trumps/triumphs:

---

19 A little forced perhaps, although they map together well. My point is not to suggest 'baptizing' nationalism, but to ask what kind of nationalism baptized people could support.

The most truly Christian state understands itself most thoroughly as 'secular'. It makes the confession of Christ's victory and accepts the relegation of its own authority. The only corresponding service the church can render to this passing authority is to help it make this act of self-*denying* recognition ... urge this on it and share with it the tasks of practical deliberation and policy which seek to embody and implement it. The church has to instruct it in the ways of the humble state. (1996, p. 219)

Even when the crucial renunciations have been made, O'Donovan's tasks of 'practical deliberation and policy' still remain. For example, in the UK context, should we be aiming at a re-covenanted parliamentary Union that will give fuller recognition and respect to its constituent nations or should we opt for a social union made up of a confederation between those parts of the UK that wish to be independent? To suggest an answer, we move in the next chapter to consider the particular case of Scotland and its relationship to the UK.

# 5

# The Evolution of Devolution

If we are to discover the character of any people, we have only to examine what it loves. If it is an assembled multitude of rational creatures and is united by a common agreement as to what it loves, then it is not absurd to call it a 'people', no matter what the objects of its love may be. Clearly, however, the better the objects of this agreement, the better the people; and the worse the objects, the worse the people.

Augustine of Hippo, *City of God*, 19.24

In this and the next chapter, I return more directly to the 'practical theology' dimension of this project, applying the work of the previous chapters to an examination of how devolution and nationalism have developed within Scotland's recent history. Recalling Jonathan Hearn's claim that '[l]iberal democracies do not so much transcend nationalism as domesticate it, routinizing its dynamic by channelling it through core political institutions', I maintain a focus in this chapter on the history and practice of the SNP within Scotland as an example of a form of nationalism that sits within what Hearn calls 'the normal functioning of democratic regimes' (2006, pp. 165–6). My intention here is not to sanctify or 'bless' the SNP's record or programme. I am enough of an Augustinian to believe that any political party will have a very mixed record of loving. However, I do want to address the arguments of Grosby, Bretherton and others that a nationalist project by definition 'repudiates civility' or is based upon 'false and destructive' models of social organization. I will do this in an Augustinian key by examining the development of the SNP, what it loves, what it prioritizes, how it seeks to mobilize, 'bind and loose' people within contemporary Scotland.[1]

---

1 After writing this I came across Ronald Turnbull's near identical formulation in a 1999 paper on Tom Nairn: 'What "doctrines", to use MacKenzie's word, are the Scots to hold, and what common purposes are their ideas to inform? Or to put this in other words, borrowing from Augustine, what are to be the objects of the Scottish

## A very short introduction to Scottish nationalism

The Scottish National Party (SNP) was founded in 1934 following a merger of two rival movements, the National Party of Scotland and the Scottish Party. It won its first Westminster seat in 1945, but held this only briefly and did not win another Westminster seat until Winnie Ewing won a famous by-election victory in Hamilton in 1967.

Any consideration of the history of nationalism in Scotland has to take account of the language of 'Home Rule', which has been owned at various times by both the Liberal and Labour Parties (and by Keir Hardie's Independent Labour Party before there was a Labour Party) in Scotland and which is today still claimed in different ways by devolutionists, federalists and supporters of independence.[2]

Tom Devine reckons medieval Scotland to have been a more heterogeneous society than either Wales or Ireland, but notes that by 1800 this had given way to 'a much more coherent sense of Scottish national identity' (1999, p. 486). During the nineteenth and twentieth centuries:

> waves of Irish, Italians, Lithuanians, Jews, Poles, Asians and English people settled in Scotland. It was the most concentrated phase of immigration since the Irish, Scandinavian and Britannic tribes had established themselves hundreds of years before and was to have a powerful and complex impact on the development of modern Scottish society. (p. 486)

The character of Scottish national identity in the nineteenth century, the great age of European nationalism in other countries of continental Europe, has been much debated. In Scotland, it seemed, this emerging nationalist script was not followed, and Devine notes Tom Nairn's and George Davie's view of 'the age

---

nation's love?' (in Bell and Miller (eds), 2004, p. 48). Clearly my project is very close to Turnbull's at this point.

2 With a referendum on independence scheduled for 2014, it's also important to recognize that a number of individuals and groups who support the YES campaign self-identify as supporters of independence, but not as 'nationalists' – the Scottish Green Party among them.

of Liberal dominance in Scottish politics between 1832 and 1914 as one of profound crisis in Scottish nationhood', with 'devastating cultural consequences' (Devine, 1999, p. 285).[3] The factors most commonly cited and debated include the economic benefits of Union and Empire to aspirational Scots and the unwillingness of the Scottish middle classes to jeopardize their stake in British imperialism at the height of its power and influence. Another factor, analysed by Davie in particular in his 1961 work, *The Democratic Intellect*, was the influence of the Disruption of 1843, when the Church of Scotland split over competing understandings of the Establishment question. Thomas Chalmers led 40 per cent of Kirk members out to form the new Free Church denomination, whose members used their stake in Victorian prosperity to build a rival 'establishment' across Scotland.[4] When considered alongside the history of earlier Presbyterian dissent, which had by the 1840s consolidated into the United Presbyterian Church, Scotland's Protestant majority was now split into three rival traditions, a majority of which were only finally reunited in 1929. Historians are still weighing and debating the consequences of these divisions,[5] including the symbolic and cultural damage done to Scotland by the fracturing of a culturally dominant Presbyterian institution, whose General Assembly had since 1707 been the closest thing Scotland had to a national parliament. The Disruption was finally triggered by the Westminster Parliament's rejection of the Kirk's 1842 Claim of Right,[6] but the potential for nationalist feeling to have arisen in response to this was dissipated by the implosion of

---

3 Ronald Turnbull comments: 'Nairn's theorization of modern Scottish history starts from the fact that in the classic age of European nationalism, 1800–1920, there was no Scottish nationalist movement worthy of the name. Scotland, so to speak, turned its back on the dominant modern political principle' (in Bell and Miller (eds), 2004, p. 37); he goes on to speak of the 'ferocity of Nairn's account' of Scottish cultural disintegration in this period (ibid).

4 The consequences are still obvious architecturally across Scotland in almost every community; New College Edinburgh and Trinity College Glasgow were originally Free Church colleges built in the mid-nineteenth century.

5 On this, see C. G. Brown, 1997. The creation of overcapacity in church buildings was one result, although this was initially masked by the fact that prior to the First World War, vigorous competition in the religious marketplace (if you accept that metaphor) was beneficial to overall levels of religious participation.

6 See n. 13 on p. 6 above for Hearn and the tradition of 'claiming right' in Scotland.

ecclesiastical life and the intellectual and social energies that were then directed into theological conflict and ecclesiastical competition.[7] Taken together, the forces of large-scale Irish immigration, Disruption in the Kirk and co-option to the projects of Union and Empire go a long way towards explaining Scotland's failure to follow a European nineteenth-century script on nationalism. More recently, historians have also focused on the persistence of relatively autonomous 'local state' institutions, arguing that these may have absorbed and contained potential nationalist demand.[8] When this factor is also included, it seems that in a then less centralized UK state the combination of local democracy (for those who were enfranchised), access to British domestic and imperial markets and careers, as well as a degree of cultural distinctiveness, was enough to blunt the appetite for political nationalism in Victorian and Edwardian Scotland (cf. Devine, 1999, pp. 287–90). Even the nineteenth-century reinvention of Scotland, with its tartanry and its hagiography of Wallace, Burns, Knox and Melville, was overwhelmingly appropriated in support of a vision of Scotland as a proud partner within the Union.

In the nineteenth century and right up until Partition in 1922, the question of Home Rule for Scotland was overshadowed by the Irish question, and the issue of distinguishing between the two causes was a live one for Home Rule supporters in Scotland (Finlay, 1994, p. 6). The salience of Irish politics for Scotland had increased dramatically following substantial immigration from Ireland during the nineteenth century, which had a lasting impact on Scottish society.[9] Scoto-Irish participation in the First World War had been blessed by the Roman Catholic Archbishops

---

7 David Bebbington describes the Disruption as 'verging on religious nationalism' (quoted in Devine, 1999, p. 291).

8 Tom Devine points out that historical judgements on these questions are still in flux, with Richard Finlay, Graeme Morton and Lindsay Paterson among those who have more recently directed attention to the role of municipal and local politics and issues of autonomy and participation available at these sub-national levels (1999, p. 287 – he uses the phrase 'local state' on p. 289).

9 Tom Devine's account of the Scoto-Irish presence in Scotland is attentive to the complexity of the dynamics of settlement, with some aspects of community life remaining 'distinct and [almost] introverted' and other parts becoming increasingly common with the majority Scots (and majority Protestant) population (1999, pp. 494–6).

and had countered doubts held by some about their loyalty to the British state. This was arguably a factor in the passing of the landmark 1918 Education (Scotland) Act, which brought Roman Catholic schools within the state system, while preserving their distinctive confessional character. In the turbulence of the 1920s, projects of both British and Scottish 'national' reconstruction were underway, alongside the continuing fallout from Irish independence and the violent convulsions of capitalism in the wake of stock-market crashes.

Home Rule for Scotland had been a Liberal policy, but disappointment over their record in Ireland, along with a widening franchise and an appetite for more radical social policies, were factors in the demise of the Liberals and the rise of a Home Rule-supporting Labour Party in Scotland.

Separate political organization for Home Rule outside of the established political parties only began in earnest in the 1920s and 1930s.[10] Even then, there were often reasons to question how earnest some of the activity was, with a quixotic, eccentric and at times neo-fascist fringe to various groups in these decades as well as a romantic communist strain running through them.[11] The remoteness of power allowed free rein to fantastic and idealist politics (and policies).

Then as now, this was also a cause that attracted some of Scotland's most gifted poets, writers and artists, with Hugh Mac-Diarmid (1892–1978) prominent among them from the 1930s onwards. MacDiarmid, one of the great poets of the twentieth century, colourfully embodies some of the contradictions inherent in the making of a distinctive strain of twentieth-century nationalism in Scotland. A founding member of the National Party of

---

10 It was anticipated by the National Association for the Vindication of Scottish Rights (1853), James Barr's 'Young Scots' (1900–20) and Roland Muirhead's Scottish Home Rule Association (established in 1918).

11 It has to be said that such infatuations of the Left and Right were very common in this period (even Lesslie Newbigin admits to being briefly impressed with fascism in his autobiography) and were not unique in any way to Scottish Nationalism. For colourful detail of early communist nationalist manoeuvres (and fantasies) in Scotland, see Timothy Neat's odd biography of Hamish Henderson (2007). Tom Devine also cites the example of Italian immigrants to Scotland forming fasci or fascist clubs in 1920s and 1930s Scotland; although, he says, 'Much of the attraction was clearly patriotic rather than ideological in nature' (1999, p. 516).

Scotland (NPS) in 1928, he was famously thrown out of the NPS for being a communist and expelled from the Communist Party for being a nationalist (see Lyall and McCulloch (eds), 2011).

This combination of nationalism, internationalism and communism or socialism would be shared by many who were influenced and inspired by the so-called Scottish Literary Renaissance[12] of the 1920s and 1930s, although some held it within Labour and alongside a politics of 'Home Rule' rather than joining the SNP.

Home Rule for Scotland was a cause native to the Liberal Party in the pre-First World War period, which came to be first owned then neglected by the ILP and Labour Party in the inter-war period. The failure of the Labour Party to offer any meaningful support for James Barr's 1927 Home Rule Bill was the final provocation for Scottish Home Rule Association activists, which led them to found their own National Party of Scotland in April 1928 (Finlay, 1994, pp. 19–22). The NPS went on to unite with the short-lived, right-wing Scottish Party[13] (founded in 1932) in the final and decisive move to consolidate nationalist organization, the formation of the SNP in 1934.

Some of the later struggles of the SNP to establish its political identity, and the pointed critiques of its political opponents up to the present time, have their roots in the mixed ideological bag of its founding members (Finlay, 1994, p. 252). It cannot rival Labour's origins as a party of labour, and it has never enjoyed the same organic links to the trade union movement. It is not hard to find quotable examples of 'the wrong kind of nationalism' in its early history, from MacDiarmid's bizarre (brief) strategic preference for the victory of fascism to various forms of Celtic ethno-cultural essentialism and numerous occasions of anti-English rhetoric. There is also some history of its being distrusted by Scotland's Roman Catholics, whose political allegiances were overwhelmingly entrusted to the Labour Party for most of the twentieth century.

---

12 Nowadays read as part of the international movement of literary modernism; see Lyall and McCulloch (eds), 2011, p. 1.

13 Richard Finlay suggests that '[i]n essence, the Scottish Party was little more than an elitist pressure group' (1994, p. 157). It was formed after a secession from the Cathcart Unionist Association (Devine, 1999, p. 325).

While genealogies have their value and a penitent approach to party history can be important both ethically and presentationally, it is more important to assess how the party developed in post-war Scotland and where it stands now in the second decade of the twenty-first century. In the introduction to a 2009 volume designed to remedy the problem, Scottish political commentator Gerry Hassan noted that '[d]espite the widespread influence of the SNP in Scottish and UK politics, the contemporary SNP has been significantly under-researched' (Hassan (ed.), 2009, p. 2).

The period from 1934 to 1939 saw the 'radicals' intent on independence subdued, as a moderate tendency led by John Mac-Cormick trimmed the party's programme in a fruitless attempt to improve its electoral fortunes, but it suffered from having 'no coherent alternative strategy of economic reconstruction to put forward in its [the Union's] place' (Devine, 1999, p. 25). By the outbreak of the Second World War, Finlay observes that 'the Scottish National Party had almost ceased to be a conventional political party' (Finlay, 1994, p. 253), while Tom Devine's verdict is that 'nationalism had ceased to be a coherent political force in Scotland' (1999, p. 326). The war years gave the 'radicals' time to regroup and they made a decisive move to gain control of the party in 1942, when Douglas Young, a lecturer in Greek at Aberdeen University, was elected chairman, defeating MacCormick's favoured candidate. MacCormick immediately resigned his membership and set up the Scottish Convention with a group of allies (Devine, 1999, p. 565). Richard Finlay concludes that this decisive victory for the pro-independence radicals over the Home Rule moderates 'established a political character which would last up until the present day' (Finlay, 1994, p. 253).

The war years also saw Labour's Tom Johnston granted a significant degree of power and autonomy at the Scottish Office (moved to Edinburgh in 1937) in the context of the National Government. Despite the lack of direct democratic control over his programme, Johnston's reputation as a Scottish Secretary has largely survived the test of time on the strength of his achievement in extending the autonomy of Scotland's political administration[14] and using

---

14 Churchill allegedly called him 'the King of Scotland' in this period (Devine, 1999, p. 552).

the 'devolved' powers to good effect. Johnston was committed to a moderate but determined programme of social(ist) planning, which included government activism in economic policy, expanded social health provision and capital spending on major infrastructure projects, most famously the electrification of the Scottish Highlands made possible through an ambitious, successful and enduring programme of hydro-electric development (see the summary in Devine, 1999, pp. 551–4).

There were complex social and political legacies for Scotland from the experience of the Second World War. In relation to nationalism, a chief one was the deep sense of its potential for evil, learned through the terrible costs of the struggle against fascistic forms of nationalism.[15] However, in the way of Derrida's *pharmakon*, it was also seen to be love of homeland and freedom that had mobilized and sustained resistance to the Axis powers. Similarly, the experience of King Tom's wartime administration was politically ambivalent. On the one hand, greater autonomy and local understanding was seen as having helped Scotland's cause. On the other hand, the Labour landslide of 1945 demonstrated that there was a growing appetite across the UK for state planning and intervention, which many in Scotland felt would be best enabled by mobilizing the power of the union state:

> While the idea of Scottish Home Rule could always find a large number willing to support it, the problem was how to determine where this came in the list of political priorities. For the Labour Party, home rule could not be easily accommodated with a greater role for British state intervention and planning in social and economic planning. Nationalisation and the Welfare State had been designed as a universal British policy to create a better and fairer British society and Scottish home rule was not relevant to this process. (Finlay in Hassan (ed.) 2009, p. 26)[16]

---

15 Although Devine notes the violent response towards the Scottish–Italian community for its strong identification with fascism when Mussolini declared war on Britain in 1940 (1999, pp. 516–17).

16 The Kirk's Baillie Commission, reflecting the work done in the Oxford 1937 Conference on Church, State and Society, was strongly supportive of the Beveridge proposals.

The legacies of the war years therefore included a strengthening of *both* British patriotism *and* Scottish national identity, including a surge of popular enthusiasm for a greater degree of Home Rule.[17] Initially, it seemed that John MacCormick's decision to part company with the SNP had been dramatically vindicated as the Scottish Convention gave birth to a broad-based mass movement that drew representation from the Church of Scotland, trade unions and Chambers of Commerce to its Scottish National Assemblies held 1947–50 (Devine, 1999, p. 566).[18] In 1949, the Convention launched a new 'National Covenant' as a mass petition for Home Rule and attracted an impressive two million signatures. It was quietly ignored by the main political parties and the energies of the Convention movement quickly dissipated as the post-war drive for reconstruction drew Scotland into the British welfare state and the emerging political culture of Butskellism.

Noting that MacCormick's strategy had failed, Tom Devine comments that '[s]elf-government could be achieved only through the ballet box, by voters backing candidates prepared to advocate self-government' (1999, p. 567). Not that his failure meant the SNP he had left was any more successful. There was a brief moment of drama on Christmas Day 1950, when four students removed the Stone of Destiny (historic Coronation Stone of Scottish monarchs) from Westminster Abbey, replacing it later in Arbroath Cathedral.[19] After 1950, it seemed that the whole Home Rule question had gone into the wilderness. The SNP had adopted a new constitution in 1946, which Chris Harvie describes unflatteringly as 'less a programme than a set of values. Influenced

---

17 The ambivalence of nationalism and the need to distinguish between 'good' and 'bad' nationalisms is well illustrated here in that masses of people found themselves simultaneously drawn to and repelled by its different forms during wartime.

18 Cf. Neville Davidson's autobiographical account in Davidson (1978) of attending the 1949–50 Assemblies, being invited to lead an opening prayer for the 1,000 delegates at the 1950 Assembly and giving a speech on spiritual renewal to the Covenant Committee in 1951.

19 On this, see Neil Ascherson's discussion in *Stone Voices* (2002) and the 2008 film *Stone of Destiny*, as well as James Robertson's fictional account in *And the Land Lay Still* (2010). This novel represents an interesting alternative to existing factual/historical writing for outside observers and younger generations to start in seeking a sympathetic though not uncritical understanding of how nationalism developed in post-war Scotland.

by social credit, populism and Catholic distributism, it repudi-
ated size, centralism and the concentration of economic power in
private or state hands' (1994, p. 169).[20]

There are intriguing signs here of an attempt to distinguish the
SNP ideologically from a more statist vision of socialism, but it
did them no good at the ballot box. Throughout the 1950s and
1960s, SNP membership remained very small and the party made
no electoral impact. Scottish voters relied overwhelmingly on
Labour or the Conservatives to make their voices heard, switch-
ing between them as necessary with little thought for third-party
options or for the Home Rule agenda. This was the high-water
mark of post-war unionism, with rising economic prosperity and
enhanced health and welfare provision being credited by Scottish
voters to their place within a British economy and society.

## The 'national popular'? Cultural renewal + retrieval

Despite the complete lack of electoral success, there is a line of
thought that sees the 1950s and 1960s as crucial for the renewal of
nationalist politics in Scotland. The historian Christopher Harvie
is among those who have documented this, along with journalist and commentator Neil Ascherson. It is also given a powerful
fictional treatment in James Robertson's 'landmark' novel *And
the Land Lay Still* (2010). With nationalist politics a political
sideshow and the Scottish electorate uninterested, those who did
care for such things devoted themselves to a broader campaign of
cultural renewal and retrieval. In this they were consciously picking up the mantle of the Scottish renaissance of the 20s and 30s,
but also adding a new attention to traditional and local forms of
popular culture in a way which moved beyond the more elitist
and vanguardist vision of MacDiarmid.

In his 1990 autobiography, singer-songwriter Ewan MacColl
recalled Hugh MacDiarmid's rejection of the idea that folk songs
could be considered great poetry and stated his own conviction

20 'The work of a group of members around Dr Robert McIntyre', by now SNP
leader, he had won a by-election in 1945 and held Motherwell for 21 days as the
first ever SNP MP. This document is interesting in the context of this book for its
mention of Catholic distributism.

that '[w]hen it comes to dealing with the real world, the world in which people live, work and die, the traditional song-makers and singers are ... far superior to their classical counterparts' (1990, pp. 281–2).[21]

An ally and collaborator of MacColl's who shared this vision and who was one of the key protagonists in this drive for cultural renewal was the folklorist, poet and songwriter Hamish Henderson. Henderson was a colourful and complex figure, who combined moments of artistic and critical genius with a capacity for monstrous self-importance, worsened in later life by his developing alcoholism.[22] Like MacDiarmid, whom he admired but with whom he had an uneasy relationship, Henderson believed in the power of poetry and art within revolutionary struggle. Both men were famously polyglot, committed internationalists in relation to culture and politics, communists, radical socialists *and* Scottish nationalists.

Henderson worked as an interpreter and interrogator for the British Army in North Africa and Italy during the Second World War and developed a deep interest in the work of Italian Marxist Antonio Gramsci, whose *Prison Letters* he translated between 1943 and 1951. With his translations not fully published until the 1970s, Gramsci's influence in Scotland can be traced in references in MacDiarmid's poetry and Henderson's critical writings, but Neil Davidson suggests:

> More important than these passing references, however, was the inspiration Henderson drew from Gramsci in what he called 'the fostering of an alternative to official bourgeois culture, seeking out the positive and "progressive" aspects of folk culture' (H. Henderson, 1996, p. 14).

This inspired both his work with the School of Scottish Studies

---

21 I owe this reference to Timothy Gorringe (2004, p. 52, n. 22). Gorringe is a rare theologian who has given serious attention to English and Scottish folk and traditional cultures.

22 Timothy Neat's adoring biographies (2007 and 2009) reproduce (mostly uncritically) many examples of such self-importance and indeed add to them through their own claims for Henderson's (verging on cosmic) significance. Read through gritted teeth, they remain indispensable sources of information on Henderson and, via their access to the Henderson archive and interview material, on the times.

at Edinburgh University and his contribution to the Scottish
folk revival. But perhaps his single greatest intervention in this
respect was contributing to the establishment of the Edinburgh
People's Festival in 1951, which he described as 'Gramsci in
action' (H. Henderson, 1980, pp. 13–14).

In particular, Henderson was influenced by Gramsci's focus on
culture as a site of revolutionary struggle and by the notion of the
'national popular', which he found in the *Prison Notebooks*.[23]
Christopher Harvie notes that '[i]nto a country which had since
1843 avoided political dialectic, "revisionist" Marxism irrupted
in the mid-1950s ... the New Left's Marxism paid unprecedented
attention to the effect of the political and cultural superstructure
on the economic base' (1998, p. 164).[24] As important as whether
Henderson or MacDiarmid or Harvie (or later Ken Currie[25])
got Gramsci 'right' (see Davidson, 2010) was the way in which
Gramsci's influence produced a broader halo effect of viewing the
cultural as political and vice versa. Neil Davidson also observes
that in this period 'the onset of the Cold War saw an assertion
of the idea of national culture as a repository of popular "folk"
values against the threat of American commercialisation and con-
sumerism' (p. 2).

From the 1950s onwards, a significant strand of the cultural
'running' within Scotland was increasingly being made by a small
group of artists, critics and cultural commentators whose work
conceived and incubated a distinctive left-wing articulation of
nationalist politics. Largely ignored by English writers and critics,
their status and influence within Scotland was to prove crucial.
In the third phase of cultural renewal, coming in the 1980s and

---

23 There are parallels to be drawn here with the brief reference in Dietrich Bonhoeffer's prison writings to 'religionless Christianity'; in both cases, the words of the
martyrs were extensively quoted, glossed and made use of by those who came after
them, leading to running academic disputes about who had correctly interpreted the
master's legacy.

24 Harvie (following George Davie?) names the Disruption of 1843 as marking
'that fateful point at which Scotland seemed to withdraw from European intercourse
and talk to itself' (1998, p. 158).

25 Glasgow-trained artist from North Shields, who painted Diego Rivera type
portraits of working-class women and men. See in particular *The Self-Taught Man*
(1986) in which the burly male figure in the painting sits reading a book by Gramsci.

1990s after the failed devolution referendum of 1979, the stature of MacDiarmid, Davie and Henderson has only continued to grow.[26] For all of their foibles and weaknesses, they were seen to have helped to rescue Scottish culture from its sentimental 'kailyard'[27] and politically 'subaltern' condition and encourage it to take itself seriously again.[28] In terms of the ethics of nationalism, which is the central concern of this book, this point is crucial for understanding the extent to which nationalism has become a kind of ethical imperative for so many on the Left.

Understanding this trajectory is helpful for clarifying the fault lines of disagreement within contemporary Scotland. The vast majority of left-of-centre intellectuals today endorse the cultural case made by MacDiarmid, Henderson and others and appreciate its political dimensions, but not all agree on the political and constitutional implications. Some believe that Scottish culture can best develop within the broader and more open context of devolution, with others believing that only independence will create the conditions necessary for artistic and cultural renewal.

## Scotland in the 1960s

If the 1950s and 1960s were 'days of small things' for the SNP and political nationalism, they saw a slow and steady process of growth, change and consolidation of its ideological identity. Under the influence of key strategists like Ian MacDonald and the leadership of Arthur Donaldson and William Wolfe, the party organization was steadily improved, with a rapid expansion of local branches in the early 1960s, driven by a more socially diverse membership (Devine, 1999, p. 572).[29] Belying its earlier

---

26 Chris Harvie speaks of 'the great organizing force of the intellectual revival of the 1980s, Professor Cairns Craig' (in Bell and Miller (eds), 2004, p. 54).

27 For readers unfamiliar with this term, it was applied disparagingly by left-wing writers and critics from the 1920s onwards to what were seen as small-minded, sentimental and mawkish depictions of Scottish life.

28 The subaltern reference echoes another Gramscian concept, more recently deployed by Gyatri Spivak in 'Can the Subaltern Speak?' (2007).

29 'Between 1962 and 1968 party membership increased from 2000 to 120,000 and the number of SNP branches rose from 40 in 1962 to near 500 in 1968, comfortably exceeding Labour' (Hutchison, 2000, p. 119).

ideological eclecticism, the SNP was also consolidating its identity as a 'social democratic' party. At the 1963 party conference, Chris Harvie notes that the party 'went left on issues like disarmament and land nationalisation' (1998, p. 75), although Tom Devine suggests that the SNP retained a 'classless' appeal, which was attractive to new voters and aspirational voters without firm party affiliations (1999, p. 577).

While the rising affluence of the 1950s had kept the Home Rule issue quiet and kept Conservative and Unionist support high, the 1961 Toothill Report recognized that there were structural problems with the Scottish economy and presaged a series of government initiatives through the 1960s designed to remedy these.[30] This was also the era in which the military muscle of the Union led a Tory and then Labour government to base the submarine-mounted Polaris nuclear deterrent at the Holy Loch in Scotland (Devine, 1999, p. 578).

Labour's (narrow) win in 1964 after what Wilson dubbed '13 wasted years' was completely dependent at the UK level on their dominance in Scotland, where they won almost twice as many seats as the Conservatives, with the Liberal recovery from near parliamentary extinction in Scotland still amounting to only a rump of four seats.[31] Labour won again and more convincingly in 1966, increasing their majority in Scotland again, but the first signs of shifting tectonic plates came in November 1967, when Glasgow solicitor Winifred (Winnie) Ewing won a remarkable by-election for the SNP in the Labour heartland of Hamilton, with 46 per cent of the vote.

---

30 From first the Churchill/Eden/Macmillan/Douglas-Home Tory governments (1951–64) and then the Wilson Labour governments (1964–70). This was the era in which the economic muscle of the Union gave Scotland new industrial capacity at Ravenscraig, Linwood, Bathgate, Longannet, Dounreay (1966) and Invergordon (1968); the era of the Scottish Development Department (1962), the Central Scotland Plan and the Highlands and Islands Development Board (1965) (see Devine, 1999, pp. 572–3).

31 A UK majority of six was achieved via a majority in Scotland of 21. The Liberal result was of course the product of the highly distorting first-past-the-post electoral system.

## After Hamilton

Hamilton was a political earthquake that changed politics in Scotland, moving the SNP from joke to threat overnight and beginning a serious and often bitter rivalry between them and Labour. Edward Heath, leader of the Tory opposition, responded within months with his 1968 'Declaration of Perth' in which he committed the Conservatives (many of them dissenting) to a devolved Scottish assembly. Harold Wilson and Labour responded a year later with a Royal Commission on the Constitution chaired by Lord Crowther. While the threat level had increased and the other parties were now taking nationalist challenges seriously in both Scotland and Wales, the dominant view across both parties was still that this was a bandwagon that would lose momentum and a threat that could be managed out of existence.

Despite the false reassurance of a poor SNP result in the 1970 General Election,[32] this was not to be and after another sensational by-election win in Govan 1973, by Margo MacDonald,[33] the decisive electoral breakthrough for the SNP followed in February 1974, when they won seven seats and 22 per cent of the Scottish vote. The ideological changes of the early 1960s had been reinforced in the intervening years and Gerry Hassan notes: 'In the 1970s the SNP had self-proclaimed centre-left policies: its February 1974 manifesto called itself a "programme of social democracy", while the October 1974 manifesto was subtitled "A Programme for Social Democracy"' (in Hassan (ed.), 2009, p. 4).

The SNP had also boosted its radical credentials in one other key respect, while Labour had swiftly abandoned its unilateralist position, the SNP developed a strong anti-nuclear weapons position in the 1960s and has held to it ever since, marking a clear contrast with Labour from that time on and further inflecting its own brand of nationalism in contrast to British post-imperial defence policy.

---

32 Which led Ted Heath to drop the Tories commitment to devolution, on the grounds that the nationalist threat was receding.

33 The presence of high-profile woman 'winners' in the 1960s and 1970s has been a significant feature of the SNP, which has continued to prove its openness to women in leadership through the rise of Nicola Sturgeon.

Reaction to the 1974 election result was swift and, for Labour, a messy and divisive process. The new Labour government instantly reversed its manifesto position and made a hasty commitment to enact devolution. At the second 1974 election, the SNP did even better, leaving the Tories trailing in third place, as they secured 30 per cent of the vote. The fact that their seat total increased only to 11, behind the Tories 16 despite beating them in the popular vote, deepened the party's commitment to securing proportional representation for future elections. But the SNP were becoming the second force in Scottish politics, after Labour, and, crucially, were now second to Labour or the Conservatives in 42 constituencies.[34]

## Explaining the rising nationalist vote

Across the spectrum of historians, political scientists and political commentators there is a wide degree of consensus that the rise of electoral support for the SNP from the late 1960s onwards has been greater than the rise of support for either nationalism or independence. A vote for the SNP has often not been a vote for independence,[35] but a protest vote against both Labour Party establishments and Westminster governments of both hues (who have been seen to take Scotland for granted) and an 'advocacy vote' for those who were seen as most committed to defending Scottish interests within the UK. Again, there is a strong degree of agreement that a good deal of what was being protested was the changing economic condition of Scotland from the mid-1960s

---

34 Between the elections, Labour had experienced an internal party debacle on the devolution issue, with their Scottish executive rejecting all the options for constitutional change set out in a Spring 1974 White Paper from the British Labour Party. The Scottish Labour Party was still not united or settled in its will to see devolution. There were severe tensions between the desire of some Scottish activists to resist appeasement and fight the nationalist threat on traditional socialist terms and the anxieties of a British leadership, which feared it might never win another UK majority unless Labour responded to Scottish aspirations for greater Home Rule. A 'bloody' Special Conference was held in August 1974 in Glasgow, when the issue was hammered out in a series of bitter debates and the British party line was finally enforced via the trade union block vote.

35 Devine reports that in 1974 support for independence stood at a mere 12 per cent.

onwards. Labour in power, with the redoubtable Willie Ross at the Scottish Office, delivered rising levels of public expenditure between 1964 and 1970 and this continued under the first Heath government until 1973. When trouble came, it reflected two grim realities. A 1960s faith in planning was severely weakened by the failure of flagship projects and what now looks like poor judgement in tackling the historic imbalances of the Scottish economy,[36] as well as struggles to balance UK budgets and contain inflation. An economic strategy built on the assumption of endless supplies of cheap oil hit the buffers when OPEC shocked the world economy with price rises in 1974. The rise in oil prices followed soon after large-scale discoveries of oil in the North Sea, a factor that was used skilfully by the SNP to make 'crude' electoral capital from 1971 onwards[37] and a key factor behind their success in that year's elections. When Edward Heath led the Tories back to power after the second 1974 election, they were a minority government in Scotland for the first time. A Liberal revival in England was not matched in Scotland. The Conservative Party was already well into an extraordinary long-term decline in support within Scotland, from the dizzy heights of 1955, when they had won over 50 per cent of the total vote.

A further, less tangible strand of identity politics is also widely seen as significant. The 1960s, despite the strategy of holding on to an 'independent' nuclear deterrent, had been a decade of some humiliation for British foreign policy, which was already reeling from the pace of post-war decolonization. The Empire was gone and the colonies were going. As the Empire changed, so did Britishness and its meaning. Britain's move to join the EEC in 1973 reflected a pragmatic recognition of changing trade patterns and a new economic interdependence within Europe. There was little sign in the UK of the social and cultural idealism that had accompanied the economic self-interest of the original founding nations. Nonetheless, it opened new fronts in relation to sharing of sovereignty at different levels of government and set debates

---

36 The fate of Upper Clyde Shipbuilders in 1971 and the subsequent 'work-in' dramatized the dilemmas over whether old heavy industries had a future in a changing international market.

37 The slogan was crude on crude: 'It's Scotland's Oil!'

about nationalism within a new international and institutional context.

These four factors – economic decline, North Sea oil, a decline in Britain's international standing and entry into the EEC – were all key drivers of nationalist support at the polls. Labour won in 1974 with a new set of commitments to devolution and published its proposals for a Scottish assembly in 1975, just as the country began to sail into troubled economic waters. Tom Devine comments:

> The government had by now become widely unpopular and did not possess either the moral authority or the power in parliament [it was now dependent on a parliamentary pact with the Liberals] to manage effectively the most important constitutional change in the United Kingdom since the emergence of the Irish Free State in 1922. (1999, p. 587)

The government was forced to concede a referendum on the assembly proposals and this was then subjected by opponents of devolution, including Labour opponents, to a further requirement that unless 40 per cent of the electorate as a whole were in favour, the proposed new Scotland Act would fall. The referendum in March 1979 was a turbulent affair, with almost all Tories opposed and with Labour in Scotland still deeply divided. Scottish Labour MP Tam Dalyell famously raised the West Lothian question as an unacceptable by-product of asymmetric devolution: it being the 'question' of whether Scots MPs should be able to vote on issues for England, which English MPs could not vote on for Scotland. The SNP supported a Yes vote but scorned the weakness of the powers to be given to the assembly, as did some Labour dissidents who formed a breakaway Scottish Labour Party. The outcome was good for no one. Yes outweighed No by 51.6 per cent to 48.4 per cent of those voting,[38] but the Yes vote was only 32.9 per cent of the Scottish electorate as a whole and well short of the 40 per cent threshold. The Scotland Act fell and devolution was dead in the water, a defeat resented by those who felt they had won, and a pyrrhic victory for those who had lost

---

38 Turnout was only 63.8 per cent.

the popular vote. The Labour government then fell at the hands of an SNP tabled vote of no confidence, a bitter recrimination for Labour's failure to deliver devolution, which has ever since been the occasion for bitter recriminations by Labour against the SNP as 'Tartan Tories' who let Thatcher in. The SNP lost 9 of its 11 seats at the subsequent general election.

## *Fin de siècle* – the Thatcher years and the road to devolution

The West Lothian question was always a fair one, highlighting an inconsistency and even a potential injustice in advocating devolution for Scotland but not for England. The trouble was that if some measure of Home Rule for Scotland was to be pursued, the remedy would have to lie with adjusting the settlement for England, since the rest of the UK (RUK) apart from England would all come to pursue devolution in some form. In Scotland, the West Lothian question was rivalled and in time outweighed by what we could call the Thatcher question. Margaret Thatcher had, as Tom Devine says, 'a radical agenda for curing Britain's ills in which constitutional change had no part' (1999, p. 588). She was elected with majorities of 43, 144 and 102 in 1979, 1983 and 1987 respectively. In Scotland, the Tories won 22, 21 and 10 seats out of 71 in the same elections.[39] As the Conservatives' radical agenda of privatization, restriction of employment rights, sale of council housing and cuts to public spending was rolled out, the Scottish economy took a hammering, with a list of high-profile industrial closures[40] and soaring unemployment. Thatcherism was accused of being an approach to government and policy-making that favoured the South-East and Midlands of England (p. 594) and, despite admiration for Margaret Thatcher among a minority of the population, this fuelled a deep, widespread and bitter hostility to 'the lady' and her governments within Scotland. This was exacerbated by a rash decision to introduce the wildly unpop-

---

39 http://www.parliament.uk/documents/commons/lib/research/rp2003/rp03-059.pdf.

40 Famously articulated in The Proclaimers' 1987 song 'Letter from America': 'Methil no more, Irvine no more, Bathgate no more, Linwood no more'.

ular Poll Tax in 1987, and to do so in Scotland a year before it was introduced in England. Tom Nairn has observed that 'during the Thatcherite 1980s, an uncompromisingly British Union was stressed as never before' (in Bell and Miller (eds), 2004, p. 20). Despite (or because of?) this, the Thatcher question came to be characterized in terms of a 'democratic deficit', which was now expressed in national terms: Scotland voted Labour, but under the current constitutional settlement it got Conservative rule. The perception of a democratic deficit deepened between 1979 and 1997, through almost two decades and four general elections in which Scotland voted consistently and overwhelmingly[41] for parties of the centre and left, but was ruled by Conservative governments. It was a period that destroyed the Conservatives' electoral base for first-past-the-post elections north of Berwick and ended in a rout at the 1997 General Election, after which they had no MPs left in Scotland. These were years that saw Labour in Scotland finally unite around a commitment to devolution which commanded clear support across the party.[42] It was also a period that further reinforced the left-leaning identity of the SNP, as Gerry Hassan says:

After the 1987 election the party began to become more comfortable asserting a social democratic outlook. The party's identity became genuinely anchored on the centre-left, reflecting wider changes in Scotland and the fusing of the national dimension and centre-left politics. (in Hassan (ed.), 2009, p. 4)

## Culture becoming politics 1979–97

The wider changes within Scotland of which Hassan speaks reflected two decades of cultural and political activism that saw a mobilizing of 'civil society' groups around a range of key issues, including the constitutional question. The journalist and com-

---

41 At least 68 per cent of votes were cast for Labour, SNP and Lib Dems in this period.

42 Tom Nairn: '[the post-97 government] had no choice but to satisfy the demands of the Scottish and Welsh party contingents, by now firmly converted to "home rule"' (in Bell and Miller (eds), 2004, p. 22).

mentator Neil Ascherson wrote in his memoir, *Stone Voices*, that in the 1980s 'Politics stood still, but Scotland was moving' (2002, p. 41):[43]

> Scots who stayed in Scotland did a great deal of singing, writing, composing and painting in these years. With the political leadership lying face down in the rubble, there was nobody to preach about the art required by a renascent nation. As a result, an explosion of creativity took place, much the most remarkable period in culture since the 'Scottish Renaissance' of the 1920s. (p. 116)

Here we return to the disputed history of Gramsci reception in Scotland, as clearly some commentators understood then and still believe, that a whole range of cultural sites were becoming sites of political struggle and contestation.[44] This is exemplified in Chris Harvie's account of 'the ambiguity of a formerly "stateless" entity whose culture *had to become* its politics' (in Bell and Miller (eds), 2004, p. 53). The political machinations and machine politics around the 1979 referendum were an abrupt end of political innocence for my generation of young people in Scotland, but what followed were three decades that, for all their unevenness and loss, saw some strong currents of cultural and political renewal running. There have been signs, in many places, of Scotland taking itself more seriously and developing a new calculus of cultural value. Moving beyond the pioneering minorities of the 1950s and 1960s folk revival, the traditional and folk music world in Scotland has gone through a steady rise and expansion, with new centres of excellence, greater cultural visibility and exciting fusions and collaborations taking place.[45]

43 Tom Nairn suggests that 'the breaking up process was held back in Britain for eighteen years' during the Thatcher era (in Bell and Miller (eds), 2004, p. 21).

44 So Hearn: 'the recovery of Gramsci's thought has been highly influential on the British left and particularly in Scotland' (2000, p. 2). But see Neil Davidson's essay on Gramsci in Scotland for the fine detail of the argument on the left/among critical theorists about what Gramsci really meant and who (in Scotland) has or has not understood him/been true to his legacy (2010).

45 A notable cultural and political firework in 1973 was John McGrath and 7:84 theatre company's remarkable *The Cheviot, the Stag and the Black, Black Oil*, broadcast on TV in 1974. Since 1994, Glasgow's Celtic Connections winter festi-

Another cultural landmark was the explosion of Alasdair Gray's remarkable novel *Lanark* onto the Scottish literary scene in 1981. In a memorable and much cited passage, Gray not only named an unease widely felt among Scots, but set out a manifesto for a new generation of Scottish writers:

> 'Glasgow is a magnificent city,' said McAlpin. 'Why do we hardly ever notice that?' 'Because nobody imagines living here,' said Thaw ... 'Think of Florence, Paris, London, New York. Nobody visiting them for the first time is a stranger because he's already visited them in paintings, novels, history books and films. But if a city hasn't been used by an artist, not even the inhabitants live there imaginatively.' (Gray, 1981, p. 243)

Gray's insight touched a nerve for many who read it and it has been widely seen to apply to Scotland as a whole, representing and naming an alienation that needed to be addressed, not because it could simply be overcome but because it could be engaged and explored. From a Christian perspective, I suggest that the atheist Gray has named a spiritual alienation. There are good reasons why Christians are enjoined to be 'sojourners' and strangers, 'resident aliens', but the inability to live imaginatively in our own cities or countries is not one of them. The prophetic imagination that looks for a city with foundations is one in which an eschatological perspective insists upon imaginative engagement in the here and now. Without imaginative engagement with our own instantiation of Babylon/Jerusalem, we cannot effectively seek its welfare or rebuild its walls. Instead, we live there in a condition of detachment, lacking the imagination to pray or prophesy. The call of discipleship should produce its own dynamics of alienation and belonging, but they will be grounded in the power of litur-

---

val has developed into an exciting model of how enthusiasm for 'national' music can promote and almost insist upon a dynamic musical internationalism. Rather than greater awareness of the value of what is close to hand acting as a wall, it has become a window through which to look with interest and relish towards other cultures. Traditional musician and Gaelic singer Mary Ann Kennedy's *Global Gathering* programme on BBC Radio Scotland fulfilled a similar function in its confident willingness to move between contemporary Gaelic, Breton and Punjabi musical idioms within a single programme.

gical imagination not in the weakness of cultural imagination. In that sense, Irvine Welsh's 1993 *Trainspotting* as a howl of lament for an opiated, alienated Babylon/Edinburgh represents a positive response to Gray's call.

Culture as politics in late-twentieth-century Scotland wrestled with the regime of Thatcherism, but it was also straining to absorb and interpret a wider historical narrative.[46] The events of 1989 and the break-up of the Soviet Union in 1992, for all the disavowals and disengagements that had gone before from revisionist Marxists and socialists, were still sobering moments freighted with political symbolism for those on the Left. They were also moments in which nationalism came to the fore within Europe, demonstrating both its anti-imperial credentials and its atavistic potentials.

## Scotland in theory[47]

The period saw the arrival of two unexpected and original books, which appeared in Polygon's *Determinations* series edited by Cairns Craig, *The Eclipse of Scottish Culture* (1989) and *Scotland after Enlightenment* (1997). In *Eclipse*, Craig Beveridge and Ronald Turnbull offered a deconstructive reading of Scotland's intellectual traditions, in particular its historiography, which drew on the postcolonial theory of Frantz Fanon and his understanding of 'inferiorism', by which Fanon denoted the colonized coming to internalize and 'live out' an image of themselves as inferior to the colonizing power (Beveridge and Turnbull, 1989). *Scotland after Enlightenment* continued the identification and rejection of inferiorist and imperialist themes, but it countered these with a series of essays rereading key themes from Scotland's intellectual tradition. The analysis is strongly influenced by the

---

46 In the 1980s, Pope John Paul II's visit to Scotland, the Falklands War and the Miners' strike, Chernobyl, Lockerbie, the fall of the Berlin Wall and the end of apartheid. In the 1990s, Gulf War I, the Rwandan genocide, the Dunblane massacre, the Northern Irish peace process. The fabled oil was flowing, but there were doubts about who was benefiting. For a trenchant assessment of the story of Scotland's oil, see Harvie, 1995.

47 This subheading is borrowed from Bell's and Miller's edited 2004 collection.

work of Alasdair MacIntyre and the 'after' in their title echoed his seminal 1981 *After Virtue*. One of their most controversial and still least welcomed proposals was directed at the need for a reassessment of the cultural and intellectual influence and value of Scotland's Protestant and Calvinist religious traditions. Other critics and commentators within Scotland, especially secularist ones, who have relished the critique of inferiorism in their work, have been less comfortable with the idea that the widespread deprecation of these intellectual traditions might also be an example of that tendency. Overall, their work has had an uneven reception. Some have accused it of myopic valorization of 'native' traditions, while others have welcomed its main arguments as an overdue corrective. An example of its influence within a general review of twentieth-century Scottish literature would be the recent judgement of poet and literary scholar Roderick Watson, Professor Emeritus of English at the University of Stirling , who identifies as an aspect of Scottish culture lacking proper recognition 'the best of what might be called the Presbyterian intellectual inheritance in Scotland'. It has, he suggests, been 'undeservedly obscured or denied, because the popular imagination has been so easily distracted (and understandably repelled) by the worst excesses of Calvinism' (Watson, 2007, p. 6). There are signs therefore that Beveridge and Turnbull's work, along with that of Cairns Craig who is also sympathetic to MacIntyre, is beginning to offset the brash anti-Calvinism that has been in vogue since the early twentieth-century excoriations of MacDiarmid and others more inclined to hymn Lenin than the Christian deity.[48]

## Claiming Scotland[49]

Returning to the more conventional political narrative, while the newly converted assembly chamber on Edinburgh's Calton Hill sat gathering dust in the aftermath of the failed first referen-

---

48 Compare the titles of Hugh MacDiarmid's 1931/1935 collections of poetry *First/Second Hymn to Lenin* with Fearghas MacFhionnlaigh's poem *Laoidh nach eil do Lenin/A Hymn Which Is Not To Lenin*, excerpt in Storrar and Donald (eds), 2003, p. 232

49 The title of Jonathan Hearn's impressive study published in 2000.

dum, the culture as politics strand moved towards convergence with electoral politics by means of a series of trans-partisan initiatives. In the wake of the referendum defeat and the election of the first Thatcher administration, a new body, the Campaign for a Scottish Assembly (CSA), was created in 1980. Out of that came a drafting committee, which prepared the 1988 Claim of Right for Scotland,[50] leading in 1989 to the establishment of the Scottish Constitutional Convention, which finally published its blueprint for devolution, *Scotland's Parliament, Scotland's Right*,[51] on St Andrew's Day 1995. This was a period in which the looser, dialogical workings of a wide constellation of artists, writers, academics and columnists provided a stimulus to, running commentary on and critique of a new mode of political organization, the like of which had not been seen since the immediate post-war activities of the Scottish Convention. Jonathan Hearn analyses this process in relation to 'the public sphere', 'civil society' and theories of the 'New Class', suggesting that 'the post 1960s rise of nationalism had seen a corresponding flourishing of a new national intelligentsia actively engaged in Scottish political and cultural issues linked to the home rule cause' and that, from the 1980s, 'civil society' became a label of self-ascription for middle-class intellectuals and activists in Scotland.[52] An important challenge to a democratic deficit internal to this process came with the production of *A Woman's Claim of Right in Scotland* in 1991. Introduced by radical Kirk minister Kathy Galloway and Judith Robertson, it responded strongly to the lack of women's voices and perspectives in the Constitutional Convention (only 10 per cent) and the 'staggering' under-representation of women in the Westminster Parliament (only 5 per cent) (Woman's Claim of Right Group (ed.), 1991, p. 1). A key contention of the book

50 See full text of the Claim, along with 15 commentaries (all written by men!) in Dudley Edwards (ed.), 1989.

51 Text online at http://www.almac.co.uk/business_park/scc/scc-rep.htm.

52 See Hearn, 2000, pp. 77ff., quote from p. 91; cf. McCrone, 1992, p. 143, 'Scotland's professional classes – lawyers, doctors, teachers, churchmen [*sic*] – while socially conservative, embody the institutional survival of distinctive Scottish "civil society" and can be considered as keepers of native institutions', quoted in McGarvey and Cairney, 2008, p. 24; most bluntly, Richard Finlay suggests, 'The construction of the idea of civic Scotland was a polite way of saying that the Scots hated Thatcher' (2004, p. 367).

was that 'while women are seriously under-represented in representative democracy, they are enormously engaged in participative democracy' (p. 5). Isobel Lindsay noted the key proposal made to the Convention by the STUC Women's Committee for a 50/50 gender balance among MSPs (p. 9). The final Convention document claimed that 'one of the key principles of the Convention's vision is that there should be equal representation of men and women in the parliament'.[53]

## Enacting the Convention

From the 1980s, the idea of Scottish civil society combined the ambitions of a new intelligentsia with the agencies of a range of older Scottish institutions and organizations and allowed scope to supplement and circumvent party politics within both Scotland and the UK. The CSA/Claim Committee/Convention operated within a space which was vigorously contested by political parties. The Conservatives overwhelmingly resisted and boycotted all three as bridges too far. The SNP kept its distance and ultimately withdrew from the Convention because it did not go far enough, having refused to table independence as one of the constitutional options. In party terms, these trans-party/multi-party spaces were dominated by the Labour Party and served as the vehicles for its redemption and reinvention of itself in relation to the Home Rule question. Labour's progress on the Scottish question beyond the deep divisions of the 1970s was driven by an increasing frustration at the contrast between their dominance within Scottish politics and their impotence within UK politics from 1979 onwards. This was exacerbated by another sensational by-election win for the SNP in Govan in 1988, where the winning candidate was Jim Sillars, a former Labour MP and activist. Sillars branded Labour's Westminster MPs the 'feeble 50' for their powerlessness, in the face of an English parliamentary majority, to prevent the imposition of Thatcherite policies on Scotland. While Labour was

---

53 Comparisons can be made with the Quebec feminist slogan of the 1990s: 'No women's liberation without the liberation of Quebec; no Quebec liberation without the liberation of women' (Fidler, 1991, p. 163).

central to the Constitutional Convention process, the presence of other political parties and of representatives from the churches,[54] trade unions, business and third-sector groups led to a proposal that, not least in its espousal of proportional representation, went beyond Labour's own previous policy position. McGarvey and Cairney observe:

> When a political consensus amongst three of Scotland's four main political parties, as well as important institutions in Scottish civic society, coalesced around the constitutional convention, Scottish constitutional change became almost inevitable. (2008, p. 28)

Rereading the Claim document and the final Convention scheme several decades later, the contrast in tone between the two is striking. The Claim breathes frustration and indignation, spelling out the dysfunctional character of the British constitutional set-up, railing against the unfettered power of 'Crown in Parliament' and warning about a crisis in the legitimacy of Westminster rule. The Convention report, on the other hand, produced seven years later, carries a firm and determined 'practical intent'.[55] Its preamble has a ring of hard-won confidence to it:

> The Convention has a diverse membership, as diverse as we could make it. Diversity and unanimity are not natural companions. It is the instinct of political parties to disagree with one another, and the instinct of civic groups like the churches, the trade unions and others to be impatient with the preoccupations of politicians. This has meant that a lot of time and effort has been required to arrive at the proposals in this document. But at the end of that process we have an agreed scheme which all the parties involved believe to be the best way forward for Scotland. The way in which that scheme has been hammered

---

54 The Convention was chaired by Canon Kenyon Wright of the Scottish Episcopal Church, and the Church of Scotland and the Roman Catholic Church in Scotland were both actively involved.

55 The first line sets the tone: 'This report is about practical intent'; http://www.almac.co.uk/business_park/scc/scc-rep.htm.

out is its strength, not a weakness. What this process has proved is that constructive consensus is achievable, even among those steeped in the ritual confrontations of British politics.

The scheme finally proposed by the Convention was given strong support by Labour Leader John Smith and Shadow Scottish Secretary Donald Dewar. Smith famously described devolution as by now representing 'the settled will of the Scottish people' (B. Taylor, 2002, p. 317). The Convention scheme, which had been part of Labour's election manifesto, formed the basis for the Scotland Act 1998, enacted as one of the early measures of the 1997 Labour government after a referendum in September 1997 saw Scots vote Yes: Yes for a parliament with tax-varying powers. This time the result was unequivocal, with 74 per cent in favour of the parliament and 64 per cent supporting tax-varying powers. Although the SNP had left the Convention process, it campaigned strongly for a Yes/Yes vote in the referendum, with only the Conservatives and a few renegade Labour supporters left to oppose the parliament in principle. It was a decisive outcome, greeted with a mixture of relief and exhilaration by activists. Conservative opposition had been rendered irrelevant by the party's utter humiliation in the 1997 General Election, when it was left with no parliamentary seats at all in Scotland.[56]

## The Parliament reconvened

The passage of the Scotland Act led, in 1999, to the creation (or reconvening as Winnie Ewing famously declared at its opening) of a devolved Scottish Parliament, elected by proportional representation,[57] with limited tax-varying powers. A key feature of

---

56 This was, of course, a consequence of the grossly unfair first-past-the-post (FPTP) system, but it is hard to feel sorry for Conservatives disenfranchised by this, since they have been such resolute defenders of it. Ironically, Conservatism in Scotland has been 'saved' by both the Parliament it opposed and the electoral system of PR that it also opposed, allowing figures such as Annabel Goldie to emerge as a significant presence within the Scottish Parliament in its first decade.

57 The scheme involves constituency votes on a FPTP basis, with proportionality achieved through the election of additional members from regional lists.

the initial design of the devolutionary settlement was a presumption that powers were devolved, unless specifically *reserved* to the Westminster Parliament.[58] Powers over health, education, transport, housing, law and home affairs and policing were devolved, while powers in relation to international relations, defence, fiscal and monetary policy, welfare, immigration and reproductive rights were reserved.

It was often suggested, between 1707 and 1999, that the General Assembly of the Church of Scotland was the nearest thing Scotland had to a parliament, gathering representatives from every parish in Scotland to consider, among other things, the well-being of the nation under God and to engage in democratic debate and voting on the motions before them. It was, therefore, perhaps fitting to see the reconvened Scottish Parliament installed on 12 May 1999 in the Kirk's Assembly Hall on the Mound, where it lodged until its new home in Holyrood was finally ready in 2004. Among the highlights of the Opening Ceremony in May 1999 were the singing of Burns' egalitarian and internationalist anthem, 'A Man's a Man for A' That', by the folk singer Sheena Wellington and the 'congregation', while the Queen, Duke of Edinburgh, Prince of Wales, Duke of Hamilton among others. looked on impassively. Before the Burns song, the Parliament and guests had heard a new poem by Iain Crichton Smith (1928–98), one of Scotland's greatest modern poets and 'a Lewis man', who was raised Presbyterian but became an atheist.

## The Beginning of a New Song (Iain Crichton Smith)

Let our three-voiced country sing in a new world
joining the other rivers without dogma,
but with friendliness to all around her.

Let her new river shine on a day
that is fresh and glittering and contemporary;

---

58 For a list of reserved and devolved areas, see McGarvey and Cairney, 2008, p. 2.

*Post-Christendom Scotland*

Let it be true to itself and to its origins
inventive, original, philosophical,
its institutions mirror its beauty;
then without shame we can esteem ourselves.

In a moving and measured speech, Scotland's first First Minister, Donald Dewar, said to the assembled company and the watching masses, 'this is about who we are and how we carry ourselves'. Later, the religious note in the proceedings was provided by a communal singing of Psalm 100 in metre to an over-elaborated and rather slow version of the tune 'Old 100th'. The event was well done and remains moving to watch.[59]

## Without dogma?

Looking back on it and re-viewing it for this book, I am more struck now than I was at the time, by this ceremony as a liminal moment at the end of Scottish Christendom. Post-Christendom Scotland cannot ignore its religious past, but neither can it bear any longer to let its civic and political present be straightforwardly framed by public prayer. This event marked the beginning of a slow relegation of religion to the status of heritage, where it could still be honoured as 'Gaelic traditional music' or 'cultural classic' but with the secular framing the religious rather than vice versa. On this occasion, this is not being done vengefully, or carelessly, or with relish, but quietly and respectfully and even, perhaps, sorrowfully. The restraint reflects a realization that for all its seeming necessity, the passing of religion from its traditional role leaves a burden for secular culture to carry, about which it secretly has its own doubts. The deep secular ecumenism of Iain Crichton Smith's words (suffused still, like so much of his poetry, with biblical and theological imagery, for example the new river of Ezekiel/Revelation) is still defining the new project by a process

---

59 Video recordings of the 1999 opening and the 2004 ceremony to open the new parliament building at Holyrood can easily be found on the internet and replayed for the benefit of any readers who have never seen them.

of subtracting or 'sublating' Christianity and its effects: without dogma/without shame. The question theology inevitably poses to the poem is whether it understands 'dogma' and whether it can live without it. Does Athens truly offer a newness and freedom from shame that Jerusalem could not? There is a dangerous thinness to the veneer of newness Crichton Smith evokes here. The only trinity that survives is a purely linguistic one, its difference to be held together by 'friendliness' and 'beauty'. All good ... and each of these three (language, friendship, beauty) too often neglected or undervalued by Christian Scotland; but whether, without dogma, they alone can bring unity and newness and banish shame? These are larger questions and harder ones.

The final poignancy of this poem lies in its hope for self-esteem; addressing what Carol Craig would subsequently term 'the Scots crisis of self-confidence' (2003). The hope (in almost Edenic terms for a new 'unashamed' state?) is one that reflects the wound, expressing the testimony of the Presbyterian atheist to the damage done by religious tyranny and political weakness. In the Assembly Hall in 1999, the echoes of the new poem had to give way to the strains of the 'Old 100th', with its different claims about origins and esteem:

Know that the Lord is God indeed;
Without our aid he did us make:
We are his flock, he doth us feed,
And for his sheep he doth us take.

By 2004, the Kirking of the Parliament was an off-stage ceremony in St Giles Cathedral and the psalmody at the Opening Ceremony for Holyrood all safely hidden in Gaelic. Edwin Morgan's 'Open the Doors' poem for the opening of Holyrood was longer, less airy and more concrete, but it too dwelt on the problem of self-esteem:

Dear friends, dear lawgivers, dear parliamentarians, you are picking up a thread of pride and self-esteem that has been almost but not quite, oh no not quite, not ever broken or forgotten.

The importance of this theme, of 'how we carry ourselves', the charge that Christianity (particularly Calvinist and Presbyterian Christianity) has been destructive of it and the hopes for renovation and repair are questions I will return to in a future chapter. From here, I move in the next chapter to offer some reflections on the experience of a parliament restored and on an era of devolution that has witnessed increased debate about nationalism and independence.

# 6

# Tasting Notes

## Scotland's Parliament 1999–2014

Since devolution there have been four elections to the Scottish Parliament, leading to two Labour-led coalition administrations in 1999 and 2003, one SNP-led coalition administration in 2007 and one SNP majority administration in 2011. The system of proportional representation was assumed by many to mean that no one party would ever win an overall majority, but this assumption was shattered by the extraordinary surge of support for the SNP in the 2011 elections, in which they won 69 seats and an outright majority.[1] Alec Salmond was returned as a Nationalist First Minister of Scotland for the second time. With the other parties and the UK government accepting the SNP majority as constituting a mandate to do this, the party immediately moved to implement its manifesto proposal for a referendum on independence, with the precise date later confirmed as 18 September 2014.

A detailed account of the first decade of the new parliament is not for this book, but as practical theology it is concerned with reflection on practice and transforming practice. In previous chapters I sketched a Christian idea of society and a theological account of nationalism and tracked the development of devolution and nationalism up to 1999. This chapter aims to apply these to a reflection on Scotland from 1999 to 2013, leaving the final chapters to apply them to a vision for Scotland's constitutional and political future. The first task, then, is the 'tasting notes' promised

---

1 The rich irony here was that the FPTP retained at Westminster to avoid the evils of weak coalition government, delivered a coalition at Westminster, while PR at Holyrood, designed to make governing majorities hard to attain, delivered a majority government.

in the title of this chapter: what have been some of the significant 'sweet' and 'sour' notes of life in post-devolution Scotland?

## Sweet notes: Reduction of the 'democratic deficit'

Perception of a democratic deficit had become a major source of grievance during the 1980s and 1990s and was a key driver of support for devolution (across parties), as well as fuelling a slow rise in support for nationalism. There is widespread agreement across party lines that the introduction of the Scottish Parliament has reduced the deficit. I say reduced and not eliminated it, because supporters of independence continue to argue that, without independence, Westminster control over reserved matters will continue to mean policies opposed by a majority of Scottish voters at a General Election can be imposed by the UK Government. In the period following the 2010 election, and particularly since the onset of campaigning for the 2014 referendum, the theme of democratic deficit has been revived by Yes campaigners, with a particular focus on the austerity policies and welfare 'reforms' introduced by the Con–Lib Dem Westminster coalition. If the 2014 referendum votes No to independence, Unionist parties, including (finally) the Conservatives, are promising enhanced devolution, with greater fiscal powers and responsibilities.

## Sweet notes: Fairer voting

Proportional representation, at both national and local level, has allowed a fairer and more democratic representation of the political opinions and choices of people in Scotland. It has ended a long period in Scotland in which the dominance of the Labour Party rested upon an electoral system that exaggerated Labour's support through its lack of proportionality (see McGarvey and Cairney, 2008, p. 53). It has enabled the Conservative Party to regain proper representation in the Scottish Parliament,[2] which is currently denied to its supporters in Westminster elections, due to

---

2 Even after a difficult result in 2011 it retained 15 Holyrood seats, with around 13 per cent of the vote.

their weakness under first past the post (FPTP). Finally, it has enabled smaller parties, such as the Scottish Socialist Party and the Scottish Green Party, to gain representation within the Parliament in a way they have struggled to achieve at Westminster.

## Sweet notes: Coalition government

Including this as a 'sweet' note may be contested by some, but in the light of the British tradition of handing large parliamentary majorities to governments with a minority of the popular vote, I want to make the case for it. The tendency within British political culture to equate coalitions with weakness rests on a willingness to give ethical approval to the fact of being able to seize majority power with a minority popular mandate. The experience of the first three minority administrations at Holyrood was that a more consensual approach to governance is possible within coalition or, as in the case of the 2007 SNP administration, from within a minority administration.[3] The tendency towards high-handed partisanship can be restrained when parties have to share power with one another. The tendency is arguably to strengthen the hand of Parliament and there are signs that, particularly under the influence of the Liberal Democrats, Scottish politics (and, since 2010, UK politics) has begun to learn the mechanics of assembling coalitions. While deals may be done behind closed doors (one of the traditional criticisms), they are immediately presented to the public so that there is a degree of transparency about the programme for government that is then agreed. In the case of the Labour/Lib Dem coalitions at Holyrood in 1999 and 2003, coalition also led to important areas of policy divergence between the Labour-led administration in Scotland and the UK Labour government. The key areas where this was seen in Scotland were in the introduction of free personal care for the elderly, the abolition of up-front student fees and the introduction of PR for local government elections; all areas where Scottish Labour ended up supporting coalition policies that diverged from Labour's UK

---

3 The Liberal Democrats and SNP could not agree coalition terms, so the SNP led a minority administration with the qualified support of Green Party MSPs.

policies being implemented in England.[4] That Scottish/UK politics is turning away from its Faustian pact with FPTP and learning the ways of power sharing and compromise is to be welcomed. It is notable that both PR and power sharing first appeared in the UK political system in the Northern Irish context, as a crucial resource in responding to bitter social divisions. This reveals, positively, their potential contribution to a view of politics as peace-building and, negatively, the way in which the winner takes all/loser must fall outcome of FPTP is intrinsically violent and lacking in concern for those whose numbers or powers are less.

## Sweet notes: Improved gender balance of MSPs

This is still unfinished business, with cause for concern about the worsening of the ratio in 2007 and only a slight advance in 2011, but I rate it sweet rather than bittersweet because it is such a significant advance on Westminster. In the four Holyrood elections, women have made up 37 per cent, 40 per cent, 33 per cent and 35 per cent of elected MSPs (compared to 17 per cent (1997) 15 per cent (2001) 15 per cent (2003) and 22 per cent (2010) of Scottish Westminster MPs; 17 per cent of Scottish MEPs in 2013, and 21.6 per cent of Scottish local councillors in 2013).[5] There is particular pressure now on the SNP and Scottish Lib Dems to improve their performance in this area. Nonetheless, Holyrood politics has in its first decade seen around double the level of representation of women that Westminster has achieved in the same period. There has also been a female presiding officer and three female party leaders. This is by no means good enough, but it is progress and represents an advance that all parties claim that they are now trying to build on.

---

4 The introduction of the ban on smoking in public places is also an example, though led by a private member's bill.

5 https://genderpoliticsatedinburgh.wordpress.com.

## Sweet notes: more diverse social/educational backgrounds for MSPs

In comparison with Westminster, where the elite pathways of private education followed by Oxbridge education still figure disproportionately, MSPs are much more likely to have been educated within comprehensive schools and, although most are university educated, only a small minority have been to Oxbridge.

## Sweet notes: Green energy targets

Since devolution, Scotland has adopted targets for the reduction of greenhouse gas emissions and the production of renewable energy that are among the most ambitious anywhere in the world. In contrast to the policy pursued by all major parties for England, the SNP government has rejected any further development of nuclear generation capacity. In a relatively cold and damp climate, which is blessed with abundant resources of wind and a long coastline, Scotland has developed a well-contextualized energy policy whose ambition is to be commended, even if its implementation will require sustained political will. All Scotland's churches support this direction of travel, arguing on theological grounds that greater sustainability is an ethical imperative.

## Sweet notes: One Scotland, many cultures

From 2002, the Scottish Executive developed a pro-social inclusion, anti-discrimination campaign called 'One Scotland, Many Cultures'. While the research evaluating the programme came to mixed conclusions as to its effectiveness,[6] my point here is to stress the way in which this liberal, pluralist view of Scottish culture has been held in common through all four post-devolution administrations. The SNP has been just as comfortable with the 'One Scotland, Many Cultures' tag as the Labour/Lib Dem administrations were, and both the Conservatives and Greens were also supportive. While neither Scottish society nor Scotland's politi-

---

6 http://www.scotland.gov.uk/Publications/2005/11/2192152/21534.

cal parties are free from, racism or wrongful discrimination, the dominant public discourse to which the vast majority of Scottish institutions have signed up is one of equality, diversity and inclusion. This is as true of nationalist and pro-independence parties as of unionist parties. The United Kingdom Independence Party (UKIP), which has the most right-wing policies on immigration of any non-fascist parties in the UK and whose members the Prime Minister once accused of being 'closet racists',[7] has virtually no support base in Scotland. No political party in Scotland and no Scottish nationalist party or grouping has embraced anything other than a strongly egalitarian, 'liberal' and anti-discriminatory stance on issues of racism and immigration. The place where anti-immigrant or anti-asylum seeker rhetoric has been most in evidence has been in the pages of London-controlled right-wing media such as the 'Scottish' *Daily Mail*.

## Bittersweet notes: Land reform

Scotland's leading land reform campaigner, Andy Wightman, notes that after the Liberal reforms of 1880–1920, mainly focused on crofters' rights, 'not until the establishment of the Scottish parliament was there to be such a sustained effort to reform landed power' (Wightman, 2013, p. 311). On the sweet side, between 1989 and 2002, Highlands and Islands communities in Assynt, Eigg, Knoydart and Gigha managed to mount successful and inspirational community buy outs of landed estates (p. 314). In 2000, the Scottish Parliament passed an act abolishing feudal tenure, and in 2003 the Scottish Parliament introduced the Land Reform (Scotland) Act 2003, Part 1 of which affirmed that there was a right of responsible non-motorized access, for recreational and other purposes, to land and inland water throughout Scotland with few exceptions.[8] Part 2 of the 2003 Acts also provided for a ground-breaking, but very limited, 'Community Right to Buy', applicable only where a rural community registers interest

---

7 http://www.independent.co.uk/news/uk/politics/ukip-are-closet-racists-says-cameron-472769.html.

8 http://www.scotland.gov.uk/Topics/Environment/Countryside/16328/Access-rights.

in acquiring title to land and when the land comes up for sale at the landowner's decision. Land reform in Scotland is to be rated bittersweet, therefore, because there is so much still to be achieved. David Cameron, Chair of Community Land Scotland, argues that Scotland stands out within Europe as having 'the most anachronistic and concentrated land ownership patterns'. He cites St Andrew's University academic Charles Warren's book, *Managing Scotland's Environment*. Warren writes:

> Half of the entire country is held by just 608 owners and a mere 18 owners hold ten per cent of Scotland. Of Scotland's private land, 30 per cent is held by 103 owners, each with 9,000 hectares [22,250 acres] or more, and 50 per cent by 343 owners. A minuscule 0.025 per cent of the population owns 67 per cent of the privately owned rural land. Thirty owners have more than 25,000 hectares [61,750 acres] each.[9]

After the 2011 election, the SNP government established a new Land Reform Review Group, chaired by a former Moderator of the Church of Scotland. Already it is clear that any meaningful reform will be opposed tooth and nail by the vested interests of those who are land-rich in Scotland. The sweetness lies in having a parliament that will once again look at issues of land reform, long ignored by Westminster.[10] The bitterness lies in who owns Scotland, in how they got it and in how tenaciously they will resist any democratization of ownership.

## Bittersweet notes: Local government reform

Despite the welcome introduction of PR for local elections, which has made the spread of councillors more representative of voters' preferences, local government in Scotland remains tarnished by its own deficits in relation to voter participation and local control. Turnouts in local elections remain very low, with the introduction

---

9 Warren quoted in David Cameron, 2013; article online at http://www.scottishleftreview.org/article/land-not-out-of-our-hands/.
10 Cf. Wightman, 2013, p. 352, 'The Land Reform Act ... had the Scottish Parliament not been established, would never have reached the statute book.'

of PR in 2004 arguably coming too late to offset a long-term trend of growing voter cynicism and apathy. The SNP administrations of 2007 and 2011 have introduced nationally led council-tax freezes, which have been highly popular with voters, but which have not been positive for local democracy. Andy Wightman argues that Scotland is over-centralized but under-governed and needs many more local authorities, with real powers over local issues, but on this he has fewer supporters than on his land reform agenda.[11] The conduct of local government election campaigns through national party organizations also tends to generate phony ideological wars on issues where more pragmatic local deliberation is needed, as parties over-compete to differentiate themselves from one another. With the exception of PR, this remains an area in need of reform and renewal.

## Bittersweet notes: Scotland's prisons

In June 2013, Professor Fergus McNeill of Glasgow University's Centre for Crime and Justice Research expressed his relief that political debates around prisons in Scotland mostly did not take the form of a race to the bottom, in terms of competition for the toughest line on 'lock 'em up and throw away the key'. His sense that there was a developing debate about how to improve Scotland's prisons and how to reduce the numbers being imprisoned was echoed by the Chief Inspector of Prisons, David Strang. Karen McCluskey of the Scottish Violence Reduction Unit spoke about the need for (secular) redemption, hope and second chances for many of those who end up in Scotland's prisons.[12] The bitterness of too many people imprisoned, most of them from Scotland's poorest communities, in conditions that still need to be improved, is only a little sweetened by the sense of a serious civil and political drive to reduce violence, reduce the prison population and improve prison conditions.

---

11 http://www.scotregen.co.uk/scotregen/global-regenerating/.

12 My own record of comments made by McNeill, Strang and McCluskey at Solas Festival in June 2013. For more information on the Scottish Violence Reduction Unit see: http://www.who.int/violenceprevention/about/participants/vru_scotland/en/index.html.

## Bittersweet notes: Participatory democracy

Some campaigners for a Scottish Parliament invested considerable hope in the creation of a Scottish Civic Forum, which would
run alongside Holyrood as a supplement to the Parliament. This
had mixed success, with many feeling that the greater accessi-
bility of the Scottish Parliament rendered it redundant and when
funding was withdrawn in 2006 the Forum folded due to lack
of popular support. The process for petitioning Parliament has
been more successful,[13] with an innovative system for allowing
e-petitions to be launched which has drawn international interest
and attention. However, to date there is little sign of it shaping
policy (McGarvey and Cairney, 2008, p. 240). There has been no
real support among the main parties for a more extensive use of
referenda as is common in Switzerland or at federal level within
the USA.

## Bittersweet notes: Performance of Scottish parliamentary committees

The Scottish Parliament was intended to be more open and consensual and a strong committee system was designed in as a key
part of this, aiming to be 'extraordinarily deliberative, rationalis-
tic, open and consensual' (Arter, 2002, p. 99, quoted in McGarvey
and Cairney, 2008, p. 97). There are perhaps two cheers to be
offered for the system in action, as it has proved to be valuable
and accessible, particularly with less contentious legislation, but
also vulnerable to grandstanding, overloading and railroading on
contentious issues.

## Sour notes: Levels of poverty and inequality remain stubbornly high

At the end of 2012, 15 per cent of the Scottish population and 16
per cent of Scotland's children were described as living in poverty
according to official UK/European measures.[14] There has been

---

13 Well over 1,000 petitions have been initiated since 1999.
14 http://www.scotland.gov.uk/Resource/0042/00424793.pdf.

almost no change in levels of economic inequality since 1998/99, with the poorest 30 per cent of Scots receiving 14 per cent of overall income in 2011/12 and the richest 30 per cent receiving 52 per cent of overall income.[15] In this key dimension of Scottish life despite reduction of child poverty and reduction of economic inequality, both being among the Scottish government's targets, devolution has not yet delivered any meaningful change.

## Sour notes: Levels of violence remain unacceptably high

Every year more than 100 people are killed in violent attacks in Scotland. The Scottish government reports that there were 51,926 incidents of domestic abuse in Scotland recorded by the police in 2009–10, with 82 per cent of incidents involving a female victim and a male perpetrator.[16] The most recent research studies of violence in relation to Scottish young people find strong correlations between levels of violence and experience of poverty, problematic parenting, abuse of drugs and alcohol and growing up in areas marked by gang organization to defend territory and reputation.[17]

## Sour notes: Decline in political participation

Voting is not compulsory in any UK election and all parties profess themselves concerned about declining levels of political participation. Party membership has been on a long-term slide, such that in 2014 fewer than 1 in 100 Scots are members of any political party, and the majority of party members simply pay their subs but take little or no part beyond that (McGarvey and Cairney, 2008, pp. 63–6).[18] Overall turnout in the 2011 Scottish parliamentary election was just over 50 per cent and turnout in

---

15 http://www.scotland.gov.uk/Resource/0042/00424793.pdf, p. 17.

16 Source: Scottish government 2010, Statistical Bulletin Crime and Justice Series: Domestic Abuse Recorded by the Police in Scotland (not all incidents were of physical abuse and not all are technically crimes), http://www.scotland.gov.uk/Topics/People/Equality/violence-women/Key-Facts.

17 http://www.scotland.gov.uk/Resource/Doc/326952/0105428.pdf.

18 Though membership of the SNP has been rising since 2003 and in 2013 was reported at 25,000 compared to c. 13,000 members of Scottish Labour.

the 2010 General Election was 64 per cent, both figures which have been seen as troubling evidence of public alienation from the political process. Political participation is higher among wealthier sections of the population and lower among those with lower incomes and lower levels of educational achievement.[19] Both low levels of party membership and low election turnout are critical issues for the future of the Scottish political system.

## Sour notes: Bitter rivalry between Labour and the SNP

The bitterness of relationships and exchanges between Labour and SNP has been a disfiguring and dismaying dimension of Scottish political culture in recent years. McGarvey and Cairney noted in 2008 that 'in ideological terms there is little to separate the two main parties ... the SNP and Labour have tended to attract support from the same social base' (p. 65). Ironically, it has been the lack of ideological difference that seems to have acerbated the sour and highly personal character of this rivalry. Douglas Alexander in 2013 was still recycling stories of being spat on by SNP supporters after an election count many years before,[20] while Alex Salmond relates stories of his father being disgusted by Labour canvassers deriding the 'Scottish Nose-Pickers'.[21] Labour and the other Unionist parties complain bitterly about the aggressive online activities of so-called 'cyber-nats',[22] while 'nats' complain about the range of hostile unionist media ranged against them. Given the range of common causes in the area of social, economic and cultural policy, the bitterness of many exchanges reflects a frantic competition for power, built on a constant competition to belittle and humiliate political opponents. This rivalry offers a graphic illustration of the need to civilize Scottish politics and to reschool society in the ethics of political discourse.

---

19 http://www.equalityhumanrights.com/uploaded_files/triennial_review/how_fair_is_britain_ch14.pdf.

20 As witnessed by me at Solas Festival in Perthshire in June 2013.

21 Profile of Alex Salmond by Tracey McVeigh in *The Observer*, 8 May 2011.

22 Though this is sometimes used tactically and aggressively as a political insult against any critique offered online, as I know from personal experience.

## Sour notes: The eclipse of Scottish banking

The financial crisis of 2008/09 proved to be a catastrophe for the Scottish banking sector, with both the Royal Bank of Scotland and Halifax Bank of Scotland (HBOS) having to be rescued from collapse by state intervention. This, combined with the discrediting of Gordon Brown's unwise claims to have ended 'boom and bust' cycles for the UK economy, was the symbolic end of a cultural conceit about prudence, thrift and sober financial management being somehow genetically encoded within 'canny' Scots and their 'sound' financial institutions. The enormous fortunes made by many working within the financial sector turned out to have been built upon 'the privatization of profit and the socialization of risk'. Champions of free markets and implacable ideological opponents of government intervention overnight became fervent advocates of state rescues of institutions that were 'too big to fail'. This was very definitely a moment of truth in which the culture and practices of the financial sector were laid bare. In subsequent years, the public watched the bizarre spectacle of the state continuing to hand out fines to institutions it had a majority stake in (effectively fining itself) for persistent mis-selling of financial products and manipulation of inter-bank lending rates. Overnight, a lingering perception of ethical surplus was exposed as covering over a major ethical deficit. If there were any lingering cultural justification for the 'canny' Scot reputation in banking, Scotland's institutions have slipped their moorings from it. Tragically, they have become just another set of hustlers in a grotesquely amoral and immoral financial system.

## Sour notes: Public health outcomes remain unacceptably low

Since 1999, academics and practitioners working in the area of public health have come to play a leading role in debates about the future of Scottish society. Scotland has one of the worst public health records in Europe, with higher mortality rates for cancer, heart disease and stroke than elsewhere in the UK and one of the lowest life expectancy rates in Western Europe.[23] Much of this has been related to the so-called 'Glasgow effect', with poor health outcomes stubbornly concentrated and clustered around Glasgow and in particular its poorest communities.[24] Scotland's lead in the smoking ban was prompted by a public health response to its high smoking/cancer/heart disease rates and is already seen to have been a successful initiative. However, levels of alcohol consumption remain 20 per cent above the UK average (hence the moves from 2011 onwards to introduce minimum pricing for alcohol), obesity and diabetes levels are increasing and one in seven of the population is on antidepressants, with over 10 per cent of over 15-year-olds making daily use of an antidepressant drug.[25]

## Sour notes: Sectarianism

While public debate in Scotland remains divided over the extent of sectarianism, academic opinion is less so. Although there are differences of opinion about how prevalent sectarian behaviour is, most researchers believe it is a diminishing problem within Scottish life, associated with particular groups and hot spots. This is in no way to diminish its vicious and sometimes deadly effects. There are no acceptable levels of sectarianism and it remains an evil to be rooted out from Scottish society. Successive Scottish governments have been at pains to show support for anti-sectarian initiatives and there are clear signs that sectarian language and attitudes have been thoroughly delegitimized across public discourse in Scotland. A sour note certainly, but one that is diminishing and one where, again, there is little difference between the main political parties. Both unionists and nationalists are united in their condemnation of sectarianism.[26]

---

23 http://www.scotpho.org.uk/population-dynamics/healthy-life-expectancy/key-points.

24 Most of Scotland's poorest communities are located in the Greater Glasgow area (as is most of Scotland's population).

25 http://www.isdscotlandarchive.scot.nhs.uk/isd/6517.html.

26 The prospect of independence raises constitutional issues about Protestant privilege, which are addressed later in the book, but these are already present within the Union settlement and could arguably be somewhat improved after independence.

## A foretaste of the future

The reflections developed above are necessarily brief. There are two reasons why I have bothered to work through them here, both of which have to do with the question of whether support for a nationalist project can be an ethical option in the specific case of Scotland. The first, negative, reason is to explore whether there are policy areas, or any areas of human life and society, where the move towards devolution and the prospect of independence might be tending to work against Christian ideas of the good society. Are there areas where the classic sins of bad nationalism are gaining ground or would gain ground, where the union has been keeping them at bay? The second, positive, reason is to explore whether there are policy areas, or any areas of human life and society, where devolution has moved and independence might move Scotland closer to a vision of the good society.

At the end of Chapter 4 I suggested that even when the case had been made for what Hearn calls a 'de-fanged' nationalism (2006, pp. 165–6), there were questions of practical policy and deliberation in play. Unless we are some kind of fundamentalist nationalist who rejects the option of ever being allowed the democratic choice to enter an incorporating, federal or intergovernmental union, the likely effects of becoming independent have to be part of our ethical reasoning. Would independence result in the impoverishment of either our population or those in the union we leave? Would independence be likely in any given case to lead to war? Would independence be likely to result in inferior treatment for people, especially vulnerable minorities, in either the new state or the state we leave? Would independence in some way do more harm than good?

My judgement is that, on balance, Scotland would be no more at risk of things turning sour than it is now and that in key areas opportunities for sweetening our society would be enhanced. I set out the case for this in more detail in the next chapter.

# 7

# Calling Time

Not enough contemporary political theology is also practical theology, because it operates at a level of remoteness and abstraction from the lived experience of the societies within which it is produced. Equally, not enough practical theology is also political theology, because it declines to engage with concrete political realities.

This book makes a gesture towards overcoming that, though still at a higher level of generality than is needed, even in the case of a wee country. It represents an attempt to think towards a manifesto and programme for political theology in Scotland, which is informed by international theological conversations and hopes to give something back to them. Theological reflection in a context of constitutional debate and reflection will hear and notice things that theology done in settled constitutional contexts will not. Equally, it will need the theoretical correctives provided by those whose work reflects different contexts and different themes, including essential continuing engagements with traditions of political theology and political theory. The last two chapters were practical theology as reflection on practice. This chapter is concerned with practical theology as a means of transforming practice. My understanding of practical theology is that, from its primary location within the Church, it reflects on practice in the Church and in the world, for the sake of the Church's witness to the *missio Dei* and as part of the Church's prayer for the coming of God's reign.

The Reformed tradition within which I serve and through which I am theologically accountable[1] has been criticized for its fantasies

---

1 I subscribe to a Presbyterian version of Stanley Hauerwas' claim that the theologian is subject to the bishop.

of social control and discipline. As a Reformed Christian, I welcome the challenge that comes from the Radical Reformation critique of the legacy of Christendom and its encouragement to the Church to be the Church, eschewing pretensions to power and rule. The Church's confession that Jesus is Lord and the Church's witness to the reign of God should be made without recourse to over-realized eschatologies or attempts to secure in human strength a victory that is already won in Christ and will be revealed in time through the sovereignty and providence of Almighty God. With that confession rightly made, however, I remain convinced of wider possibilities and responsibilities for what Duncan Forrester has called 'the political service of theology in Scotland' (in Storrar and Donald (eds), 2003, pp. 83ff.) and, in keeping with that, for the political service of Christians in Scotland. Christians have a catholic vision of their place within one humanity in creation and one Church in redemption. That vision relativizes and disciplines their commitments in every area of human life. Their practice of these claims in worship and discipleship is theologically prior to their participation in the claim-making practices of nationalism and the political activity associated with this. *In practice*, these two dimensions, discipleship and political activity, are experienced together and each has to be discerned through the other. The Church's liturgical rhythms of prayer and worship, of proclamation and listening, of baptism and communion continually reassert the priority of theology over politics.

In worship, the *ekklesia* proclaims the sovereignty of God, adores the goodness of God, confesses the fallibility of all human life, including its political dimensions, attends to the revelation of God in Scripture and responds to the presence of God in baptism and communion.

In worship, the *ekklesia* relearns the world as God's world and its people, all of its people, as beloved by God.

In worship, the *ekklesia* is formed ethically and practises and rehearses its ethics in microcosm, recognizing and blessing life in baptism, engaging in corporate confession of sin, giving and receiving signs of peace, sharing the goods of bread and wine and seeking the good of others in intercession.

When the time of worship comes to an end, with blessing and

dismissal, when the ingathering of *ekklesia* turns into the out-sending of *mission*, the people of God are sent to their domestic service, their social service, their cultural service, their political service in the world.

The intensification of worship, its gratuitousness and play, its feel for beauty and adoration, its delight in gift and relationship, its rituals of peace and absolution, these are recognized as pre-figuring a vision of life in all its fullness, as foretastes and firstfruits of an eschatological sweetness.[2] The original mission of humanity to *live*, to live in God and to know all things in God, is rejoined in daily discipleship, animated by the Spirit of God, united by the Spirit to the risen Christ.

For Christians living between the times there is a disjunctive and incongruous dimension to their living, so that we say as the writer of the letter to the Hebrews says, we do not yet see 'all things' subjected to the reign of God (Heb. 2.8–9). We are conscious, along with Paul in Romans 8, of 'creation groaning', longing for its liberation. In worship, we learn, beginning with our own lives but reaching out to every dimension of life, to pray for the hallow-ing of God's name, the coming of God's reign on earth.[3]

This space of disjuncture and incongruity, which is first of all the space of my–our own life and practice, but is also the space of social, cultural and economic life, becomes a place of calling and a place of work. The calling always precedes and summons the work. The call is to glorify and enjoy God forever in our liv-ing. The brokenness in our realization of that is not just due to our own fallenness, but to our finitude and our vulnerability to the brokenness of others as it hits our lives in both personal and systemic ways. My ability to glorify God in my life and work can be compromised by my own vanity, greed and laziness. It can also be compromised by personal and systemic actions, by

---

2 This is not exclusive to worship, although it can be argued it is essential to wor-ship. But in art, sport, friendship, sex, family life, experiences of the natural world there are also moments of profound connection through which we can glimpse and taste the redemption of all things in Christ.

3 Cf. D. Stephen Long's claim that both Torah and Lord's Prayer are social projects/social ethics, set in the context of the formation of a people. He also cites Lohfink's ethical-hermeneutical question: what form shall the people of God take? (2010, p. 38).

brutalizing or degrading treatment, by low pay, by wrongful discrimination, by my participation in economically distorting and
environmentally degrading systems of production and exchange,
by my location within structures and systems that disempower
me, by lack of educational opportunity, by lack of food or shelter
or love.

The elaboration of a Reformed political theology, which dreams
of a disciplined economy, a good society, a godly commonwealth,
is not just a fantasy of elite control by Christians desperate to get
their hands on the levers of power; although it has sometimes
been that in the past. It can also be imagined as a humble and
penitent work, inspired, as John Bell's great hymn says, 'by love
and anger' and animated by the Holy Spirit, the Spirit of holiness,
whose sanctifying work in Christians impels them to see every
area of life in relation to the liberating reign of God.

Dutch Calvinist theologian and politician Abraham Kuyper
made the famous claim that 'there is not a square inch in the
whole domain of our human existence over which Christ, who
is Sovereign over all, does not cry, "Mine!"'. Elsewhere Kuyper
offers a classic statement of the Reformed vision of Christian
vocation in the world:

> Whatever man may stand, whatever he may do, to whatever
> he may apply his hand – in agriculture, in commerce, and in
> industry, or his mind, in the world of art, and science – he is,
> in whatsoever it may be, constantly standing before the face of
> God. He is employed in the service of his God. He has strictly
> to obey his God. And above all, he has to aim at the glory of his
> God. (Kuyper, 1899, p. 63)

In contemporary European societies such as Scotland, such rhetoric will often be met beyond the churches, with surprise, scepticism
and, sometimes, hostility. Chasing the approval of aggressive
'hard' secularism is a fool's game, but that said, Christ's command
is to 'let your light shine before others, so that they may see your
good works and give glory to your Father in heaven' (Matt. 5.16).

Here we return to the case made in different ways by Nicholas
Wolterstorff and Jeffrey Stout for participation in public life in

such a way that none of us are disqualified from bringing to the table our reasons and reasoning for the public policy positions we support.

That means Christians and Christian theologians speaking in our own voices as we share our visions for the future, as we set out our ideas for public policy, as we offer our analysis of how things are and why. This will involve forms of scriptural and theological reasoning that may seem foreign and exotic to political and cultural discourses that collude in occluding their own debts to Scripture and theology. Whether that difficulty and even embarrassment at hearing explicitly Christian talk in public discourse increases or diminishes is mostly outwith the control of theologians, except that their retreat from distinctively Christian speech will only exacerbate its strangeness.

Recognizing that my ambition exceeds both my ability and opportunity in this book, in the rest of this chapter I try to sketch the outline of a Christian, 'reformed' theological vision for transforming Scotland.[4] Even when I use the restrained language of 'try', 'sketch', 'outline', this feels like a risky venture.

That it feels so is worth reflecting on. There are some obvious risks. One is *presumption*, which is a good reason for making clear that this is 'a' and not 'the' Christian vision. Theology is the work of the whole Church, it takes place within a critical, mutually correcting conversation in which all who join the conversation (including theologians) are wise to be attentive to one another in a spirit of humility and generosity.[5] Another risk is *superiority* and has to do with the difficulty of holding rightly in public to convictions about the truthfulness of Christian beliefs, including divine sovereignty and the centrality of Jesus Christ, without becoming a monster or an asshole. A risk that is harder to name is what I will call *eccentricity*, meaning by that an overdeveloped sense of distinctiveness or specialness.[6] As someone tempted by

---

4 Or, as Chris Harvie puts it in the title of a 2004 book, *Mending Scotland*.

5 There is something deeply unchristian about the idea of an incorrigible theologian.

6 This runs close to what John Howard Yoder and Stanley Hauerwas are often accused of by Reformed theologians, in their concern for the distinctiveness and faithfulness of Christian witness and their insistence that Christians should not try to 'run the world' or 'win' in history.

Anabaptism, I find eccentricity the most beguiling risk, but as someone within the Reformed tradition, I also feel the temptation of *conformity*: not least that of showing other folk on the political Left in Scotland that my theological vision has impeccable leftist credentials.

Perhaps the biggest risk is one of which much Christian social thinking in the modern era has been wary, namely that arising from the awareness that a little knowledge is a dangerous thing. Denominations like the Kirk or the Church of England, in their annual 'social theology' reports, have long had two fears: one of being seen by the relevant experts as meddling amateurs; the other of courting their own members' wrath if they press too forcefully from general Christian 'principles' or 'axioms' towards very specific policy implications.[7]

In recent Scottish practical theology, *middle axioms* have been critiqued by Duncan Forrester and defended by Will Storrar, although both agreed that the Kirk's wartime Baillie Commission represented one of that approach's finest hours (Storrar, in Morton (ed.) 1994, p. 63).[8] Their critiques circled around the problem of social theology stopping short and not saying enough (Forrester) versus the challenge of it making a substantial and lasting policy contribution (Storrar).[9] I see in that a counsel to be flexible in deciding how far to press the implications of a Christian position

---

7 Although 'middle axioms' are often associated with Archbishop William Temple, the term was first coined by Joseph Oldham in his preparatory volume for Oxford 1937, written with W. Visser 't Hooft (1937, pp. 209–10). Here the authors argue that 'it belongs to the prophetic and teaching office of the Church to expound the implications of the Christian understanding of life'. The key paragraph that coins the term reads: 'Hence, between purely general statements of the ethical demands of the Gospel and the decisions that have to be made in concrete situations there is need for what may be described as middle axioms. It is these that give relevance and point to the Christian ethic. They are an attempt to define the directions in which, in a particular state of society, Christian faith must express itself. They are not binding for all time, but are provisional definitions of the type of behaviour required of Christians at a given period and in given circumstances.'

8 In my PhD thesis I wrote that 'only John Baillie fully embraced the concept of "middle axioms". Ian Fraser and Duncan Forrester tended to emphasize the importance of concrete dialogical encounters between theologians/churchpeople and policymakers, which moved between an overall horizon of "social vision" and specific proposals for "social action"' (Gay, 2006).

9 Both conceded that it made a difference how well the approach was used.

towards detailed policy prescription and when to reserve judgement at a more general level. A detailed position may be quickly
overtaken by events or information, while a more general position
may prove its value in defining the limits or range of action that
Christians might plausibly support.

A middle axiom may, like the Baillie Commission's 1942 call
for more democratic control over the British economy, strike a
bold prophetic note, which both seems profoundly fitting for the
needs of its own time and offers a challenging rebuke to the timid-
ity of our statements today.

The need to be reflective and self-conscious about the risks of
theo-political visions, does not mean that such risks should not
be taken. There will always be value in judicious and cautious
treatments of an issue, but there are also *kairos* moments, when a
judgement must be made about a key issue or challenge.

As I finished this book, the referendum on independence for
Scotland lay exactly one year ahead. Some, but I hope not all, of
its readers will know the result by the time they read this. If the
referendum rejects independence, most commentators now pre-
dict that an enhanced level of devolution will follow, but most
also agree that it will be some time (probably decades?) before the
direct question of independence could be put again in a similar
referendum. If there is or was a vote for independence, we will be
living in interesting times after September 2014.

This moment therefore represents a contextual challenge for
political theology across the UK and Scottish political theology in
particular. It deserves to be taken with a theological seriousness
and addressed with a kind of honest and clear-headed judgement
that party loyalties and political contests often obscure.

As a constitutional issue, raising the question of a new constitution being created,[10] it has a particularly telling interface with
both church history and the history of political theology in relation to the pre-1603 and 1707 Scottish State and the post-1707
British state.

---

10 The Church of Scotland called at its 2013 General Assembly for the Scottish
government to publish a draft constitution ahead of the referendum, a call that is
likely to be resisted.

If there was ever an area of politics in which theological literacy was self-evidently necessary, it is the area of constitutional politics in this kingdom with its anointed monarch and asymmetric establishments of religion as well as its asymmetric devolution settlement.

## Constitutional evolution + devolution

One obvious but helpful approach is to set the 2014 decision in historical context:

| | |
|---|---|
| 1603 | The Union of the Crowns, James VI of Scotland becomes James I of England and Scotland. |
| 1649 | King Charles I of England is executed by Parliamentarians. |
| 1657 | Cromwell and Second Protectorate Parliament create the Commonwealth of England, Scotland and Ireland (dissolved in 1660). |
| 1707 | The Union of Parliaments creates the United Kingdom of Great Britain. |
| 1801 | United Kingdom of Great Britain and Ireland is created. |
| 1885 | Extension of Franchise – majority of adult males able to vote for the first time. |
| 1918/1928 | UK finally becomes a democracy with votes for women partially from 1918 and on equal terms with men from 1928. |
| 1921 | Irish Independence and Partition. |
| 1937 | New Irish constitution adopted, oath of allegiance to British monarch abolished. |
| 1969 | Voting age for women and men lowered to 18. |
| 1973 | UK joins the European Economic Community (EEC). |
| 1993 | European Community created by Maastricht Treaty. |
| 1998 | National Assembly of Wales created, Northern Ireland Assembly created. |
| 1999 | Scottish Parliament created; partial reform of House of Lords. |

| 2009 | Treaty of Lisbon replaces European Community with European Union. |
| 2010 | Further powers devolved to Northern Ireland Assembly. |
| 2011 | Further powers devolved to Welsh Assembly. |

I have included certain 'disruptive' elements within the constitutional timeline which would not be there in some versions of history, in particular the constitutional landmarks of majority adult male suffrage and the final achievement of a fully 'democratic' suffrage in the UK in 1928. Given the history of exclusions from the franchise on class, ethnic and gender grounds in countries like the USA and UK, and their persistence into the twentieth century, references like that of theologian John W. de Gruchy to 'countries with a long democratic tradition' (in Scott and Cavanaugh (eds), 2004, p. 444) are open to question or at least qualification.

What this timeline makes clear is that the UK's constitutional settlements have long been in process, subject to evolution, negotiation, union, devolution and dissolution.

The scope and reach of democracy has been in question for centuries, both in relation to which sections of society were allowed a vote, but also in relation to the boundaries of the state. For example, between 1878 and 1928, we moved from a nineteenth-century context in which Great Britain and Ireland operated with a franchise restricted to a minority of the most privileged males, to a twentieth-century context in which Great Britain and *Northern Ireland* operated with a franchise including almost all adult women and men and Ireland became independent.

Between 1947 and 1997, we saw first the rapid dismantling of the British Empire, beginning with the liberation of India from British imperial rule, and then the unravelling of the imperial legacy through decades of decolonization, up to the return of Hong Kong to Chinese rule. From 1973, we saw the rise of UK participation in a new era of shared sovereignty europolitics, extended by subsequent treaties of the European Union. Meanwhile, from 1969, 18–21-year-olds, both female and male, had been welcomed into the electorate.

The point of rehearsing these historical episodes is to highlight both the simple fact that UK constitutional history is one of evolution and adaptation and the sobering fact that such changes[11] trace a journey that could be described as a long and reluctant journey of repentance.

To say this is not to subscribe wholesale to a narrative of progress. It is to reiterate what was said in Chapter 3 above, that questions of theological anthropology, that is to say accounts of the nature, status and worth of human beings, underwrite all political systems, along with their inclusions and exclusions – the sweet and the bitter.

Here I stand with Reformed philosopher and theologian Nicholas Wolterstorff, who presents a Christian case for supporting liberal democracy in terms of 'the rights we have as human persons', the case for 'equal political voice' and 'the right of the people to a democratic state'.[12]

While adopting something close to Wolterstorff's defence of liberal democracy as my default position, I want to focus the discussion here on three other related questions for political theology and philosophy that are particularly relevant to the Scottish context at this moment in history: the question of national identity and the political and cultural problems and aspirations associated with independence or unionism; the question of elaborating a theo-political vision and imagination for Scotland's future; the question of the future role of religion in general and Christianity in particular within a prospective Scottish constitutional settlement.

---

11 Inevitably often fiercely resisted by those who had most power and privilege within society, including many within the churches.

12 See the essays with these titles in Wolterstorff and Cuneo, 2012. His focused attention on these issues in recent years reflects his awareness of the growing influence of the work of John Howard Yoder and Stanley Hauerwas and the currents of scepticism about liberalism, democracy and the state running within their work. It also reflects his disagreements with John Milbank about how to interpret Western traditions of human rights, as well as his running dialogue with Rawlsian perspectives in North American political philosophy. In this book I do not engage any of those three major dialogues at any depth or length, although I remain keenly aware of their importance.

## National identity and independence

I have already quoted Stanley Hauerwas' comment about liberal political theory's particular difficulty in accounting for borders. In Wolterstorff's recent writing on political philosophy, the question of borders is hardly mentioned. His discussions about the nature of liberal democracy proceed on the assumption of a pre-existent state with settled borders. Similarly, with respect to the Augustinian visions of O'Donovan, Gregory or Bretherton, the focus on 'common objects of love' manages to leave mostly obscure the question of who is doing the loving. How wide a set of lovers can we consider when we are thinking about the nature of the res publica before we are obliged to talk about res publicae (Sonnenschein, 1904)?

Liberal theorists and political theologians prefer to cope with their difficulties around such vulgar, vexing and embarrassing questions by ignoring them, and by developing their conversations about political philosophy on the assumption that border issues have been settled. Historical contexts in which borders are problematized, particularly by demands for independence or secession, are therefore unsettling and revealing moments. They lay bare assumptions that are normally kept quiet and out of sight.

Arguments from the principle of self-determination presume there is a national self, which can do the determining, leading us back to the fuzzy, dangerous territory of national definition. My position in this book is that 'nations' are approximate, relative and provisional communities, which resist both entire denial and exact definition of their existence.

This makes attempts to align them with state boundaries continually problematic. With state borders, even when they are disputed, there is a determinate character to what is claimed. This is not the case with national entities, nor should it be. Nations are coalitions and constructions assembled from resources both inherited and imagined, they are 'texts under negotiation', a term applied by Walter Brueggemann to the Bible (1993), whose meanings are continually subject to hermeneutical activity and conversation. They are 'affective communities', characterized and identified by shared patterns of love that are continually evolving and that vary in intensity over time and across populations. The objects of love are themselves very varied in character, so that they need to be considered carefully and critically, to assess whether they are liable to lead to Bretherton's false and destructive patterns of *dominium* or whether they enable what Jean Bethke Elshtain calls 'enacting projects of *caritas*'.

We need to unpack and unpick the kinds of loves carried within the life of 'nations' so that they can be assessed in relation to the 'greater' loves that are constitutive of Christian discipleship.[13] Many of these involve the love of non-exclusive 'goods', which can and should co-exist peacefully and happily. The love of landscape and of particular geographies is of this kind, as is the love of particular foods. Similarly, the love of language and dialect, of folksong and story, can be unreserved in its attachment to the local and familiar without seeking to dominate or denigrate other vernaculars.

Even a love for how people 'look' who are local to us or related to us should be something we can express wholeheartedly, as in the famous example of Stokely Carmichael's 1967 speech in Seattle: 'We have to as a people gather strength to stand up on our feet and say, "Our noses are broad, our lips are thick, our hair is nappy – we are black and beautiful! Beautiful! Yeah."' In fact, as Carmichael's speech makes clear, this kind of 'self-love' is vital because it is the opposite of an inferiorist self-loathing, where we internalize someone else's negative reading of who we are, how we sound, how we look.[14] The benign side of being 'national' is at ease with a positive, shared and concentrated set of loves for what is local, familiar and common. The dangers associated with this are captured by Canadian singer songwriter Bruce Cockburn in his 1977 anti-racist anthem 'Free to Be':

There's music in the forest/Children laugh in the school yard
On the skid row of the spirit/Hear the ranting of the Western
    Guard

---

13 Or, for non-Christians, the greater loves constitutive of their religious or humanistic commitments.

14 Full text at http://www.aavw.org/special_features/speeches_speech_carmichael01.html.

Why don't you cool out/Can it be so hard
to love yourself without thinking/someone else holds a lower
card

Grow up you/Grow up me/Grown together/Free to be.[15]

Here, the malign side of self-love comes out in true Augustinian
fashion as a parody of the good, when we are only able to value
or boost ourselves by denigrating the other: when I am only able
to love my skin or accent or culture by asserting its superiority to
yours; when I resist any 'mixing' of your DNA, accent, language
or music with mine, for fear of pollution or dilution of my distinctiveness; or when I am unable to show or seek love and hospitality
for what is distinctively mine in relation to what is distinctively
yours.

The positive vision advocated here, which I would argue is
required by Christian ethics and Christian discipleship, is of a way
of loving self and same, which does not reduce, traduce or exclude
the other.

The form of Christian cosmopolitanism invoked here does not
equate to saying that I have equal claim to call home and be at
home in every place I go in the world. Sometimes my claim on
you or yours on me might be as guest to host. The test will come
when I want to settle in your 'homeland' or you in mine, whether
temporarily or permanently. In those situations, we will be faced
with mutual responsibilities – the guest to respect the host, the
host to welcome the guest.

If I as an English-speaking Scot were to move to Sweden or Sri
Lanka and seek to make either of them 'my home', my hope for
warm welcome and equal treatment there might quite fairly be
balanced by a set of formal and informal expectations that I meet
certain conditions: seeking to learn the host language, respect
for local customs and traditions, a period of residency before I
acquire full citizenship.

However, some caveats are essential here. First, the expectations of the host must not be predicated on assumptions of

15 http://cockburnproject.net/songs&music/ftbe.html, from the album *Circles in
the Stream*.

cultural or ethnic superiority or be such as to violate the integrity of my cultural identity as guest. Second, there must also be a proper understanding of the situation in relation to power dynamics and patterns of ethnic or cultural prejudice. There could rightly be a stronger expectation on me to learn Swedish or to learn Sinhala, Rodiya or Tamil than there is on a recently arrived Somalian grandmother, whose immigration was driven by civil war, to learn English in Glasgow and develop an interest in the music of Dick Gaughan or the poetry of Robert Burns.

When all these vital ethical qualifications are made and when it is made clear that I am only endorsing a form of nationalism that is also internationalist, cosmopolitan, hospitable, porous, open to hybridity and admixing, anti-racist, civic, democratic and liberal – the question will arise as to whether this is not a *reductio* to the point where it is absurd to call the discourse in question 'nationalism'. I want to resist that.

My argument is that such a 'sweet nationalism' is also constituted by another set of loves and claims, which go beyond the modest version of a civic 'patriotism' that might be approved by Jürgen Habermas or by theologians such as Luke Bretherton and Nigel Biggar.[16]

These claims, to 'identity, jurisdiction and territory', which constitute a claim to 'independent' statehood, are based on a complex, compound set of political judgements, confessions and feelings that can imagine a project of *caritas*, to use Jean Bethke Elshtain's phrase, involving a breaking of the United Kingdom.[17]

We have already prepared the ground for the possibility of thinking this kind of 're-stating' of Scotland in the earlier discussions of decolonization and the break-up of the Soviet Union. My point here is not to equate an England-dominated UK with the various forms of imperialism involved in those examples, but simply to argue the principle in similar though opposite terms to the pro-UK 'Better Together' campaign,[18] that it is both possible

16 See Biggar's paper, 'The Value of Limited Loyalty: Christianity, the Nation, and Territorial Boundaries', *Modern Believing* 20:53 (2012), p. 4.

17 Elshtain, J. B., 'The Just War Tradition and Natural Law' in *Fordham International Law Journal*, Vol. 28, Issue 3, Article 6, p. 746.

18 'Better Together' is a cross-party pro-union campaigning group established in 2012 to campaign for Scotland to stay within the UK and vote No to independence.

and legitimate for 'national' entities to conclude that they are 'better independent'.

This has in fact become the primary basis on which the conversation about Scottish independence is being carried on, from both sides, as an argument about which is the *better* option. This language of relative merits, differing visions of how best to seek the good society in Scotland, is a form of debate that fits with the account of nation and nationalism I am proposing here. It implies that we can imagine circumstances in which political union within a multi- or plurinational state would be the 'better' option, but also circumstances in which the opposite is possible.

It recognizes the post-war context within Europe, where a series of initiatives in European political co-operation have produced structures in which sovereignty is pooled and shared by consent of national parliaments. Those parliaments remain free to withdraw from those structures if in future they judge it better to be outside them.

To propose a Scottish national identity as the basis for 'independence within Europe' and within a looser social union of The Isles is not to elevate such an identity to any kind of idolatrous position where it becomes the sole possible determinant of political legitimacy. That is not my contention. I am arguing for the more modest proposal that given the continuing resilience and significance of 'national' narratives within the life of states, where there are multiple 'national' narratives within a union state such as the UK, they can legitimately be mobilized as part of a case for dissolving the single state and replacing it with multiple states.

My argument is that such a move is not intrinsically illegitimate or unethical, but that each ethical and prudential case for 're-stating' a national community needs to be assessed on its own merits. We can relate this to Augustine's words in *City of God*, that 'the better the objects of this agreement, the better the people; and the worse the objects, the worse the people' (19.24). My contention is that a new Scottish state, formed by withdrawing from the UK, offers a *better* legitimate basis on which to seek to unite a majority of people in a democratic system around *better* 'common objects of love'.

This does, of course, assume that there are some very serious problems with the current pluri-national UK state, which are unlikely to be fixed by change short of independence. Those problems now need to be named.

## Calling time

I believe the current state of the UK should not be maintained because of a series of intractable problems, which can be variously characterized as *psycho-social*, *political*, *cultural* and *economic*.

The *psycho-social* problems arise from the nature of relationships between the various national communities within the UK. As in so many other states, this is rooted in the power relationships between majority and minority communities, and in the UK is primarily to do with relationships between England – and Wales, Scotland and Northern Ireland. Some of the problems are mundane, but are also pervasive and persistent.

For example, there is the continual tendency to equate England with Britain and or the UK. The daily irritation caused by this to those with ears to hear and eyes to see should not be underestimated. From Barack Obama talking about visiting England when he means the UK, to the hundreds of instances every day on UK-wide media, where English-only organizations, data, legislation and so on. are presented as British. It is the classic sin of a majority community, the tendency to an imperialistic over-assertion of its own identity and a complacent failure even to notice it is doing this most of the time.

But as with whites doing it to people of colour, as with men doing it to women, such examples of language and speech encode and display power. They make some visible and others invisible. When minorities are made visible within dominant modes of representation, it is often on majority terms, in order to belittle, patronize or fetishize areas of difference.

In postcolonial theory, such as the work of Fratz Fanon discussed earlier, such patterns of representation are seen to produce psycho-social patterns of inferiorism. Minorities[19] internalize their

---

19 Or oppressed peoples who may be in a majority but lack power, e.g. black South Africans under apartheid, women in most societies.

own marginalization, their own invisibility. When consciousness of the power relations involved increases, minorities begin to resist these ways of conceiving of themselves and to assert their own worth, presence, visibility and identity.

For those who identify as Scottish, such patterns of articulated resistance have been increasingly prominent over the past century, from the work of the 1920s' literary renaissance onwards. They are rarely noticed, understood or mentioned within theological discourse in the UK and rarely voiced by Scottish theologians, but they are increasingly and insistently heard within contemporary cultural discourse in Scotland.

It is significant, as noted above, that at the opening of the Scottish Parliament in 1999 Donald Dewar said, 'this is about who we are and how we carry ourselves', and at the opening of Holyrood in 2004, Edwin Morgan's poem spoke of the almost broken thread of self-esteem. The rise in support for both nationalism and independence has much to do with a justified anger against the psycho-social costs of being a minority partner within the Union.[20] Until this problem is better understood by English commentators and by English theologians, the desire and case for independence will not be adequately understood or engaged by them.

The psycho-social problem is intimately connected to the *political* problem. In parliamentary terms, while there was a unicameral first chamber, the numerical dominance of MPs from English constituencies was always vulnerable to criticism on 'national' grounds, where a majority of English MPs was able to secure a majority and pass legislation affecting Wales *or* Scotland *or* Northern Ireland which did not command majority support among MPs from those countries or from the wider population in those countries.

Devolution has definitely ameliorated and reduced that democratic deficit and, arguably, more devolution would reduce it

---

20 From the continued naming of the UK central bank as the Bank of England, to the complacent domination of coronation rituals and second-chamber representation by the Church of England, to designating Queen Elizabeth as the Second, to the appropriation of God Save The Queen and the Union flag by English sporting teams, the list of cultural mistakes is extensive and ongoing.

further. The problem persists, however, in relation to reserved matters. UK-wide political parties, with the exception of the Liberal Democrats, have proved reluctant to embrace a more thoroughgoing federal solution. A major reason for this has been the lack of party support and popular demand for either an English parliament or for English regional parliaments (see Harvie, 1991; Curtice and Heath, 2000), with the result that devolution in the UK has been asymmetrical, driven by minority nations and leading to constitutional anomalies such as the West Lothian question. While the Scottish Constitutional Convention embraced proportional representation for the Holyrood elections, and the Scottish Parliament later extended this to local government, neither English civil society nor UK Labour or Conservative parties have embraced it as a goal for English or UK elections.

The failure to reform the voting system has been matched by an abject failure to reform the absurdly undemocratic second chamber of the House of Lords, despite the obvious potential for such reform to be a key component of a federal reshaping of the UK. When these political anomalies are set alongside half a century of the Scottish electorate overwhelmingly voting for parties of the centre left, but being governed for long periods by the Conservatives, the result is the pressure to partition government along national lines which has led to devolution, to two nationalist administrations at Holyrood and now to the independence referendum. The rise of support in England for the United Kingdom Independence Party (UKIP) in 2009–13, and the prominence of anti-European discourse and sentiment within English media and public discourse, has not so far been paralleled in Scotland.

Differing policy trajectories have also begun to emerge since 1999, between Westminster and Holyrood, in relation to personal care for the elderly, student tuition fees, nuclear power and nuclear weapons, welfare and educational reform. The intractable political problem of the Union, seemingly incapable of thoroughgoing constitutional reform at the level of the UK state,[21] is that it

---

21 As I finish this book in autumn 2013, no parties have revealed substantive plans for addressing the future of devolution, the West Lothian question or reform of the second chamber.

seems increasingly unable to accommodate the preferences of the Scottish electorate.

The *cultural* problem that independence promises a way of engaging is interwoven with the psycho-social and political dimensions of Scottish life. We have seen how accounts of cultural sterility and banality, repudiations of 'kailyard' and tartanry, diagnoses of inferiorism and low self-esteem have been variously attributed: by George Davie to the Disruption; by Hugh MacDiarmid to a blend of Presbyterianism, unionism and capitalism; by Beveridge and Turnbull to cultural colonialism; by Alasdair Gray to imaginative neglect; and by Carol Craig to poverty, materialism and crises of masculinity.

That might seem an impressively diverse range of causes and scapegoats and we should hope that Scotland's artists and critics are capable of debunking and satirizing any overly simplistic diagnosis or prognosis. However, it seems only fair to recognize the ways in which the 'culture as politics' analysis of recent decades is persuasive. Debates about 'the national question' have helped to focus some crucial cultural projects. For all his excesses and foibles, the internationalist nationalism of MacDiarmid and his 'cosmic' ambitions for art made and voiced in Scotland has a striking breadth of vision and humanity. The folklorism of which Hamish Henderson was exemplar and champion was rooted in a passionate love of and deep respect for the oral culture carried within poor, working communities. The national question has allowed and encouraged a diverse articulation of Scotland as Iain Crichton Smith's 'three-tongued nation', increasingly binding support for Gaelic, Scots and English into a single vision. The current debate around independence does seem to have had a galvanizing effect. When Scotland's Makar, Liz Lochhead, was interviewed by the *Guardian* in August 2013, the piece included the following exchange:

G: Would independence be a good thing for the arts in Scotland? LL: We'll find out. A lot of artists I know are going to vote yes. I'm not so sure the union has benefited Scotland culturally: Irish playwriting, for instance, is taken more seriously than Scottish playwriting, because Ireland is an independent country. When my play *Mary Queen of Scots Got Her Head Chopped Off* was a hit in London, my agent sent it to the National Theatre. They said: 'We love this piece, but it's far too Scottish for us.'[22]

The irony in this exchange is obviously the question of whose 'national theatre' this is. That we now have a National Theatre of Scotland, albeit in a different form to the English (?) one in London, is some illustration of how devolution has helped and independence promises to help further.

The lure of independence for artists, who are probably less risk averse than the population as a whole, lies in its potential to move beyond a narrative that 'provincializes' Scotland and positions it in relation to a cultural centre that is elsewhere.

There are signs that a new cultural agenda is beginning to coalesce: Gray's call to attend imaginatively to our own country combines both with MacDiarmid's rejection of perspectives positing Scotland as 'small' and MacFhionnlaigh's confession, 'I am small and like small things; the buried seed that splits the stone, the word of truth that is heavier than the world.'[23]

Another motivation for pursuing a 'national' agenda in culture and one seen across many countries and cultures is the desire to resist the homogenizing and, above all, Americanizing cultural effects of globalization. As Scotland's folk and trad scene grows in confidence and ambition, festivals like Celtic Connections and radio shows like Ricky Ross's *Another Country* are ardent in their love for 'Americana', but receive it as another valued folk tradition, not as the accent in which all must sing or the frame in which all must appear.

These are the cultural 'gains' associated with independence and, within the theological perspective advocated here, they are real gains. It is perhaps above all in relation to theological engagement with culture and the arts that Scotland's churches have work to do in displaying the colour and tenor of their social vision. In part this is about overcoming inferiorist disdain for Calvinism.[24]

---

22 http://www.theguardian.com/books/2013/aug/21/liz-lochhead-poet-scots-makar.

23 Fearghas MacFhionnlaigh, *The Midge*, Gairm Publications, 1980.

24 A task that figures like the US novelist Marilynne Robinson can help with. Robinson delivered the Croall Lectures at New College, Edinburgh, in September 2013.

In greater part it is about the churches repenting of past mistakes and articulating a new theological vision for art and culture in Scotland.

The fourth intractable to which it is argued independence offers the best response is the question of Scotland's *economic* future. The economics of independence in opposition to unionism represents one of the most hotly contested areas of the debate.

From the late seventeenth century onwards, the promise of the Union, and later the Empire, to deliver enhanced prosperity for Scotland was one of its strongest selling points. In the mid-twentieth century, the orthodoxy of most on the left was that only the power of the union state could deliver the security of the welfare state and raise the living standards of the poorest.

The debate was transformed from the 1970s onward by the discovery of North Sea oil, the rise of inflation and the painful decades of recession that witnessed the savage decline of Scotland's manufacturing sector and the rise of unemployment. Thatcherism and EU membership moved the UK economy decisively into a post-nationalization era, at least until the banking collapse of 2008.

Scotland's economy shared in the boom and bust of the Blair–Brown years, which ended with the collapse and nationalization of key financial institutions based in Scotland.

By 2013, the future of the economy was a much more open question. The remainder of the oil revenues was still in play, along with accusations that while little Norway had prudently created a sovereign wealth fund with a proportion of its oil revenues, various UK governments had squandered theirs.

Increasingly, critics were arguing that the UK economy, under both Labour and the Conservatives–Liberal Democrats, had become dangerously unbalanced both sectorally and geographically. The eclipse of the manufacturing sector by the service economy was being questioned, with particular concerns about a bloated financial services sector operating with short-term, predatory instincts. Deep concerns were voiced about an overheated housing market built on cheap credit, which was failing to deliver decent and affordable housing and which was vulnerable to abrupt 'corrections' and contractions. The UK economy was seen to be driven by and pandering to the needs of the south-east of England and the City of London.

The publication in 2009 of *The Spirit Level: Why More Equal Societies Almost Always Do Better* by Richard Wilkinson and Kate Pickett (2009) provoked significant debate about levels of inequality within the UK.

While arguments raged about how far Labour or Conservative administrations had reduced or aggravated inequality during their terms in office, the deeper lesson of the book was that under both right and left the UK had failed to address growing economic and social inequality. Measured against the more equal Nordic societies, the UK's record looked particularly bad and this as a full 13 years of Labour government drew to an end.

Meanwhile, that devolution in Scotland had made relatively little difference to the Scottish economy vis-à-vis that of the UK was seen positively as confirming that a Scottish parliament was capable of managing the economy and negatively as confirming that its very limited fiscal powers were an obstacle to enabling more dynamic performance.

The SNP's economic credibility was damaged by First Minister (and former economist) Alex Salmond's rash endorsement in a 2008 speech at Harvard University of an 'arc of prosperity' made up of Ireland, Iceland and Norway, along with a vision of Scotland, the 'Celtic Lion', joining in said arc as an independent country.[25] Salmond's analysis was widely ridiculed after the crash of 2008/09, when Ireland and Iceland did particularly badly, leading to running jibes about the 'arc of insolvency'.

Given the ambivalence of the brief account I have given, I remain cautious about suggesting independence will bring enhanced prosperity. Access to fiscal powers, even when offset by the restraints of a currency union, whether Sterling or Eurozone, will provide more options for economic management, but macroeconomic policy-making in a globalizing world of highly mobile capital remains a fraught and demanding task.

The intractable problem to which I believe independence offers the best solution is not increasing Scotland's wealth, but sharing

---

25 http://www.scotland.gov.uk/News/Speeches/Speeches/First-Minister/harvard-university.

and distributing it more equitably. There are grounds on which we might hope for radical changes to the way the Scottish economy is structured and regulated. I would argue there is an overwhelming case for working towards that end.

In 2013, a powerful manifesto for change has begun to circulate in Scotland, under the banner of *The Common Weal* and has been attracting interest across the political spectrum.[26] Whether this vision can flourish, grow its support base and be refined through a broad and open process of dialogue remains to be seen. If it achieves this, it will have successfully resisted being overtaken by the sectarianism of the Left. I hope many in the churches will engage with its arguments, but I also hope that church people will develop and discuss their own visions for economic and social development in Scotland, without being overtaken by their own sectarianisms.

The record of 50 years in which a majority of voters in Scotland have voted consistently for one or other social democratic parties gives me some grounds for hoping that an independent Scotland could become a more equal Scotland, with significantly lower rates of poverty. I do not see meaningful progress on this being achieved within the United Kingdom as it is currently constituted.

Not only that, I believe that a strong Scottish drive towards this, post-independence, might serve as a model for the rest of the UK (RUK), emboldening and inspiring those in England, Wales and Northern Ireland who long for radical economic change.

When I contemplate an independent Scotland, I don't imagine a golden era in which the Scottish economy is always growing and in which per capita income is always higher than that in England. But for richer or poorer, I do dare to imagine a fairer and more equal Scotland. That would be economic honey from the Celtic Lion, however loud it may roar among the nations.

## Augustine's better objects

A practical political theology may advocate a perfectionist vision, without losing its Augustinian or Reformed reservations about

---

26 http://scottishcommonweal.org.

perfectibility.[27] The work of practical political theology in pointing towards better objects of love is one part of the prayer of the Church for God's will to be done on earth. It is theology's work in progress of learning to desire the kingdom (cf. Smith, 2009).

In the previous chapter, I identified sweet and sour elements of contemporary Scottish political and cultural life. In the discussion above I argued that the creation of a Scottish nation-state could offer a better way to tackle intractable psycho-social, political, cultural and economic problems.

In what follows, I claim that it should be the burden of the Scottish churches and of a Scottish contextual theology to advocate a transforming vision of Scotland's future, in which constitutional change is embraced as a means to pursue virtue in Scottish society. We will, I believe, be better placed as an independent state to pursue better objects.

27 The phrasing is Eric Gregory's (2008).

# 8

# Transforming Scotland

In Chapter 3, I outlined an ecumenical account of political theology in terms of narrative, discipline and witness. Here I want to explore something of what that could look like when developed as a vision of transforming practice.

The primary theo-political narrative which should direct social transformation in Scottish life is the idea of the Common Good. Given its clearest and most systematic articulations within Catholic social teaching since the Second Vatican Council, the Common Good is an ecumenical theme that should be received and promoted by Reformed and Anabaptist theologians. It is rooted in a biblical vision of theological anthropology, which affirms the dignity and value of each and all within society and which finds in the doctrine of the *imago Dei* a radical presumption in favour of the equality of all people, regardless of their gender, ethnicity, health, ability to learn, wealth or status.

I suggested at the outset that the ideas at the core of this book should 'preach', should be viable for Christian education and catechism. The Common Good meets these criteria, and it needs to become more visible and audible within the work of Christian theologians and churches in Scotland.

We should teach our children that this is a focal narrative for Christian political concerns: the idea of a society in which all are valued, all are loved, all are fed and cared for, all are called to fullness of life.

We should encourage them and one another to find areas of agreement in seeking this, with people of other faiths and with secular humanists, but we should be clear that for us it is rooted in the heart and character of a loving Creator, in the life and teaching of Jesus Christ and the life-giving power of the Holy Spirit.

As Christian disciples we are charged with relearning ourselves and the world through following the Jesus we meet in the Gospels, whose radical commitment to the poor and marginalized, to peacemaking and nonviolence, to healing and forgiveness, summons us to a life of love and service. Commitment to the Common Good, understood as sharing in the *caritas*-love of God for all people in society, should also extend to sharing in God's anger against injustice and oppression.

For the churches, this narrative is implicit within their theology, but needs to be made explicit in their teaching and proclamation. It should not become a social gospel, detached from spiritual concerns, but should be understood as the outworking of core spiritual and theological convictions.

It should not be identified uncritically with a particular political ideology or with the programme of any one political party, but should be continually 'audited' through dialogue within the Church regarding its faithfulness to Scripture and our creeds and confessions.

It should not be elevated to a place beyond critique and criticism, but exposed to dialogue within and beyond the Church about its capacity to speak to the lives of people in Scotland, especially the lives of the poorest.

While it is a focal narrative, it should not be allowed to remain at a level of generality where it can be invoked by everyone in support of everything. Churches need to risk moving towards explicit social teaching about what the Common Good will look like in particular times and places.

In educational and formational terms, the challenge is for churches to develop more detailed 'axioms', which express a prophetic voice within society. Such axioms will be provisional and open to refinement and reformulation. They will need to be continually tested by referring them to church teaching and confessions. They will also be tested by reflecting on them in the light of concrete liturgical encounters with Scripture and sacrament and in the light of concrete pastoral encounters with women, men and children across Scotland.

In arguing for this, I mean no disrespect to the valuable work done through church councils and commissions on a regular or occasional basis. My fear for them is twofold, however: that too often their reports neither engage the hearts and minds of people within the churches, nor make compelling practical–legislative proposals to politicians and decision-makers outwith the churches. Political occasions like the independence referendum are *kairos* moments, which call for *kairos* visions, contextually apt expressions of theo-political imagination.

## A narrative of the common good

A Christian vision for transforming Scotland will aim at:

- a society committed to seeking and pursuing the Common Good, insistent on the dignity and worth of every member of the body social and of their valued place within the commonwealth
- a society with very low levels of poverty
- a society with significantly lower levels of wealth and income inequality
- a society in which women are equal and empowered in every area of life
- a society in which men are less violent and more nurturing
- a society in which children are loved and cherished, kept safe from abuse and exploitation and given access to excellent opportunities for education and formation, regardless of ability to pay
- a society in which there are few unwanted pregnancies and fewer terminations of pregnancy
- a society in which land and ownership is widely distributed, with a presumption of access to the land and an increasing percentage of land held in common, public or co-operative ownership
- a society that cares for the earth and the environment, minimizing pollution and maximizing sustainability
- a democratic society with high levels of political participation
- a society organized around principles of subsidiarity, with decisions taken at appropriate levels, maximizing local power in so far as it is conducive to the Common Good

- a mutual society that encourages and supports co-operation, profit-sharing and stake-holding
- a society in which there is work for all that is limited, meaningful, valued and well rewarded
- a society in which 'wealth creation' is not the only criterion by which the value of work is assessed
- a society in which leisure is enabled, creativity is encouraged, the arts are valued
- a society in which there are homes for all, which are warm, dry, healthy and affordable
- a hospitable society, which welcomes guests, migrants, asylum seekers and refugees
- a healthy society in which levels and measures of public health improve towards the best in Europe
- a society in which those with disabilities are given maximum opportunity and support
- a caring society with strong national health and care services as well as generous and empowering welfare provisions
- a safe society with low levels of crime, especially violent crime
- a free society with low levels of state surveillance and restriction
- a redemptive society with a lower prison population
- a society free from racism and wrongful discrimination, which celebrates unity in diversity, valuing both old and new cultural traditions
- a society committed to fair and friendly exchange, peacemaking, fair trade, development and emergency aid in its international relations
- a society that in its international relations seeks to hold partner states to high standards of justice, and by its own practice has the moral authority to do so
- a society that rejects the use of and threat to use nuclear weapons
- a society in which there is a presumption of freedom of belief, practice and expression except when this is incompatible with the Common Good
- a society that glorifies and enjoys God.[1]

---

1 I hope it is obvious that my aim is to contribute to a broader project here, not to claim that this is the last word – all lists can be improved and most leave out something they shouldn't have.

## Notes for a *Third Book of Discipline*[2]

A Christian vision of Scotland looks for a society whose freedom and well-being is secured by the ethical formation, education, positive enabling, negative restraint and, ultimately, lawful coercion of its citizens.

The report of the Church of Scotland's Commission on the Purposes of Economic Activity said this:

> Christian reflection on economics takes with full seriousness the ways in which human beings fail to live out this vocation [to love God and neighbour]. From a consideration of human sin and human limitations, flows an understanding of the need for law, governance, regulation and sanction in the sphere of economics as in other spheres of life, to promote justice and to preserve freedom. However, an understanding of human capacities to do wrong and to make mistakes also means a recognition that all projects to discipline and shape society for good, may be ineffectual or may have unwelcome and unforeseen consequences. Questions of regulation, planning, management and policy making need to avoid the extremes of a cynicism which underestimates, undervalues or undermines human dignity and capacity for right action. Equally they need to avoid the naïveté which overestimates the capacity of human beings to do the right thing and overstates the capacity of human beings to manage complex systems or anticipate future events.[3]

A Christian social vision for Scotland needs to be integrated into Christian preaching, catechism and education. It will seek to form women and men who understand and own their high calling to

---

2 What follows is a sketch that I hope will become the basis of a future multi-author collaborative project to develop a distinctive Christian social policy manifesto – an unofficial *Third Book of Discipline* offered as a contribution to democratic policy debates on Scotland's future. The title should not be taken too seriously; it is a provocative attempt to reclaim the broad social vision of sixteenth-century Reformed theology, not an illiberal Christian bid for power or control. See also below.

3 From the longer version, available online via the Church of Scotland website, Church and Society page.

personal and social holiness, but it will also seek to form disciples, who are profoundly realistic about human fallibility and finitude, both their own and that of others. Disciples should be people committed to the ongoing work of updating and refining Scotland's *Third Book of Discipline*, which today can stand as a metaphor for the body of planning, law and regulation produced by local and national government, as well as professional bodies and quangos. Drawing on both Catholic social teaching (see Hand, in Storrar and Donald, 2003) and a Reformed understanding of stewardship and vocation across the whole of life they will see their discipleship and Christ's lordship extending across every area of life in Scotland.

## Ministries of state and society

The language of ministry, which is shared across traditions of Church and State, reflects Christian understandings of work done in the service of God and neighbour. Using this language here is a deliberate attempt to recall the ethical and vocational basis of policy-making and public administration. It also reflects the division of government into a variety of 'ministries': prime, first, minister for ..., civil service and so on, while supplementing this with an understanding that governance involves a variety of ministries undertaken by non-governmental actors within the public realm.

### Economic ministries – finance, business and tax

The financial crisis that began in 2008 was exacerbated by failures of regulation and by widespread ethical failures. Recklessly over-leveraged banks lent recklessly, while hedging their risks by means of financial instruments they did not properly understand and that were not fit for purpose. They also engaged in systematic mis-selling of insurance products and systematic manipulation of inter-bank lending rates.

A greed- and testosterone-fuelled culture was encouraged by reckless patterns of incentivization to ignore ethical and prudential restraints. Venture capital companies developed predatory patterns of takeover and asset stripping, supported by weak regulation and fiscal regimes that encouraged short-term investment and profit-taking. Accountancy and auditing firms colluded with businesses to engage in systematic tax evasion and avoidance, as well as lawful but anti-social tax mitigation. Payday loan and credit card companies emerged who were charging usurious rates of interest, with APRs of over 4,000 per cent.

A Christian vision for serving Scotland's financial sector looks to rebuild a culture of probity, which is sustained by a rigorous culture of regulation and enhanced requirements for transparency. It will make a positive ethical case for fair taxation and seek to stigmatize anti-social behaviour by naming and shaming offenders. It will seek legal limits on usury, with a statutory maximum for interest rates and will actively establish and promote new sources of affordable credit for those on low incomes.

A Christian vision for serving Scotland's corporate sector will emphasize the ethical and social responsibilities of companies, which are granted the rights and protections of limited liability by the societies in which they operate. It will emphasize their duty to contribute to the Common Good by paying a fair rate of tax and support the work of revenue authorities in penalizing offenders. While it may support government in some comparative adjustment of corporation tax, to incentivize companies to locate in more remote locations with higher transport costs, it will not support a race to the bottom in which very low corporation tax rates encourage patterns of manipulation and deception by multinational companies.

A Christian vision for fiscal policy would encourage a new era of corporate evolution by emphasizing the responsibilities that come with society's conferral of incorporated status and by new ways of incentivizing the pro-social company. Companies which incorporate pro-social practices that contribute to the Common Good could be offered lower bands of corporation tax or higher tax reliefs. This would incentivize behaviours such as:

- profit-sharing – the 'John Lewis' model
- employee ownership and shareholding
- employee representation in governance

- payment of the living wage
- manufacture or sale of fair-trade goods
- production or sale of free-range and organic foods
- use of 'green' packaging
- use of 'green' energy
- limiting ratios of maximum to minimum remuneration.

Scotland could pioneer a new national drive to alter and enhance business culture, supporting a new era of ethically ambitious and pro-social economic development by rewarding and incentivizing corporate virtue. Since much of this would not be compulsory, sceptics or refuseniks could continue to run old-style companies, allowing for the efficiency and effectiveness of new approaches to be evaluated in real time.

## Legal ministries – land reform

A Christian vision, inspired by the Scriptures of the Old Testament, looks beyond the historical dominance of landed 'gentry' in Scotland, to imagine a more equitably landed society and people.

In Jim Hunter and Andy Wightman we have our own Isaiah and Amos figures, combining rigorous historical analysis with a prophetic passion for change.[4]

With the most inequitable distribution of land in Europe, Scotland needs a new era of land reform that will enable and incentivize more democratic and productive patterns of land-holding. It needs to address the scourge of massive sporting estates with absentee or aristocratic owners and monocultural forestry estates held as tax shelters by footballers and pop stars. It needs to support tenant farmers in acquiring freeholds and enable ordinary people to develop new patterns of crofting, 'hutting' and small-holding. It needs to address an over-inflated housing market and reform the under-regulated land-banking, site-banking practices of the property/construction industry. Finally, it needs to address the political cowardice and dissembling that surrounds the recent history of how property valuation is related to local taxation.

---

4 Among James Hunter's many publications is *Towards a Land Reform Agenda for a Scots Parliament*, Perth: Rural Forum Scotland, 1996.

A Christian social vision will press for disciplines that will achieve these ends: reformed succession laws, well-targeted land-value taxes, enhanced community rights to buy and fiscal incentives for community land-holding and land use, including for wind farms. When it encounters howls of pain from vested interests, it should reread Wightman's *The Poor had No Lawyers* (2013) and remind itself why this issue, so resonant of Old Testament prophecy, is still an urgent matter for the Christian conscience today.

## Justice ministries – policing and criminal justice

'In heaven the police will be British', or so the old joke runs. Law enforcement is a difficult area of social policy discussion that is often neglected by political theology. Liberals worry that public discourse is too easily swayed by right-wing 'hang 'em, flog 'em' rhetoric, while conservatives complain of a lack of tough love and concern for victims.

The obvious correlations between maleness, poverty, low educational attainment and offending signal that crime prevention is also a social justice issue. These are areas already devolved to the Scottish Parliament, which has recently overseen the creation of a single national police force in 2013. Scotland's largest city, Glasgow, has an unenviable record for violent crime, but the innovative work of its Violence Reduction Unit gives hope for new patterns of positive policing. A leading Scottish criminologist spoke in 2013 of his perception that public debates around policing and sentencing in Scotland were less punitive and more open to restorative justice, community service and non-custodial alternatives to prison than similar debates in England.[5]

As one of the few practical, political theologians who has engaged with this area, Duncan Forrester's work on criminal justice stresses the value and relevance of Christian theological convictions about forgiveness, mercy and redemption (1997). There are reasons to be optimistic about where policy in these areas is moving within Scotland and signs that, despite relative

---

5 Professor Fergus McNeill, speaking at Solas Festival on 23 June 2013; personal record.

theological neglect, Scotland's churches and their members remain active in support of offenders and their families.[6]

## Educational ministries

In the course of even the strongest anti-Calvinist, anti-Presbyterian rhetoric, pause is still routinely made to honour Knox's and the Reformers' commitment in the original *First Book of Discipline* (1560) to expanding educational provision through 'a school in every parish'.

Scotland's education system developed under Presbyterian hegemony for more than three centuries until the decisive reform of 1918, when Roman Catholic schools were brought into the state system, with protections for their distinctive governance and ethos.

On this most divisive of social policy questions, I stand with those who defend faith-based education and with those who argue that the principal driver of sectarianism is poverty, not the existence of Catholic schools. I also find myself among a small minority of Presbyterians who are actively supportive of the development of more faith-based schools, both for other religious traditions and for non-Roman Catholic Christians. On this issue, I look enviously at the English situation, where Church of England schools exist side by side with Roman Catholic schools in the state system.

Presbyterians in Scotland presumed for too long that the state system was 'theirs', with little prescience about the future, and are now set to be left high and dry as the tide of religious affiliation and participation goes out. Such a view will leave many of my co-religionists cold and will enrage the shrill elements of militant secularism, who compare faith schools to 'child abuse'.

Looking forward, my strongest wish and prayer (although I am not hopeful it will happen) would be for a new era of ecumenical faith-based education in Scotland, where new ways of sharing and developing the legacy of Roman Catholic schools could not only allow educational formation in a 'catholic and reformed'

---

6 http://www.faithinthroughcare.org; http://www.voxliminis.co.uk; http://www.swscja.org.uk/church-of-scotland-hosts-prison-visitor-centres-seminar.html.

ethos, but could also enact a living witness against the evils of sectarianism.

My position on this issue reflects a pessimism about how Scotland's public institutions will respond to growing secularization in coming decades. I hope both that I am proved over-pessimistic about this and that others will devise innovative and persuasive ways to promote Christian formation within non-faith-based mainstream education.

When all that is said, however, the most pressing theological and ethical issues for Scotland's education system are those connected to increasing educational opportunity and achievement for children from Scotland's poorest families.[7]

It is of course one of the proud achievements of Scotland's Roman Catholic schools that they have done just that, for a community that for historical reasons contained many children from poor families (Paterson, 2003, p. 148).

In one of Scotland's too rare moments of political ecumenism, the 2011 report by Professor Susan Deacon, a former Labour MSP and Scottish government (Health and Community Care) minister to the SNP government on the crucial role of Early Years Education in overcoming social disadvantage, has been widely welcomed across the political spectrum.[8]

The old correlations between poverty, especially urban poverty, and educational attainment remain shamefully persistent and the haunting epithet 'born to fail' recurs frequently within these conversations. As with public health and crime, education is inseparably linked to questions of social and economic justice. Until we can create a more equal society, with fewer children raised in poverty, we will struggle to raise educational achievement for 30–40 per cent of our children.

## Ministries of health – a SNHS

Media commentators from the USA watched in some bafflement at Danny Boyle's euphoric tribute to the National Health Service

---

7 http://www.sccyp.org.uk/news/in-the-news/poverty-and-educational-attainment.

8 http://www.scotland.gov.uk/Resource/Doc/343337/0114216.pdf.

during the Opening Ceremony of the London Olympics. It was not culturally plausible for many in a US audience, but it was an apt expression of public esteem and affection across the UK. High-quality health care free at the point of need remains a crucial ministry for Scotland's future as does a stronger response to Scotland's daunting public health challenges. Devolution has already enabled Scotland to pioneer responses to its specific problems with smoking rates and alcohol consumption. The vision of a SNHS is of a social body in which none says to the other, we don't need you. The prominence of acts of healing within the gospel records continues to catechize all with ears to hear about the importance of responding to sickness and suffering, wherever it occurs. The current pressures towards marketization of the NHS south of the border and the contrasting trajectory of devolved health policy in Scotland represent an opportunity to compare and contrast outcomes in future. Whatever the future divergence in policy and governance, close and collegial co-operation between an ENHS and a SNHS should continue.

## Ministries of defence + peacemaking

In the period 2011–13, Unionist commentary on the future of defence within an independent Scotland sometimes appeared to swing between casual derision about a Navy comprised of two fishery protection vessels and thinly concealed panic about what RUK would do with Trident in the event of a Yes vote.[9]

While seldom at the forefront of the public debate in Scotland or the UK, the question of defence displays the contrast between unionism and independence like no other issue. Wartime experiences and memories, along with experiences of serving in the armed forces, are still potent sites of 'Britishness' for many Scots. Independence for Scotland is represented by critics as hastening the final demise of Britain's global influence, potentially leading

---

9 See the highly sceptical June 2013 report from pro-unionist think tank The Scotland Institute, http://www.scotlandinstitute.com/wp-content/uploads/2013/06/Defence_Report_-_Scot_Inst.pdf; c.f. http://www.telegraph.co.uk/news/uknews/scotland/9616006/Britains-enemies-will-exploit-Scottish-independence-to-cut-UK-power.html.

to the loss of the UK's permanent seat on the UN Security Council and threatening its status as a nuclear power. The fall from influence was first dramatized by the 1956 Suez crisis, but in practice Britain has continued through subsequent decades to imagine itself in a global role of sorts.[10]

Independence would involve a radical re-imagining of Scotland's role in world affairs. In contrast to having a key role in this global policing function, pro-independence campaigners openly speak of shifting to a more 'Nordic' role in international affairs and suggest a Scottish defence budget comparable to that of Norway or Sweden. The disciplines of independence would therefore involve an abrupt end to the Scottish stake in maintaining British exceptionalism.

It is the SNP's and Scottish Green Party's commitments to a non-nuclear weapons defence policy that most clearly reveal the reduction in international power and influence being contemplated. Scotland will, in defence terms, simply become small, in a way that the UK has never allowed itself to. In becoming militarily small, Scotland may or may not take RUK down with it, but RUK's sense of itself would never be the same. Even to experiment with the vocabulary of the 'English Army' or the 'English Nuclear Deterrent' is, for 'British' ears, to reveal how intimately Britishness has been bound up with imagining and legitimating our history of mobilizing for attack and defence. Somehow, Britain has managed to preserve something of the aura of its past military and naval might in the traditions and identities of its armed services. Distant echoes of empire and proud memories of war against fascism still attach to its military capacities and lend them weight.

I stand with the position of my own Church of Scotland, which has since 1983 adopted the position through resolutions of its General Assembly, that, by their nature, nuclear weapons are inherently evil and to use them or threaten their use is ethically

---

10 Its chosen role in the sad saga of post-1945 armed conflict has almost always been to act alongside the USA, although the Falklands War in 1982 was a more independent venture. Britain's role in the two Gulf Wars (1990–91 and 2003–11), in the Balkan conflicts in the 1990s, in the Afghanistan conflict from 2001 and in Libya from 2011, demonstrates the UK state's ongoing commitment to costly involvement in international conflicts.

indefensible. It is time to put their possession and the threat of their potential use behind us and to learn new disciplines of peace-making as a small country in a troubled world.

## Ministries of witness

According to my large-scale, broad-brush model of ecumenical political theology, while Roman Catholics encircle the world in encyclicals and Reformed Protestants dream of disciplining society, Anabaptists work to create disciplined examples of virtuous living that bear witness to the encircling gospel. Their examples work from the ground up, not the top down.

This third 'type' of political theology[11] is an important correct-ive to more pessimistic 'realist' perspectives, because it exemplifies Eric Gregory's point about the value of perfectionist approaches that remain clear-eyed about perfectibility. In the face of weary reproaches, such as the traditions of political theology often asso-ciated with Reinhold Niebuhr about not expecting too much from people in society, the theology of the Radical Reformation urges and inspires people to do small things, to remake society in microcosm, to make prototypes of godly societies in their own neighbourhoods. A Christian and humanitarian vision, with high ideals of mutuality, care for the poor or equality, has in the past been given concrete expression in institutions and organizations ranging from savings banks and building societies, to mutual aid and insurance organizations, to co-operatives, social enterprises and fair-trade networks. The existence of these examples and their 'voluntary' character acts as a counter witness against those who argue that ethical principles are too idealized to be put into practice and economic and social practices too unruly to be dis-ciplined by principle.

The political ministry of witness seems to me to be particularly important for what, in some respects, is a 'post-ideological' polit-ical landscape. I can already imagine hearing various friends on the Left groan at that expression and anticipate their protests that

---

11 These are ideal types differentiated boldly and baldly for heuristic purposes; in practice there are many cross-overs.

I am just blind to the ways in which neo-liberal ideology continues to dominate contemporary living. I don't, however, accept that this is the case.

Despite its having been widely attacked in the routine practice of political bickering, I remain impressed by the power of David Cameron's 2005 contention that 'there is such a thing as society. It's just not the same thing as the state.'[12] As well as being a clever way of trying to distance himself from Thatcherism, it also works well as a rebuke to 'Old Labour' and 'Hard Left' imaginaries. It resonates with a range of dissident political perspectives, from the humane end of small-government conservativism in the USA, to aspects of anarchist and Green thinking, to Red Tory/Blue Labour enthusiasm for ideas of a 'complex society'. Socialists and social democrats, who put all their faith in statist solutions too easily develop a cynicism about change that is local or small-scale as representing a form of false consciousness.

Anabaptist theology, forged through centuries of persecution for its refusal to bear arms and centred on the crucified Lord, carries both a 'realist' sense of human evil and a commitment to the value of personal and local witness to counter-cultural ways of living. In holding these tensions, it speaks both to political realists' temptation to cynicism and to political idealists' temptation to naivety.

---

12 Quote from Cameron's 'victory' speech after being elected party leader: http://news.bbc.co.uk/1/hi/uk_politics/4504722.stm.

# 9

# Constitutional Questions

It is part of the peculiar history of the UK and, for some, part of its peculiar charm that it has no single written constitution. It is very unlikely that this could be carried over into an independent Scotland. Not only is it long-standing SNP policy to produce a written constitution, but there appears to be a broad consensus that, if independence were to come, it would be desirable to produce one.[1]

The Church of Scotland called in 2013 for the Scottish government to publish a draft constitution in advance of the referendum, but this seems unlikely to happen, not least because recent examples of constitution-making or revision elsewhere in the world suggest a broadly based process, overseen by civil society groups and drawing on wide public consultation.[2] Despite its being a political innovation, I do not expect the process of constitution-making to generate undue anxiety within Scotland. Given the dominance of liberal democratic norms in public opinion and discourse, the central features of the constitution are likely to be relatively uncontroversial, with the exception of the status of the monarchy and the role of religion.

It should be clear from the concerns of this book that I do not believe theological reflection should be confined to 'religious' questions. However, given my belief that large sections of any

1 New constitutional drafts are beginning to be published alongside the SNP's existing draft version. A Constitutional Commission charity was founded in 2005, although it does not yet have broadly based support, while a Scottish Constitutional Futures Forum was set up in 2012 by academics from the five Scottish law schools.

2 The SNP will publish its own preferred version in time, but is likely to submit this to a future Constitutional Convention. It will want to be seen to back a broadly based and non-partisan process and is unlikely to risk alienating public opinion by being perceived to exert any improper influence.

future constitution would be the subject of a wide consensus, I will restrict my comments to these two areas in which religious questions are most explicitly in play. Although of major importance, the issue of religious freedom is also uncontroversial and is already present within the list of human rights commitments in all extant drafts.

In both areas we need to see, first of all, how the Scottish polity got itself into this, that is to say our present peculiar historical situation. Not everyone will accept all the details of these sketched historical accounts, but my purpose here is not at all to write a formal constitutional history, simply to establish a few navigational bearings.

## The monarchy

The monarchy occupies a fascinating space within British and Scottish political culture. No major political party, with the exception of the Green Party and Scottish Green Party, is committed to republicanism, although outside the Conservative Party and UKIP other parties are likely to contain large numbers of republicans. This is for the simple reason that the monarchy remains popular with a majority of the British public and to embrace republicanism would be a vote-loser. The campaign group Republic accepts that polls in the UK put support for republicanism at around 20 per cent.[3] The monarchy represents an area of political inertia, with few politicians believing that the amount of energy and political capital required to reform it, far less abolish it, is worth expending. It is the policy of the SNP to retain the Union of the Crowns of 1603 and maintain what is called a 'social union' with RUK, while withdrawing from the parliamentary union of 1707.

The most controversial features of the monarchy in the contemporary UK, which would remain so in an independent Scotland, which adhered to the Union of the Crowns, are the role of the monarch as Supreme Governor of the Church of England and Defender of Faith and the restrictions on Roman Catholics and

---

3 http://www.republic.org.uk/What%20we%20want/In%20depth/Public%20 Opinion/index.php.

women succeeding to the throne (assuming that any foreseeable Scottish Parliament would indeed adhere to the Union of the Crowns).

The difficulties in reforming succession law relate to the need to consult and secure the agreement of all governments in territories that continue to recognize the British monarchy as also theirs.[4] The Succession to the Crown Act, which gained Royal Assent in the UK on 25 April 2013, replaced male primogeniture with absolute primogeniture and removed restrictions on heirs to the throne marrying Roman Catholics. However, the ban on a Roman Catholic sovereign remained, as did the requirement that the monarch be in communion with the Church of England.[5] The continuation of restrictions perceived to be discriminatory towards non-Anglicans and non-Christians was because of the implications of change for the established status of the Church of England, another high-inertia zone in UK politics.

The role of the monarchy in UK life is, for well-known historical reasons, asymmetrical and even inconsistent in the area of religion. A strange pragmatic fiction obtains, whereby the monarch when in Scotland behaves as, and is treated as, a member of the Church of Scotland. In England it is very much otherwise.

The monarch has no role in the governance of the Church of Scotland.[6] He or she is always represented at the Kirk's General Assembly, sometimes in person but usually by an appointed Lord High Commissioner. Following accession to the throne, the monarch, in conformity to the 1707 Treaty of Union, takes an oath before the Privy Council, 'swearing and subscribing' to 'inviolably maintain and preserve the ... Settlement of the True Protestant Religion with the Government Worship Discipline Rights and Privileges of this Church [of Scotland]'.[7]

---

4 http://services.parliament.uk/bills/2012-13/successiontothecrown.html.

5 They do not have to be 'members' of the Church of England at accession, but must be baptized and communicant members of a Church subscribing to trinitarian doctrine, who are in good standing with their own church. See http://www.ucl.ac.uk/spp/publications/unit-publications/133.pdf.

6 'Provided that it acts within the law of the land, the Assembly has the power to pass resolutions which can have effect without Royal Assent'; summary on http://www.royal.gov.uk/MonarchUK/QueenandChurch/QueenandtheChurchofScotland.aspx.

7 Treaty of Union 1707: http://www.legislation.gov.uk/aosp/1707/6.

If we follow the most likely constitutional scenario under which independence might come to pass, we are faced with a Scottish state, which continues to be a constitutional hereditary monarchy, with a Head of State 'in the line of Elizabeth I, Queen of Scots'.[8]

How the Head of State would be offered the Scottish Crown remains unclear. It seems inherently implausible that in the event of independence the successor to the current queen can be crowned as King of Scots by the senior bishop of the Church of England, a church not established or represented in Scotland.

The situation as it stands is already unsatisfactory, with the entire ceremony a product of Anglican hegemony and presumption. The coronation service of the current monarch was an ecumenical disaster,[9] while the presentation of the Honours of Scotland[10] to her in Edinburgh was a ceremonial flop.[11] There is an urgent need for fresh thinking here, but little sign so far that anyone at either Buckingham Palace, Lambeth Palace or 121 George Street is attending to it.

It is not so hard to see why. The ceremonial around monarchy can have a bizarre, Ruritanian feel to it, which is helpfully obscured by the 'authority' of precedent and tradition preventing the logic of the rubrics being made visible or debatable. Giving it a fresh articulation in the twenty-first century is not an easy task and not a task many people are yet interested in. However, if we are not to have an independent Scottish republic, and if the implications of independence are to be thought through, then such nettles will have to be grasped.

Like many of us, I suspect, I have highly ambivalent feelings about the monarchy. On the one hand, I am sympathetic to the view that the whole idea of a hereditary monarchy is nonsense on stilts, and if we were starting over (which is of course what independence means for republicans in Scotland) I would never want such a system. On the other hand, in keeping with what

---

8 So the draft text proposed by the Constitution Commission on its website, finally overturning the grievance of those annoyed by her being styled Elizabeth II!

9 The Archbishop of Canterbury refused to give communion to the Moderator of the General Assembly.

10 That is, the Scottish Crown Jewels/Regalia.

11 The young Queen was badly advised and wore an outfit considered not fitting for the dignity of the occasion; this was interpreted as a slight to Scottish dignity.

has been said before about complex space, the rituals around the monarchy, even though dominated by Anglican hierarchy and flummery, express profound truths of political theology. They represent part of what Oliver O'Donovan bravely argues is the positive legacy of Christendom, understood as a history of how Christianity has left its mark on Western culture (O'Donovan, 1996, p. 228). Above all, what the coronation ritual expresses and dramatizes is the confession that human sovereignty exists under divine sovereignty, that authority comes from God and is accountable to God.

Unless and until the powers that be in England gird up their loins to disestablish the Church of England or to reform radically its links to monarchy, sharing a monarch with England will mean Scotland sharing a Protestant Christian monarch. That remains an uncomfortable reality for Scotland's large Roman Catholic community and Scotland's small militantly secularist community. The trouble with arguing for the symbolic unifying role of monarchs in the life of the nation comes when they symbolize only some traditions and cultures in a pluralist society.

## Recognizing religion?

A related but distinct constitutional question has to do with the recognition of religion in an independent Scotland. The SNP's policy (for the short term at least) of not rocking tradition's boats unless absolutely necessary has been a practical strategy of political management designed not to open unnecessary fronts, while pursuing the main strategic objective. The task of academics, the media and wider civil society is to interrogate the silences as well as the speeches. It therefore speaks to the issue that there has been no suggestion from the SNP government of repealing the Protestant Religion and Presbyterian Church Act 1707, the statute which secures the Reformed and Presbyterian polity of the Church of Scotland, irrespective of Union. Nor is it yet suggested to prevent the monarch taking an oath on accession to defend the 'rights and privileges' of Presbyterianism or to repeal the 1921 Church of Scotland Act, the statute that recognizes the

Kirk as 'a national church, representative of the Christian faith of the Scottish people'. If these things were not done, then we would either have a situation where the status quo ante independence still prevailed (if the new constitution was silent on the questions at stake), or one where the provisions of the new constitution superseded these previous acts on the basis of its status as the new fundamental law of the state.

Under its existing unwritten constitution the UK, and Scotland within it, remains officially a 'Christian' state, with the Head of State required to say 'I will' when asked at the Coronation:

> Will you to the utmost of your power maintain the Laws of God and the true profession of the Gospel? Will you to the utmost of your power maintain in the United Kingdom the Protestant Reformed Religion established by law?[12]

While the establishment of the Church of England is clear in law, as is the disestablishment of the Church in Wales (under the 1914 Welsh Church Act) and the Church of Ireland (under the 1869 Irish Church Act), the constitutional position of the Church of Scotland is more ambiguous. The 1707 Protestant Religion and Presbyterian Church Act (in terms that were also inserted into the Treaty of Union) refers explicitly to the Church of Scotland as 'the Church of this Kingdom as now by Law established'.[13]

It is language that was designed to lock in a Presbyterian settlement after a turbulent and bloody century. During that century Scots Presbyterians had felt assailed by Anglicizing pressures to accept Episcopalian polity and liturgy. Beyond this, the terms in which both church confession and monarchical succession were to be protected reflected a still visceral suspicion of potential attempts to restore Roman Catholicism.

But what kind of establishment was this and what did establishment mean in Scotland when compared to what it meant in England? John Robertson suggests that the shadow of Hobbes hung over the 'erastianism' of the Union settlement: 'As enacted by the two parliaments, the Union established both the Presbyterian

---

12 http://www.ucl.ac.uk/spp/publications/unit-publications/133.pdf.
13 http://www.legislation.gov.uk/aosp/1707/6/paragraph/p1.

and the Anglican churches on terms clearly incompatible with the jure divino pretensions of many of their clergy' (Robertson, in Dickinson and Lynch (eds), 2000, p. 39).

It was not just that the theology and jurisprudence of establishment were debatable, the whole institutional structure through which it was imagined and experienced was radically different in England and Scotland. There was no settled experience of how to enact Presbyterian establishment in pre-Union Scotland, where the power of the monarchs had formed a greater part of the power of the state.

Working out what it meant in relation to a more parliamentary state in the eighteenth century also meant testing it against the new Union state. The first tests came almost immediately when the Westminster Parliament passed first of all the Patronage Act and then the Toleration Act, both coming into force in 1712 and both being seen by their opponents as going against the Treaty of Union.[14] This ensured that, in practice, Presbyterian establishment in Scotland would continue to be experienced as a contested and disputed relationship, albeit in a less bloody form than had been practised in the previous century.

Presbyterian church history, along with the theology and political theology accompanying it, can be famously hard for insiders, let alone outsiders or non-specialists, to understand and interpret.

In the eighteenth century, after the final, doomed gesture of the '45 rebellion, issues of toleration gradually became less significant, but issues of patronage became more problematic. Dissatisfaction with the principle and practice of establishment was one of the forces behind schisms within the Kirk, which led to the emergence of a range of seceding Presbyterian churches.

By the time Thomas Chalmers emerged as a key Evangelical leader in the nineteenth century, toleration was no longer the main issue. Episcopalians were an accepted minor tradition within the landscape of Scottish Christianity and Chalmers famously supported Catholic emancipation. The meaning of establishment,

---

14 'An unsympathetic Anglican English Tory party saw no reason to defend the privileges of a Presbyterian Church of Scotland' (Murdoch, in Dickinson and Lynch (eds), 2000, p. 43).

however, was changing. In this new era, establishment needed to be performed differently.

The vision of Chalmers and the Evangelicals, who remained strongly critical of Episcopalian and, even more so, Roman Catholic theology and practice, was of a less punitive and more positive performance of establishment. It was to be seen less as a negative means of suppressing dissent or denying civil rights to other traditions and more as a positive account of the state's duty 'to maintain true religion' (Scots Confession, 1560) and to see 'all the ordinances of God duly settled, administrated, and observed' (Westminster Confession, 1646). Establishment was still to be about self-preferment, but less about punishment of the other.

In order to ensure its better performance of this positive role, two major changes were necessary on the part of the state. It had to remove the offending obstacle of patronage and it had to demonstrate its practical commitment to supporting the advance of true (that is, Church of Scotland) religion in a booming Georgian/Victorian era of rapid industrialization and urbanization. The state's refusal after a decade of dispute and debate to address the General Assembly's claims on either count evoked the 1842 Claim of Right and provoked the 1843 Disruption.

It is crucial to understand that the Disruption was not provoked by a rejection of the establishment principle, but by the passionate conviction that because the state was not performing its side of establishment properly, the Church of Scotland had become a fatally compromised space within which to maintain true religion. The Disruption was a rebuke to the state for failing to recognize and support true religion in Scotland and a rebuke to those who stayed within the Church of Scotland for tolerating such a travesty of establishment.

This is what lies behind Thomas Chalmers' moderatorial address to the founding General Assembly of the Free Church of Scotland:

> We hold that every part and every function of a commonwealth should be leavened with Christianity, and that every functionary, from the highest to the lowest, should, in their respective spheres, do all that in them lies to countenance and uphold it.

That is to say, though we quit a vitiated establishment, we go out on the Establishment principle; we quit a vitiated establishment, but would rejoice in returning to a pure one. To express it otherwise: we are the advocates for a national recognition and national support of religion – and we are not Voluntaries. (*Proceedings*, 1843, p. 12, emphasis added)

By the mid-nineteenth century, the religious unity of Scotland was profoundly fractured. Presbyterianism was divided into three main blocks: the *United Presbyterian Church*, a union of eighteenth-century seceders who (mostly) opposed establishment; the *Free Church*, who rejected the current 'vitiated' form of establishment, and the *Church of Scotland*, who were working to reform the current form of establishment. Alongside them were the growing number of Episcopalians and Roman Catholics. The latter in particular were still struggling for recognition and rights within Scottish society. Both Episcopalians and Roman Catholics were also hostile to the Church of Scotland's power and privilege and the record of those being used against them.

As these variously sized churches jostled for power and advantage within Scotland, the establishment principle was being challenged and contested across the whole of the UK in the second half of the nineteenth century.[15] The rise of Roman Catholicism and Protestant Dissent in England, along with the fracturing of Presbyterianism in Scotland, meant that both the Church of England and the Church of Scotland had become minority traditions within their respective countries. In the end, the Church of England survived the disestablishment campaign, and its complex, neo-gothic relationship with the UK state has continued to evolve pragmatically, with a decreasingly Anglican parliament increasingly persuaded that the governance of the Church of England is primarily a matter for the Church of England. During its periodic enquiries into its own constitutional position, the position of the Church of Scotland post-1921 has been frequently cited.[16]

---

15 'During the great age of European nationalism, Scottish religion took centre stage' (Harvie, 1994, p. 14).

16 Although in each case deemed not suitable for the Church of England, the Scottish formula is viewed as a hugely important marker and statement of principle. See Cranmer et al., 2006, details of which appear in note 17 below.

One of the best recent discussions of these different forms of establishment is a paper by Frank Cranmer, John Lucas and Bob Morris.[17] One of the things they capture particularly well is the unprecedented character of the 1921 Church of Scotland Act, based on the Church of Scotland's Articles Declaratory (Cranmer et al., 2006, p. 62; see also Murray, 1993). They suggest that 'those coming across it for the first time may be surprised by its content'.

To explain their suggestion we need to enter a tangled and then partially untangled web of denominational union and readjustment. From 1847, the fragmentation of Presbyterianism gave way to what Callum Brown calls 'a reversal of pluralization' (1997, p. 47). Some seceding congregations united into the United Presbyterian Church in 1847, while other congregations joined with the Free Church in 1852. The reversal came about when in 1900 there was a major consolidation, in which most of the Free Church united with most of the United Presbyterian Church to form the United Free Church. The formation of the United Free Church complicated the Free Church's traditional 'Chalmers' position on establishment, with the new united denomination now containing significant numbers opposed to the principle of establishment. Five years of bitter litigation between the United Free and the (wee) Free Church (the remnant who had stayed out of the 1900 union) were finally resolved via a 1905 Act of Parliament, which distributed the contested assets of the former United Free denomination between the two successor bodies. This cleared the way for a new round of negotiations to begin in 1909 over potential union between the United Free Church and the Church of Scotland.

It is these negotiations that, after a shattering decade including the First World War and the Russian Revolution, would finally lead to the production of the Articles Declaratory, the passing of the 1921 Church of Scotland Act and the 'Glorious Union' of 1929. The crucial debates around how to cope with the deeply divisive issue of establishment took place within these negotiations.

---

17 Published in 2006 by The Constitution Unit, Department of Political Science, UCL, London, http://www.ucl.ac.uk/spp/publications/unit-publications/133.pdf. The paper is titled 'Church and State – A Mapping Exercise'.

For all the complexity and emotional turbulence of fission and reunion there were two underlying poles of principle. On the one hand, there was a determination to resist *erastianism*, on the other a determination to avoid *voluntarism* and to call the state to its proper vocation under God. To recognize the complexity of institutional narrative that such a basic polarity can generate is to go a long way to understanding Reformed Presbyterianism in its Scottish incarnation.

What seems extraordinary a century later[18] is not so much that the two uniting churches agreed on the Articles Declaratory, but that they persuaded the state to agree to them. The churches strained to reach agreement on a meticulously worded compromise, which turned on eschewing the language of establishment altogether and consigning it to the past. Those opposed to it knew they could not excise it from the historic legislation, but they insisted it was left there.

For those who supported the establishment principle, as well as the term 'establishment' remaining intact in statute, there were other reassurances. Article I affirmed the historic trinitarian orthodoxy of the Kirk, its commitment to Scripture and its Catholic and Reformed identity. Article II affirmed its commitment to the Westminster Confession and to Presbyterian governance. Article III saw the crucial area of innovation, where both parties had compromised around a new formula:

> This Church is in historical continuity with the Church of Scotland which was reformed in 1560, whose liberties were ratified in 1592, and for whose security provision was made in the Treaty of Union of 1707. The continuity and identity of the Church of Scotland are not prejudiced by the adoption of these Articles. As a national Church representative of the Christian Faith of the Scottish people it acknowledges its distinctive call and duty to bring the ordinances of religion to the people in every parish of Scotland through a territorial ministry.

---

18 Substantial agreement was reached in 1914, but implementation was delayed by the outbreak of war (Murray, 1993, p. 23).

Instead of claiming establishment, the epithets of choice were now 'national' and 'representative'. It laid claim to a 'distinctive' popular and territorial vocation to 'the people in every parish'.[19] It did not claim Scotland as 'a Christian nation', but spoke of the faith of the people.

If that was the compromise that replaced establishment in binding the Church to the state, the 'disestablishing' formula that freed it from the state appeared immediately after in Article IV:

> This Church as part of the Universal Church wherein the Lord Jesus Christ has appointed a government in the hands of Church office-bearers, receives from Him, its Divine King and Head, and from Him alone, the right and power subject to no civil authority to legislate, and to adjudicate finally, in all matters of doctrine, worship, government, and discipline in the Church, including the right to determine all questions concerning membership and office in the Church, the constitution and membership of its Courts, and the mode of election of its office-bearers, and to define the boundaries of the spheres of labour of its ministers and other office-bearers. Recognition by civil authority of the separate and independent government and jurisdiction of this Church in matters spiritual, in whatever manner such recognition be expressed, does not in any way affect the character of this government and jurisdiction as derived from the Divine Head of the Church alone or give to the civil authority any right of interference with the proceedings or judgments of the Church within the sphere of its spiritual government and jurisdiction.

Article V affirmed the Church's inherent right to frame, adopt, interpret and modify its doctrinal standards. Article VI articulated the relationship of Church and state:

> This Church acknowledges the divine appointment and authority of the civil magistrate within his own sphere, and maintains

---

19 Anglican theologian Wesley Carr has spoken of an 'earthed' understanding of establishment, which has some resonances with this 'territorial' vision (Carr, 2002, quoted in Cranmer et al., 2006, p. 9).

its historic testimony to the duty of the nation acting in its corporate capacity to render homage to God, to acknowledge the Lord Jesus Christ to be King over the nations, to obey His laws, to reverence His ordinances, to honour His Church, and to promote in all appropriate ways the Kingdom of God. The Church and the State owe mutual duties to each other, and acting within their respective spheres may signally promote each other's welfare.

Taken as a whole, it was an extraordinary blend of compromise and claim, of adaptation and assertion. It was recognized legally by what Colin Kidd describes as 'the peculiar Church of Scotland Act 1921', which 'was, however, a most unusual piece of legislation, for it appeared to be a sort of concordat between state and the Kirk, a phenomenon unheard of in British constitutional practice'.[20] Kidd's verdict echoes the earlier conclusion of Vernon Bogdanor that the Act was 'in effect a treaty between Church and State' (1995, p. 237, quoted in Cranmer et al., 2006, p. 61). Both Cranmer et al. in their mapping essay and Colin Kidd in his later study of *Political Thought in Scotland* (2008, p. 123) refer to the legal opinions of Ronald King Murray, Lord Advocate under Labour in the 1970s. Murray's comments on the 1921 Act are trenchant and provocative:

By this remarkable statute the UK Parliament has admitted the legislative sovereignty which the General Assembly has always claimed in the ecclesiastical sphere, and, by implication, it seems to have conceded that there is in at least one respect in which the UK Parliament is not sovereign. This power of ecclesiastical legislation is a very real mark of freedom, but not at all a mark of disestablishment. For what established church could ask for a greater measure of state association than to share with the civil authority the legislative power of the state? (Murray, 1958, pp. 160–1, quoted in Cranmer et al., 2006, p. 63)

---

20 Colin Kidd, 'The Union and the Constitution', September 2012 paper, published online at http://www.historyandpolicy.org/papers/policy-paper-137.html#S4.

In recent years, as some high-profile court cases have raised questions about the scope of 'spiritual independence', the Kirk has preferred to speak softly about its powers under the 1921 Act. Duncan Forrester asked whether its independent jurisdiction in matters spiritual was more than a quaint survival: 'My own opinion is that despite its questionable relevance at present, in other possible circumstances, facing a future hostile government, the Church of Scotland Act 1921, might at least ensure that the courts provided some protection' (1999, p. 87).

The Act is certainly a little known constitutional phenomenon and the assessments of its scope and uniqueness quoted above give a clear indication why Cranmer, Lucas and Morris speak of its being viewed with a degree of 'envy' by a succession of Anglican commissions considering the future of their own establishment, even if they did not feel the formula was a good fit for the Church of England (Cranmer et al., 2006, p. 62).

On the formula adopted in the Third Article, a succession of New College divines, Will Storrar (1990), Duncan Forrester (1999) and David Fergusson (2004), have expressed reservations about its wording. They have questioned both the phrase 'national church' and the idea of the Church of Scotland representing 'the Christian faith of the Scottish people'.[21]

The counsel of Storrar and Fergusson that the Kirk repeal its Third Article, as a gesture of penitence for past intolerance and openness to rethinking its future, was rejected by the Church's recent Special Commission on this Article, whose report to the 2010 General Assembly defiantly reaffirmed the principles it enshrined, against the clear advice of three of its best theological minds.[22]

A final historical note might be to observe that the 1918 Education Act, in its provision of state support for Roman Catholic education, extended its own small degree of 'establishment' to a non-Presbyterian, non-Protestant denomination in Scotland, along with its own guarantees of spiritual independence. The

---

21 Forrester is, however, more inclined to see some positive aspects to 'the Christian faith of the Scottish people' phrase (1999, p. 88).

22 http://www.churchofscotland.org.uk/__data/assets/pdf_file/0014/3470/ga10_reports_specarticle.pdf; or Reports To The General Assembly 2010.

living legacy of that decision will also be under scrutiny as the conversation goes forward.

## Establishing the future constitutional status of religion

With the coming referendum on independence and open discussion of the possible contents of a new written constitution for Scotland, the 1921 Act will be exposed to fresh scrutiny.[23]

My own feelings about this harbour some of the same ambivalence as my feelings about monarchy do. The political theology of Scottish Presbyterianism, while it has had its shameful episodes, has also long borne witness to the belief that there is an 'outside' to politics, an 'outside' to the state. There is not only a sovereignty of the people to be reckoned with, but a sovereignty of the good.

In Melville's justly famous words, there are 'twa kings and twa kingdoms in Scotland'. Talk of the 'spiritual independence' of the Church (without absenting it from the usual run of the fiscal's writ in civil matters) has held open the thought that the state is not a self-sealing, all-encompassing sphere, but rather that it has limits that can and must be thought beyond, must be 'transcended'. Everything is political, but politics is not everything.

It is something like this to which the current ritual of coronation bears witness. When the monarch is anointed, prayed for, presented with orb and sword, Scripture and sceptre, the ritual being enacted affirms that power comes from God and is accountable to God. When it is next seen in anything like this classic form it will likely come as something of a shock to a more secular Britain or RUK, just because the rites are so overtly and deliberately religious.

My point here is not to defend monarchy or establishment, but to claim that events such as coronations (or inaugurations) are meant to be 'big picture' moments, when the values, beliefs and virtues of a society are dramatized and celebrated. They act as bridges from the past to the present. They express hopes for

---

23 Though not by the faint hearted as the preceding discussion shows. There are signs that some doughty militant secularists are up for the fight.

continuity and progress in the future. They try, in frames that, however gilded, are always broken, to insist that power must give way to virtue and they try to express the sovereignty of the good.

If there were to be a vote to create a new Scottish state, I believe that we would continue to need rituals that show that it and its politics have an 'outside', that the state aspires to ideas of the good that transcend the workings of power, even the power of a democratic majority. David Fergusson's warning in 2004 about the dangers of 'hard secularism' remains prescient:

> A secular liberalism based upon autonomy provides a basis that is much too thin to sustain public life. Moreover a constitution which attempts to keep religion out of public life may result in many of the absurdities and anomalies that blight debates in the USA about the interpretation of the First Amendment. Behind arguments for equality there lurks a new form of establishment, the establishment of the secular which prohibits the intrusion of religious convictions in public debate. (2004, p. 187)

Supporters of independence for Scotland are fond of looking to Norway for inspiration. There is a country that, it can be argued, is allowing establishment to evolve, honouring its past traditions while offering recognition and respect to its present diversity. Its revised constitution acknowledges its historical debt to both Christian and humanist traditions.

Whether or not Scotland votes or has/has not voted for independence in 2014, questions about the place of religion within a constitutional settlement will not go away. The 1921 Act will rightly continue to frustrate, fascinate and challenge the debate today, but it and its formulas, especially those of Article III, were designed to solve the social and theological problems of an earlier era.

Establishment has long been a contested and debatable condition, capable of assuming different forms in different countries and different eras. Examples of evolving patterns of establishment in other countries continue to be useful for the debates within Scotland and England, even if we continue to leave the 'E' word to one side in crafting new formulas.

Where the 1921 Act was designed to heal the intra-Presbyterian wounds of the Disruption and of earlier secessions, the main issues to be addressed by any new formulation a century later are those of ecumenism, inter-faith relations and secularization. These are very different issues and they need to be addressed in different terms.

One of the conceptual shifts in the Articles Declaratory that is still valuable today is the shift from the language of establishment to that of recognition. This will be a key term for whoever drafts any future constitution. The hope has to be that Protestant and Roman Catholic Scotland, Christian and Multi-Faith Scotland, Religious and Secular Scotland can find common ground around a rubric of recognition without discrimination.

Recognition need not mean crude equalization. It can still take account of majority traditions while showing due respect and esteem for minority traditions. It can still take account of history, without losing sight of the need to right wrongs and to welcome new voices. It can still allow focal practices and rituals to be performed with integrity, while supplementing them with new ones, in which new actors can speak and act from their own traditions.

In refusing to support any project for dying on the hill of 'establishment' I also believe that Scotland's churches should resist any idea of simply replacing the 1560 or 1707 style establishment of Presbyterianism with the establishment of a year zero, hard-secularist world-view. They should resist it firstly because it remains part of the mission of the Church to call the state, as the Sixth Article Declaratory puts it, 'to render homage to God, to acknowledge the Lord Jesus Christ to be King over the nations'. Oliver O'Donovan points to this in *The Desire of the Nations*:

> The most truly Christian state understands itself most thoroughly as 'secular'. It makes the confession of Christ's victory and accepts the relegation of its own authority. The only corresponding service the church can render to this passing authority is to help it make this act of self-denying recognition. It may urge this on it and share with it the tasks of practical deliberation and policy which seek to embody and implement it. The church has to instruct it in the ways of the humble state. (1996, p. 219)

They should also resist any abrupt establishment of secularism because it does violence to the legacy of tradition, where tradition is understood as an extended argument in time about the nature of the good. There are non-decadent forms of conservatism, whose arguments about the wisdom of continuity deserve to be heard alongside radical demands for what is oppressive to be swept away today.[24]

Finally, the establishment of secularism should be resisted because I do not believe it is yet what most people in Scotland want to see. That will of course have to be tested by a democratic vote sometime in the future and none of my arguments for resisting secularism are presented in opposition to the need for full and proper democratic process to prevail. My concern is that people of faith within Scotland, both Christians and those who adhere to other religions, should make the case within public debate for a constitutional settlement that by democratic agreement bears witness to that which transcends democracy, to the sovereignty of the good. In doing so, they would arguably be sustaining the spirit of the 1921 Act, in so far as their witness would recognize, but not establish or create what they are bearing witness to.

As a final exercise in political imagination, consider a Scottish Constitution that began like this:

## The Scottish Constitution

### Article I – Sources of Law

- This constitution, without compromise to equality under the law or to the rightful jurisdiction of the law, recognizes that Scotland's people acknowledge different sources of law, right, truth and goodness, to which they believe our positive laws, including this constitution, are both accountable and subordinate, even when enacted by due democratic process.
- This constitution recognizes the value and wisdom of the Christian tradition and its long influence upon Scotland. In

---

24 Fergusson quotes George Lindbeck: 'I once welcomed the passing of Christendom ... but now I am having uncomfortable second thoughts' (2004, p. 190).

particular, it acknowledges the belief of many of Scotland's people that the state is accountable to God, from whom its power and authority derives.

- It recognizes also the value and wisdom of other religious traditions and of secular, humanistic world-views and the differing accounts they may give of the ultimate sources of law and the good.
- This constitution establishes neither religion nor secularism, but acknowledges their varied traditions of thought and belief, welcoming the insights and wisdom they may bring to democratic deliberation and to the civic and ceremonial life of the nation.
- This constitution expresses the democratic consensus of the people of Scotland on basic laws and fundamental rights.

# Conclusion

*I am not Atlas;*
*there is nothing on my shoulders but my head.*
*I cannot raise the world.*
*I cannot raise Scotland.*
*And to tell the truth, it is with difficulty sometimes*
*that I raise my head.*
*But who knows that if I raise my head a little*
*I might not raise Scotland a little?*
*And in raising Scotland a little*
*I won't raise a little the world?*

(Fearghas MacFhionnlaigh, *The Midge*)

Parts of this book have been writing themselves in my head ever since as a student I read *The Midge* in the magazine *Cencrastus*, a journal of 'Scottish and International Literature, Arts and Affairs', in autumn 1982. The whole has been written more on the move than I would have liked, but there will be a number of books on Scotland published in 2013 and 2014 that have that feel to them. Independence referendums concentrate the mind. They are once in a generation events. They deserve to be the subject of theological reflection.

Looking back through that faded green issue of *Cencrastus*, with articles by Will Storrar, Michael Hechter, Christopher Harvie, Ian Hamilton Findlay and Lindsay Paterson, two things are striking. One is how few women wrote for that issue; only a couple of brief reviews were penned by women. The other, more positive reaction is to the feel of the thing – the ethos of it, if you like. There was a combination of seriousness about Scottish culture and language, an interest in radical politics, a clearly internationalist perspective and, in this issue at least, an openness to theological ideas, in both Will's article and Fearghas's poem.[1] The editorial spoke of 'creeping nationalism' in the ranks of the Labour Party being mirrored by 'creeping socialism' in the ranks of the SNP and a growing unity of interest emerging that would thrust devolution to the forefront of Scottish politics again.[2]

I found it an impressive and inspiring combination back then and still do today. I wanted to write this book because of the tension I have felt over the years between the ethical instincts I have carried about Scottish nationalism as a Christian and the visceral hostility to nationalism that I often encountered among theologians or in theological writing. This book was an opportunity to reflect on that tension and to think through how far my support for a nationalist party was consistent with my Christian theology.

The ethical tensions over nationalism are real ones, and they have not been sufficiently explored within political theology.[3] The legacy of two world wars and the rise of fascisms were a horrific testimony to the power of toxic nationalisms to channel fear and hatred, racism and lust for power. In the post-war period, the imperial nationalisms at the heart of the grim and bloody history of colonialism have been unmasked and indicted, although their legacies continue to fuel conflict and misery for millions around the world. A theological critique must name and face these evils unflinchingly. There should be no hint of spin or mitigation.

The tensions arise because projects of thinking beyond nationalism have their own demons to confront. The ideas of perpetual peace associated with Kantian cosmopolitanism, which fed Marxist dreams of international socialism, became the house 'religions' for new kinds of imperialism and created their own litanies of oppression and murder. The history of the Church's confession of 'catholicity' is also associated with great sins, where attempts were made to enforce this identity on others or treat those seen

---

1 Described here by Derick Thompson/Ruaraidh MacThomais as 'probably the most exciting and interesting long sustained poem to be published in Gaelic this century', *Cencrastus* 10 (1982), p. 28 – what was published was the poet's own English translation.

2 *Cencrastus* 10 (1982), p. 3.

3 Because it has not paid enough attention to positive accounts to perceive such tensions.

to be outside of it as, in various ways, disposable, enslaveable, torturable, damnable.

The rehabilitation of nationalism in the postcolonial and post-Soviet eras has been an ambivalent one, often acknowledged grudgingly by those whose own secured power and settled state borders left them to project 'nationalism' on to others, while quietly ignoring their own claims and how they had been secured. The paradox of nationalism both being implicated in the cause of imperialism and seeming essential to its downfall remains. Those who deplore nationalism need to explain why the ambitions of colonized people to secure independent statehood are philosophically incoherent. Or they may need to rethink what they mean by nationalism.

So the tensions around nationalism remain severe and pressing. My agreement with Jonathan Hearn that 'nationalism' is normal is only a preliminary move, designed to overcome a false pathologizing. In itself it does not take us far. Sin is normal. My argument has been that there are no other games in town, so we need to learn to play this one well. We need to work at its rules and to find other ways to play it.

The book has worked with beastly metaphors, picking up Hearn's 'defanging' and Keating's 'tiger-riding' comments along the way. To anticipate the criticisms of some reviewers, those two metaphors have the advantage over mine from Judges, that for them the beast is still alive. Granted; but without pressing the image too far, there are ways of understanding and exercising power that have to be refused outright, that have to be 'killed' if you like. There is a breaking open of nationalism that has to take place if it is to become part of 'the ways of the humble state' (O'Donovan, 1996, p. 228). I name the crucial renunciations it has to make as imperialism, essentialism and absolutism – the world, the flesh and the devil. Any nationalist who refuses to make those renunciations, if they claim to be a Christian, deserves to be condemned, as the supporters of apartheid finally were, as a heretic.

The trouble with ancient constitutional rituals is that they are almost always contaminated with the genteel violence of aristocratic privileges and exclusions. The trouble with modern constitutions is that, outside of the language of human rights, which is both powerful and valuable, they lack ways of bearing witness to the 'outside' of politics, to the power of God and the sovereignty of the good.

After the necessary renunciations have been made and rituals of adherence to right, law and democracy enacted, everything still hangs on how particular nationalisms are enacted and performed. There are no blank political cheques to be written to power.

The idea of being a nation, is a dangerous one, much abused in the past, which will be abused again in the future. But so is the idea of being a man. The claims to identity, territory and jurisdiction which are constitutive of nationalism need to be constantly subjected to a hermeneutic of suspicion. That is why the ongoing, never-finished work of political theology in developing an account of the good society is so important within and beyond the Christian community. The grand narratives of what people and societies are for, the enabling and restraining disciplines of legislation and regulation and the enacted witness of virtuous examples are all vital parts of a process of catechism and prophecy which the church owes to the state. Its potential for hubris and hypocrisy in these areas is always being tested by the warning that it has nothing more to share with the world than what it is sharing with itself.[4]

The potential legitimacy of nationalist projects does not mean that the goal to be sought is one final rigid pattern of objectively separated entities. Nations are made by negotiations, both internally and externally. The practice of 'politymaking' can be kept open to possibilities of union and independence. Plurinational union states may create new and positive understandings of shared nationality or they may develop overarching identities which come to be resented and resisted by their constituent nations. Independent states may decide to enter international unions of different kinds. The ethics and the wisdom of such political decisions will need to be weighed on a case by case basis. What ends do they serve? Whose interests are advanced and whose are damaged? Will this hinder or advance the cause of peace?

I have argued for the need to 'taste and see' the sweet and sour notes of various political arrangements, for an Augustinian audit

---

4 Wallis 1981, 130.

of what constitutes 'better objects of love'. In the case of Scotland, I suggest it will be better placed as an independent state to pursue better objects. I have set out the outlines of such a case in this book, but only as a way of taking part in a broader conversation within the churches, Scotland, the UK and the international community of theologians. The conversation is crucial – the conclusions can only be reached together.

## Converging on 'the secular'

If non-religious or non-Christian readers have stayed the distance, respect to you for doing so. The sound of an unapologetically theological voice in the public square should not be taken as a sign that the speaker does not want to reach agreement with others. My resistance to the establishment of a 'secularist' world-view does not mean that I want to see religious domination of public life. My hope is that relationships between religious and secular Scotland will not be set up as a zero sum game and that constitutional debates will not aim at a secularist year zero, setting aside the gifts of Scotland's Christian past and present to its public life and rituals. The goal, which I believe can be a widely shared one, should be to construct a democratic, pluralist future that does not seek to erase its past or push past the still significant, even if changing, religious commitments of its people in the present.

## Raising heads and hopes

Sniffing the air, a year out from the referendum, there are signs around of a new vibrancy and enthusiasm in Scottish culture, some of it linked to the prospect of political change. I hope some of that will survive whatever the outcome. I have no interest in being a dead-hand Presbyterian trying to squash the naive idealism of a rising generation.

In writing this book I have been struck again by Charles Taylor's account of Calvinists dreaming they could change the world. It poses the challenge of how to live out a Reformed understanding of Christian identity. I like the idea of a realism about human capacities for evil and misjudgement being combined with a rigorous insistence on pursuing the good. I also like the idea of being a Reformed Christian, informed by Catholic social teaching and inspired by Anabaptist practice. There are friends and whisky to help with sorting out the contradictions.

As I finish this book, the well-known Scottish author and broadcaster Lesley Riddoch has published her own manifesto for Scottish renewal, unashamedly titled 'Blossom'. While she quotes Hugh MacDiarmid's well-loved poem about 'the little white rose of Scotland', my own thoughts about an ending for this book have in recent months been bound up with lines from another much longer MacDiarmid poem, *A Drunk Man Looks at the Thistle*:

> O Scotland is
> THE barren fig.
> Up, carles, up
> And roond it jig.
> Auld Moses took
> a dry stick and
> Instantly it
> Floo'ered in his hand.
> Pu' Scotland up,
> And wha can say
> It winna bud
> And blossom tae.
>
> A miracle's
> Oor only chance.
> Up, carles, up
> And let us dance!

(Hugh MacDiarmid, from A Drunk Man Looks At The Thistle, 1925)

In Luke 13.6–9, the barren fig in Christ's parable is given a reprieve of one more year, when it can be dug around and fertilized, to see if it might yet bear fruit. Even if we have other very different ideas about how to look for miracles, it might do Scotland's

Presbyterian 'carles' no harm to let themselves be pulled further into the dance and mend the cultural gap between congregation and ceilidh.

There are days when many of us find it hard, in MacFhionn-laigh's words, to raise our heads. To write a book is an act of hope for the future. This is my attempt, to raise my own head a little, in the hope that it will raise Scotland a little and, as good internationalist nationalist, it may also raise the world a little. A Christian Vision of Scottish Identity, to invoke Will Storrar's project, is one that longs to see Scotland bud and blossom, that is passionate about pursuing the Common Good and about seeking life in all its fullness for all Scotland's people.

My claim, then, is that a theological construal of nationalism along the lines I have suggested can support a case for independence as a better option for Scotland (and England). The hope is for a future state in which Scotland's lion rampant is not a cruel or pitiless beast, but a state in which we, like Samson, can get honey from the lion, and about which we can tell this theo-political riddle:

> Out of the eater, came something to eat.
> Out of the strong came something sweet. (Judges 14.14)

# Bibliography

Adams, N., Pattison, G. and Ward, G. (eds), *The Oxford Handbook to Theology and Modern European Thought*, Oxford: Oxford University Press, 2013.

Anderson, B., *Imagined Communities*, London: Verso, 1991.

Arter, D. (2002) 'On Assessing Strength and Weakness in Parliamentary Committee Systems: Some Preliminary Observations on the New Scottish Parliament', *Journal of Legislative Studies*, 8, 2, 93–117.

Ascherson, N., *Stone Voices: The Search for Scotland*, London: Granta, 2002.

d'Ancona, M. (ed.), *Being British: The Search for the Values that Bind the Nation*, Edinburgh: Mainstream, 2009.

Augustine, *City of God*, trans. and ed. R. W. Dyson, Cambridge: Cambridge University Press, 1998.

Beetham, D., *The Legitimation of Power*, Basingstoke and New York: Palgrave Macmillan, 1991.

Bell, E. and Miller, G. (eds), *Scotland in Theory*, Amsterdam: Rodopi, 2004.

Berrigan, D., *The Word Made Flesh*, Maryknoll, NY: Orbis Books, 2004.

Berry, W., *What Are People For?*, London: Rider, 1991.

Beveridge, C. and Turnbull, R., *The Eclipse of Scottish Culture*, Edinburgh: Polygon, 1989.

Beveridge, C. and Turnbull, R., *Scotland after Enlightenment*, Edinburgh: Polygon, 1997.

Bhabha, H. (ed.), *Nation and Narration*, London, Routledge, 1990.

Biggar, N., 'The Value of Limited Loyalty: Christianity, the Nation, and Territorial Boundaries', *Modern Believing* 20:53:4 (2012).

Biggar, N. and Hogan, L. (eds), *Religious Voices in Public Places*, Oxford: Oxford University Press, 2009.

Billig, M., *Banal Nationalism*, New York: Sage, 1995.

Bobbio, N., *Democracy and Dictatorship*, Minneapolis, MN: University of Minnesota Press, 1989.

Bogdanor, V., *The Monarchy and the Constitution*, Oxford: Clarendon Press, 1995.

Bonhoeffer, D., *The Cost of Discipleship*, trans. R. H. Fuller, rev. edn, New York: Macmillan, 1960.

Bourdieu, P., *The Logic of Practice*, Cambridge: Polity Press, 1990.

Bradstock, A. and Rowland, C. (eds), *Radical Christian Writings: A Reader*, Oxford: Blackwell, 2002.

Breckenridge, C. et al. (eds), *Cosmopolitanism*, Durham, NC: Duke University Press, 2002.

Bretherton, L., *Christianity and Contemporary Politics*, London: Routledge, 2010.

Brown, C. G., *Religion and Society in Scotland Since 1707*, Edinburgh: Edinburgh University Press, 1997.

Brown, C. G., *Religion and Society in Twentieth-Century Britain*, Harlow: Pearson Education, 2006.

Brown, F. B., *Good Taste, Bad Taste and Christian Taste*, Oxford: Oxford University Press, 2003.

Brown, S. J., *Thomas Chalmers and the Godly Commonwealth in Scotland*, Oxford: Oxford University Press, 2003.

Brubaker, R., *Nationalism Reframed: Nationhood and the National Question in the New Europe*, Cambridge: Cambridge University Press, 1996.

Brueggemann, W., *The Land*, Philadelphia, PA: Fortress, 1977.

Brueggemann, W., *The Prophetic Imagination*, Philadelphia, PA: Fortress, 1978.

Brueggemann, W., *Genesis*, Atlanta, GA: John Knox Press, 1982

Brueggemann, W., *The Prophetic Imagination*, Minneapolis, MN: Augsburg, 1983.

Brueggemann, W., *The Hopeful Imagination*, Philadelphia, PA: Fortress, 1985.

Brueggemann, W., *Texts Under Negotiation*, Minneapolis, MN: Augsburg, 1993.

Brueggemann, W., *An Introduction to the Old Testament: The Canon and Christian Imagination*, Louisville, KY: Westminster John Knox Press, 2003.

Butter, P. (ed.), *The Complete Poems of Edwin Muir*, Aberdeen: Association of Scottish Literary Studies, 1991.

Calvin, J., *Commentaries*, Philadelphia, PA: Westminster John Knox Press, 1958.

Carr, W., 'Crown and People: Reflections on the Spiritual Dimensions of Establishment', lecture delivered at Westminster Abbey, 16 September 2002.

Cavanaugh, W. T., *Theopolitical Imagination*, London and New York: T & T Clark, 2002.

Christensen, D. L., 'Nations', in *The Anchor Bible Dictionary*, vol. 4, New York: Doubleday, 1992, pp. 1037–49.

Clements, K., *Faith on the Frontier: A Life of J. H. Oldham*, Edinburgh: T & T Clark, 1999.

Cohen, R., *Frontiers of Identity: The British and the others*, London/New York: Longman, 1994.

Craig, C., *The Scots' Crisis of Confidence*, Edinburgh: Big Thinking, 2003.

Cranmer, F., Lucas, J. and Morris, B., 'Church and State: A Mapping Exercise', London: Constitution Unit UCL, 2006. Available at http://www.ucl.ac.uk/spp/publications/unit-publications/133.pdf.

Curtice, J. and Heath, A., 'Is the English Lion about to Roar? National Identity after Devolution', in R. Jowell et al. (eds), *British Social Attitudes: The 17th Report*, London: Sage, 2000, pp. 155–74.

'T. S. Eliot reviews influence of the Bible', *Daily Princetonian*, 58:38 (24 March 1933).

Davidson, N., *Beginnings But No Ending: An Autobiography*, Edinburgh: Edina, 1978.

Davidson, N., 'Gramsci's Reception in Scotland', *Scottish Labour History* 45 (2010), pp. 37–58.

Davie, D., *A Gathered Church: The Literature of the English Dissenting Interest, 1700–1930*, London: Routledge, 1978.

DeBerri, E. et al. (eds), *Our Best Kept Secret: The Rich Heritage of Catholic Social Teaching*, 4th edn, Maryknoll, NY: Orbis Books, 2003.

Devine, T. M., *The Scottish Nation 1700–2000*, London: Penguin, 1999.

Dickinson, H. T. and Lynch, M. (eds), *The Challenge to Westminster: Sovereignty, Devolution and Independence*, East Linton: Tuckwell, 2000.

Dudley Edwards, O. (ed.), *A Claim of Right for Scotland*, Edinburgh: Polygon, 1989.

Eliot, T. S., *The Idea of a Christian Society*, London: Faber & Faber, 1939.

Elshtain, J.B., 'The Just War Tradition and Natural Law' in *Fordham International Law Journal*, Vol 28, Issue 3, Article 6, p. 746.

Ellul. J., *The Presence of the Kingdom*, London: SCM, 1951.

Ellul, J., *The Meaning of the City* (Fr: *Sans Feu ni Lieu* 1970), Grand Rapids, MI: Eerdmans, 1970.

Fergusson, D., *Church, State and Civil Society*, Cambridge: Cambridge University Press, 2004.

Fidler, R., *Canada Adieu? Quebec Debates its Future*, Lantzville, BC: Oolichan Books and the Institute for Research on Public Policy, 1991.

Finlay, R. J., *Independent and Free: Scottish Politics and the Origins of the SNP 1918–1945*, Edinburgh: John Donald, 1994.

Finlay, R. J., *Modern Scotland 1914–2000*, London: Profile, 2004.

Finn, D. K., *The Moral Ecology of Markets*, New York: Cambridge University Press, 2006.

Forgacs, D., 'National Popular: Genealogy of a Concept', in S. During (ed.), *The Cultural Studies Reader*, London: Routledge, 1993.

Forrester, D. B., *Christian Justice and Public Policy*, Cambridge: Cambridge University Press, 1997.

Forrester, D. B., '*Ecclesia Scoticana* – Established, Free or National?', *Theology* 102:806 (1999), pp. 80–9.

Forrester, D. B. and Gay, D. (eds), *Worship and Liturgy in Context: Studies of Theology and Practice*, London: SCM Press, 2009.

Gay, D., 'Scotland, Church and World', unpublished PhD thesis, Glasgow, 2006.

Gay, D., *Remixing the Church*, London: SCM Press, 2011.

Geertz, C., *The Interpretation of Cultures*, New York: Basic Books, 1973.

Gellner, E., *Thought and Change*, London: Weidenfeld & Nicholson, 1964.

Gorringe, T., *Furthering Humanity: A Theology of Culture*, Aldershot: Ashgate, 2004.

Grabill, S. J., *Rediscovering the Natural Law in Reformed Theological Ethics*, Grand Rapids, MI: Eerdmans, 2006.

Graham, E., *Transforming Practice: Pastoral Theology in an Age of Uncertainty*, London: Mowbray, 1996 and Eugene, OR: Cascade, 2002.

Gray, A., *Lanark*, Edinburgh: Canongate, 1981.

Gregory, E., *Politics and the Order of Love: An Augustinian Ethic of Democratic Citizenship*, Chicago, IL: University of Chicago Press, 2008.

Grosby, S., *Nationalism: A Very Short Introduction*, Oxford: Oxford University Press, 2005.

Gustafson, J., 'The Sectarian Temptation: Reflections on Theology, the Church, and the University', *Proceedings of the Catholic Theological Society of America* 40 (1985), pp. 83–94.

Gutiérrez, G., *The God of Life*, New York: Orbis Books, 1991.

Hall, Stuart, 'The Question of Cultural Identity', pp. 274–316 in: Hall, David Held, Anthony McGrew eds., *Modernity and Its Futures*, Cambridge: Polity Press, 1992.

Harrison, B. W., 'The Power of Anger in the Work of Love', in A. L. Loades (ed.), *Feminist Theology: A Reader*, London: SPCK, 1990.

Harvie, C., 'English Regionalism: The Dog that Never Barked', in Bernard Crick (ed.), *National Identities: The Constitution of the United Kingdom*, Oxford: Blackwell, 1991.

Harvie, C., *Scotland and Nationalism*, London: Routledge, 1994.

Harvie, C., *Fool's Gold: The Story of North Sea Oil*, London: Penguin, 1995.

Harvie, C., *No Gods and Precious Few Heroes: Twentieth-Century Scotland*, 3rd edn, Edinburgh: Edinburgh University Press, 1998.

Hassan, G. (ed.), *The Modern SNP: From Protest to Power*, Edinburgh: Edinburgh University Press, 2009.

Hastings, A., *The Construction of Nationhood: Ethnicity, Religion and Nationalism*, Cambridge: Cambridge University Press, 1997.

Hauerwas, S., *Sanctify Them in The Truth: Holiness Exemplified*, Nashville, TN: Abingdon Press, 1998.

Hauerwas, S., *After Christendom*, Nashville, TN: Abingdon Press, 1999.

Hauerwas, S., *The Peaceable Kingdom*, London: SCM Press, 2003 [1983].

Healy, N., *Church, World and the Christian Life*, Cambridge: Cambridge University Press, 2000.

Hearn, J., *Claiming Scotland, National Identity and Liberal Culture*, Edinburgh: Polygon/Edinburgh University Press, 2000.

Hearn, J., *Rethinking Nationalism: A Critical Introduction*, Basingstoke: Palgrave Macmillan, 2006.

Henderson, H., '"It was in you that it A' Began": Some Thoughts on the Folk Conference', in E. J. Cowan (ed.), *The People's Past*, Edinburgh: Polygon, 1980.

Henderson, H. (ed.), *Antonio Gramsci: Prison Letters*, London: Pluto, 1996.

Henderson, I., *Scotland: Kirk and People*, Edinburgh/London: Lutterworth, 1969.

Howard, T. and Packer, J., *Christianity: The True Humanism*, Vancouver: Regent College, 1999 [1985].

Hughes, D., *Castrating Culture*, Milton Keynes: Paternoster, 2001.

Hutchison, I. G. C., *Scottish Politics in the Twentieth Century*, Basingstoke: Macmillan, 2000.

Inglish, D. and Delanty, G. (eds), *Cosmopolitanism: Critical Concepts in the Social Sciences*, 4 vols, London: Routledge, 2011.

Jackson, C., *Restoration Scotland 1660–1690: Royalist Politics, Religion and Ideas*, Woodbridge: Boydell Press, 2003.

Jeanrond, W., *A Theology of Love*, London: T & T Clark, 2010.

Jobling, D., *1 Samuel*, Collegeville, MN: Liturgical Press, 1998.

Keating, M., *Plurinational Democracy: Stateless Nations in a Post-Sovereignty Era*, Oxford: Oxford University Press, 2001.

Kidd, C., *Union and Unionisms: Political Thought in Scotland 1500–2000*, Cambridge: Cambridge University Press, 2008.

Kojecky, R., *T. S. Eliot's Social Criticism*, London: Faber & Faber, 1971.

Koyama, K., *Water Buffalo Theology*, Maryknoll, NY: Orbis Books, 1999.

Kreider, A., *Social Holiness*, Eugene, OR: Wipf & Stock, 2008.

Kuyper, A., *Calvinism: Six Stone Lectures*, Edinburgh: T & T Clark, 1899.

Lane, B. M and Rupp, L. J., *Nazi Ideology before 1933*, Manchester: Manchester University Press, 1978.

Lévinas, E., *Ethics and Infinity*, Pittsburgh, PA: Duquesne University Press, 1985.

Lilla, M., *The Stillborn God*, New York: Alfred A. Knopf, 2007.

Liverani, M., 'Nationality and Political Identity', in *The Anchor Bible Dictionary*, vol. 4, New York: Doubleday, 1992, pp. 1031–6.

Long, D. S., *The Divine Economy*, London: Routledge, 2000.

Long, D. S., *Christian Ethics: A Very Short Introduction*, Oxford: Oxford University Press, 2010.

Long, D. S. and Fox, N. R., *Calculated Futures*, Waco, TX: Baylor University Press, 2007.

Lyall, S. and McCulloch, M. P. (eds), *The Edinburgh Companion to Hugh MacDiarmid*, Edinburgh: Edinburgh University Press, 2011.

McAfee, N., 'Feminist Political Philosophy', in Edward N. Zalta (ed.), *The Stanford Encyclopedia of Philosophy* (Winter 2011), http://plato.stanford.edu/entries/feminism-political/.

MacColl, E., *Journeyman*, London: Sidgwick & Jackson, 1990.

MacDiarmid, H., *Collected Poems*, Manchester: Carcanet Press, 1993.

MacIntyre, A., *After Virtue*, 2nd edn, Notre Dame, IN: University of Notre Dame Press, 1984 [1981].

Manzo, K. A., *Creating Boundaries: The Politics of Race and Nation*, Boulder, CO: Lynne Rienner, 1996.

Mason, R. (ed.), *Scots and Britons: Scottish Political Thought and the Union of 1603*, Cambridge: Cambridge University Press, 2006.

Mason, R. A. and Smith, M. S. (trans. and ed.), *George Buchanan's Law of Kingship*, Edinburgh: Saltire, 2006.

McCrone, D., *Understanding Scotland: The Sociology of a Stateless Nation*, London: Routledge, 1992.

McCrone, D., *The Sociology of Nationalism: Tomorrow's Ancestors*, London: Routledge, 1998.

McCrone. D., 'Cultural Capital in an Understated Nation: The Case of Scotland', *British Journal of Sociology* 56:1 (2005), pp. 65–82.

McGarvey, N. and Cairney, P., *Scottish Politics: An Introduction*, Basingstoke: Palgrave Macmillan, 2008.

McGrath, A. E., *The Open Secret: A New Vision for Natural Theology*, Oxford: Blackwell, 2008.

Mendieta, E. and Vanantwerpen, J. (eds), *The Power of Religion in the Public Sphere*, New York: Columbia University Press, 2011.

Milbank, J., *Theology and Social Theory*, Oxford: Blackwell, 1990.

Milbank, J., *The Word Made Strange*, Oxford: Wiley, 1997.

Milbank, J., 'Against Human Rights: Liberty in the Western Tradition', *Oxford Journal of Law and Religion* 1:1 (2012), pp. 203–34.

Miller-McLemore, B. (ed.), *The Wiley-Blackwell Companion to Practical Theology*, Chichester: Wiley, 2012.

Moltmann, J., *The Spirit of Life*, London: SCM Press, 1992.

Morton, A. (ed.), *God's Will in a Time of Crisis: A Colloquium Celebrating the 50th Anniversary of the Baillie Commission*, Edinburgh: CTPI, 1994.

Moyaert, M., *Fragile Identities: Towards a Theology of Interreligious Hospitality*, Amsterdam: Rodopi, 2011.

Murray, D., *Freedom to Reform: The 'Articles Declaratory' of the Church of Scotland 1921*, Edinburgh: T & T Clark, 1993.

Murray R. K. [Lord Murray] 'The Constitutional Position of the Church of Scotland': Public Law, 1958.

Nairn, T., 'Internationalism and the Second Coming', *Daedalus* 122:3 (1993), pp. 155–70.

Nash, K. and Scott, A. (eds), *The Blackwell Companion to Political Sociology*, London: Blackwell, 2004.

Nation, M. and Wells, S. (eds), *Faithfulness and Fortitude: A Festschrift for Stanley Hauerwas*, Edinburgh: T & T Clark, 2000.

Neat, T., *Hamish Henderson: A Biography, Vol. 1: The Making of the Poet*, Edinburgh: Birlinn, 2007.

Neat, T., *Hamish Henderson: A Biography, Vol. 2: Poetry Becomes People*, Edinburgh: Birlinn/Polygon, 2009.

Newlands, G., *Theology of the Love of God*, London: Collins, 1981.

Niebuhr, R., *Moral Man and Immoral Society*, New York: Scribner, 1932.

Nouwen, H., *Lifesigns: Intimacy, Fecundity, and Ecstasy in Christian Perspective*, New York: Doubleday, 1986.

Nussbaum, M. C., 'Kant and Stoic Cosmopolitanism', *Journal of Political Philosophy* 5:1 (1997), pp. 1–25.

O'Donovan, O., *The Desire of the Nations*, Cambridge: Cambridge University Press, 1996.

O'Donovan, O., *The Ways of Judgment*, Grand Rapids, MI: Eerdmans, 2005.

O'Donovan, O. and J. L., *From Irenaeus to Grotius: A Sourcebook in Christian Political Thought*, Grand Rapids, MI: Eerdmans, 1999.

Paterson, L., *Scottish Education in the Twentieth Century*, Edinburgh: Edinburgh University Press, 2003.

Polanyi, K., *The Great Transformation*, Boston, MA: Beacon Press, 1944/1957 [2001].

Reicher, S. and Hopkins, N., *Self and Nation*, New York: Sage Publications, 2001.

Robertson, J., *And the Land Lay Still*, London: Hamish Hamilton, 2010.

Said, E., *Culture and Imperialism*, London: Chatto & Windus, 1993.

Sanneh, L., *Translating the Message*, New York: Orbis Books, 1989.

Scott, P. and Cavanaugh, W. (eds), *The Blackwell Companion to Political Theology*, Oxford: Blackwell, 2004.

Seerveld, C., *Rainbows for a Fallen World*, Toronto: Tuppence Press, 1980.

Seerveld, C., *In the Fields of the Lord: A Calvin Seerveld Reader*, ed. C. Bartholomew, Toronto: Piquant/Tuppence Press, 2000.

Senst, A. M., 'Regional and National Identities in Robert Frost's and T. S. Eliot's Criticism', *CLCWeb: Comparative Literature and Culture* 3:2 (2001), http://docs.lib.purdue.edu/clcweb/vol3/iss2/10.

Sillars, J., *Scotland: The Case for Optimism*, Edinburgh: Polygon, 1986.

Skinner, Q., *The Foundations of Modern Political Thought*, 2 vols, Cambridge: Cambridge University Press, 1978.

Smith, J. K. A., *Desiring the Kingdom*, Grand Rapids, MI: Baker Academic, 2009.

Smith, R. M., *Stories of Peoplehood: The Politics and Morals of Political Membership*, Cambridge: Cambridge University Press, 2003.

Sonnenschein, E. A., 'The Plural of Res Publica', *The Classical Review* 18:1 (1904), pp. 37–8.

Song, R., *Christianity and Liberal Society*, Oxford: Clarendon Press, 1997.

Spencer, P. and Wollman, H. (eds), *Nations and Nationalism: A Reader*, Edinburgh: Edinburgh University Press, 2005.

Spivak, G., 'Can the Subaltern Speak?', in Rosemary Morris (ed.), *Can the Subaltern Speak? Reflections on the History of an Idea*, New York: Columbia University Press, 2007.

Storrar, W., *Scottish Identity: A Christian Vision*, Edinburgh: Handsel, 1990.

Storrar, W. and Donald, P. (eds), *God in Society*, Edinburgh: St Andrew Press, 2003.

Stout, J., *Democracy and Tradition*, Princeton, NJ: Princeton University Press, 2004.

Swartley, W. M., *Slavery, Sabbath, War and Women*, Scottsdale, PA: Herald Press, 1983.

Taylor, B., *Scotland's Parliament: Triumph and Disaster*, Edinburgh: Edinburgh University Press, 2002.

Taylor, C. *Sources of the Self*, Cambridge, MA: Harvard University Press, 1989.

Taylor, C., *A Secular Age*, Cambridge, MA: Harvard University Press, 2007.

Thompson, J. A., *Deuteronomy*, Leicester: Tyndale Press, 1974.

Tournier, P., *A Place for You*, New York, HarperCollins, 1968.

Tutu, D., *The Rainbow People of God*, New York: Doubleday, 1994.

Vallely, P. (ed.), *The New Politics: Catholic Social Teaching for the Twenty-First Century*, London: SCM Press, 1998.

van Ree, E., 'Lenin's conception of socialism in one country, 1915–17', *Revolutionary Russia* 23:2 (2010), pp. 159–81.

Venn, C., 'Altered States: Post-Enlightenment Cosmopolitanism and Transmodern Socialities', *Theory, Culture & Society* 19:1–2 (2002), pp. 65–80.

Verhey, A., *Remembering Jesus: Christian Community, Scripture and the Moral Life*, Grand Rapids, MI: Eerdmans, 2002.

Visser 't Hooft, W. A. and Oldham, J. H. (eds), *The Church and Its Function in Society*, London: George Allen & Unwin, 1937.

Wallis, J., *The Call to Conversion*, New York: HarperCollins, 1981.

Walter, T., *A Long Way from Home*, Exeter: Paternoster, 1979.

Ward, G. (ed.), *The Postmodern God: A Theological Reader*, Oxford: Blackwell, 1997.

Watson, R., *The Literature of Scotland: The Twentieth Century*, Basingstoke: Palgrave Macmillan, 2007.

White, L., 'The Historical Roots of Our Ecologic Crisis', *Science* 155:3767 (1967), pp. 1203–7.

Whyte, I., *Scotland and the Abolition of Black Slavery, 1756–1838*, Edinburgh: Edinburgh University Press, 2006.

Wightman, A., *The Poor Had No Lawyers: Who Owns Scotland and How They Got It*, Edinburgh: Birlinn, 2013.

Wilkinson, R. and Pickett, K., *The Spirit Level: Why More Equal Societies Almost Always Do Better*, London: Allen Lane, 2009.

Witte Jr., J., *The Reformation of Rights*, Cambridge: Cambridge University Press, 2007.

Wolterstorff, N., *Art in Action*, Grand Rapids, MI: Eerdmans, 1980.

Wolterstorff, N., *Justice: Rights and Wrongs*, Princeton, NJ: Princeton University Press, 2010.

Wolterstorff, N. and Audi, R., *Religion in the Public Square*, Lanham/London: Rowman & Littlefield, 1997.

Wolterstorff, N. and Cuneo, T., *Understanding Liberal Democracy: Essays in Political Philosophy*, Oxford: Oxford University Press, 2012.

Women's Claim of Right Group (ed.), *A Woman's Claim of Right in Scotland*, Edinburgh: Polygon, 1991.

Wright, C., *Living as the People of God: The Relevance of Old Testament Ethics*, Leicester: InterVarsity Press, 1983.

Yack, B, 'The Myth of the Civic Nation' in Beiner, R., ed. *Theorizing Nationalism*, New York: SUNY, 1999.

Yoder, J. H., *Body Politics*, Nashville, TN: Discipleship Resources, 1992.

Yoder, J. H., 'See How They Go with Their Face to the Sun', in *For the Nations: Essays Evangelical and Public*, Eugene: Wipf & Stock, 2001.

Young, R. J. C., *Postcolonialism: A Very Short Introduction*, Oxford, Oxford University Press, 2003.

# Index of Names